Green IT
FOR
DUMMIES®

**by Carol Baroudi, Jeffrey Hill,
Arnold Reinhold, Jhana Senxian**

WILEY

Wiley Publishing, In...

D1434617

Green IT For Dummies®

Published by
Wiley Publishing, Inc.
111 River Street
Hoboken, NJ 07030-5774
www.wiley.com

Copyright © 2009 by Wiley Publishing, Inc., Indianapolis, Indiana

Published by Wiley Publishing, Inc., Indianapolis, Indiana

Published simultaneously in Canada

For general information on our other products and services, please contact our Customer Care Department within the U.S. at 877-762-2974, outside the U.S. at 317-572-3993, or fax 317-572-4002.

For technical support, please visit www.wiley.com/techsupport.

Wiley also publishes its books in a variety of electronic formats. Some content that appears in print may not be available in electronic books.

Library of Congress Control Number: 2009924156

ISBN: 978-0-470-38688-0

10 9 8 7 6 5 4 3 2 1

WILEY

About the Author

Carol Baroudi has been writing For Dummies since 1993 and feels especially lucky to work on this project. Her day job as an industry analyst and research director in the IT security practice at Aberdeen Group affords her a great way to meet fabulous folks from the computer industry, many of whom have rallied to make this book possible in a timely manner. By night she's a graduate student at the University of Massachusetts with an assistantship in the Office of Sustainability. As an undergrad she studied Spanish and computer science at Colgate University. She started her computer career as a software developer, logged many years as an information architect, and has followed emerging technologies in the U.S. and Europe for the last decade. She's interested in opportunities to discuss green and sustainability so please feel free to write to her at carol_baroudi@yahoo.com.

Jeffrey Hill has been involved with the computer industry since 1980 in technology roles in software, software companies, and the commercial printing industry. He helped develop an on-demand printing and fulfillment system for financial documents and has worked with the U.S. Agency for International Development. He currently works as a senior research analyst at the Aberdeen Group covering such topics as virtualization, cloud computing, business continuity and disaster recovery, data archiving, and of course, green IT.

Jeff has an MBA from Northeastern University and studied English at Tufts University. Contact him at Jeffrey.Hill@verizon.net.

Arnold Reinhold has over 30 years experience in the computer industry. He has done cool stuff in spacecraft guidance, air traffic control, computer-aided design, computer-aided manufacturing, and machine vision. He was one of the founders of *Automatix*, a robotics pioneer. Recent writing includes *E-Mail For Dummies*, *Internet For Dummies Quick Reference*, and *Switching to a Mac For Dummies*, all from Wiley Publishing.

Arnold studied mathematics at CCNY and MIT and management at Harvard. You can check out his home page at www.arnoldreinhold.com.

Jhana Senxian leads the Sustainability and Corporate Responsibility practice at Aberdeen Group and directs a strategic research partnership with the United Nations on private sector involvement in Sustainable Consumption and Production (SCP). She is a Harvard-trained social anthropologist with over ten years of international experience in professional research, analysis, writing, and training including fieldwork and collaboration with business, government, academic, and cultural entities in the U.S., Europe, and Africa.

Jhana has an M.A. from Harvard University (Ph.D. forthcoming, 2009) and a B.A. from Brandeis University.

Dedication

Carol dedicates her part of this book to our new president, Barack Obama, and to the people of the United States who elected him — thanks for giving us a chance to right things. And to Josh, my parents, Brian, and Sucia, with all my love.

Jeff dedicates his part of this book to his darling (and patient) wife, Susan Elliott, and talented stepson, Eli Ross. He says, "I wish that my brother Barry could have lived to see this book, and I'm pleased that my mother Evalyn and my sister Sherry will."

Arnold dedicates his part of this book to his parents, Max and Grete, of blessed memory, and to Josh and Barbara.

Jhana dedicates her part of this book to Sharon, Donna, Ren, Becky, Gramsci, and Zora — without your love and support, nothing would be possible.

Author's Acknowledgments

We gratefully acknowledge the many generous people whose help and support made this book possible. Thanks to the encouragement and support of Aberdeen Group management — Steven Gold, Andrew Boyd, and Vik Muiznieks — who understand the importance of our mission, and to Deb Casey, Joe Snowden, Marc Collura, and Dave Boynton.

A special thanks to Judith Tracy of the IBM Corporation who rallied vast resources to come to our aid. Thanks to other IBMers including Rich Lechner, Chris O'Connor, Cameron O'Connor, Vik Chandra, Chris Spaight, Jay Dietrich, Michael Hogan, Logan Scott, Wayne Balta, David Anderson, Roger Schmidt, Andy Wachs, Bola Oyedijo, Wendy, Kellogg, Jeff Hittner, Charles Jenkins, Lena Stark, Jane Snowden, Christopher Dittmer, Eva Lau, and Bill Neale.

Thanks to Brian Fry of Rackforce, Bob Houghton, Jim Mejia of Redemtech, Jim Regan, and Paul Vetter. Thanks to Brian Cowie of the CIT Paper Group, both for his contribution to this book and for what he's doing for sustainability.

Thanks to our friends at Cisco — Mark Leary, Lisbet Sherlock, and Neil Harris.

Thanks to Larry Vertal at AMD who has been involved since an early foray into green IT and who has cheered us on ever since. Thanks to Peter Doggart of Crossbeam.

Thanks to Sun Microsystems — Dave Douglas, Alex Dethier, Sebode Tafad, and Mark Monroe.

Thanks to Jose Iglesias, Mike Spink, Bruce Naegal, Caroline Dennington of Symantec, Will Layton of Copan Systems, Craig Nunes of 3PAR, Larry Cormier of LeftHand Networks, Stephen Yeo of iGel, and Christina Guilbert.

Our thanks to the folks at Wiley — Mary Bednarek, Amy Fandrei, and Becky Huehls.

Publisher's Acknowledgments

We're proud of this book; please send us your comments through our online registration form located at http://dummies.custhelp.com. For other comments, please contact our Customer Care Department within the U.S. at 877-762-2974, outside the U.S. at 317-572-3993, or fax 317-572-4002.

Some of the people who helped bring this book to market include the following:

Acquisitions, Editorial

Project Editor: Rebecca Huehls

Acquisitions Editor: Amy Fandrei

Copy Editors: Jen Riggs, Tonya Cupp

Technical Editor: Tom Raftery

Editorial Manager: Leah Cameron

Editorial Assistant: Amanda Foxworth

Sr. Editorial Assistant: Cherie Case

Cartoons: Rich Tennant
(www.the5thwave.com)

Composition Services

Project Coordinator: Patrick Redmond

Layout and Graphics: Samantha K. Allen, Carl Byers, Reuben W. Davis, Melissa K. Jester, Sarah Philippart

Proofreaders: Broccoli Information Mgt.

Indexer: Potomac Indexing, LLC

Special Help: Barry Childs-Helton, Susan Christopherson, Jodi Jensen

---

Publishing and Editorial for Technology Dummies

Richard Swadley, Vice President and Executive Group Publisher

Andy Cummings, Vice President and Publisher

Mary Bednarek, Executive Acquisitions Director

Mary C. Corder, Editorial Director

Publishing for Consumer Dummies

Diane Graves Steele, Vice President and Publisher

Composition Services

Debbie Stailey, Director of Composition Services

Contents at a Glance

Table of Contents

Introduction

●　●

*W*e have passion, conviction, urgency, and necessity. We know that most people don't understand what's in their power to change. Our explicit goal is to enable you to better understand the basic issues around green information technology (IT) and to equip you to take those initial steps. We were changed by writing this book and hope reading it changes you. Time is short; the subject desperately important.

Whether yours is a small organization trying to cut costs, a medium-size organization fighting for your survival in harsh economic times, or a larger organization face to face with power constraints and industry regulations, we hope this book will ground you with what you need to know and empower you to move forward. The folks we've met who've already begun this journey are passionate about what they're doing and proud of what they've done. Many of them are working overtime because they too feel the urgency.

Whether you're an IT manager, a C-level executive, a facilities/operations person, or just someone who wants to understand the implications of information technologies in consumption of power, in finding more efficient processes and cutting costs, and in impacting the planet, we hope you find this book useful.

About This Book

Information technology (IT) is an enormously complex field. It's amazing enough that your applications run, that people can actually use them to get their work done, and that your systems stay up 24 hours a day, 7 days a week, 365.25 days a year. Green considerations add another layer to that complexity and bring new disciplines that IT people normally don't study in depth. All most of us know about heating, ventilation, and air conditioning (HVAC), for example, is the phone number to call to alert facilities when the computer room gets too hot. We bring the basic information you need to find more efficient and environmentally responsible ways to meet your IT business goals and to leverage IT to move your entire organization in a greener direction. Green IT isn't just about energy efficiencies but also about operational efficiencies that can improve the whole of your IT.

Think of this book as a reference to the big picture of green IT. If you already have ideas about where you want to start your green IT initiatives, peruse the Table of Contents or take a gander at the Index and jump straight to your topics. You can of course read this book cover to cover, but chances are you'll pick and choose and come back to topics over time. It matters less where you start than that you start, and we wish you the best in your journey.

Conventions Used in This Book

We point out many useful resources on the Internet — we trust you've heard of it. In the text, Web addresses are shown in this typeface: www.dummies.com

Foolish Assumptions

We assume you have some connection with the IT world and that terms like server, processor, network, and desktop conjure up electronic meanings. We make no assumption about where you work or what your title is. IT and facilities managers may be the most direct audiences for this book, but anyone involved with an organization — for example, individual contributors, senior management, bean counters, analysts, and outside investors — will find this book valuable.

We also make no assumption about the size of your organization. Simply put, there is no business without IT. Where there's IT, IT can be greener. We provide steps to help every size organization. Some of what we cover applies to organizations with large, looming data centers, but we also provide help for humbler IT setups. Much of the foundational thinking needed to understand how to green your own environment applies to everyone.

Finally, we make no assumption about your politics. Some people have deep distrust of environmentalists; others think all corporations are evil planet destroyers. We're not here to point fingers at anyone. Most of the things we recommend in this book have tangible financial as well as environmental benefits.

How This Book Is Organized

We've divided this book into six sensible parts. Each is pretty much self-contained, so you can feel free to skip about.

Part I: Understanding the World of Green IT

In this part, we tell you what green IT is and why it's so important. We give you reasons and ways to get started as well as examples of real world organizations that have already embraced green strategies and are realizing the benefits.

Part II: Getting a Running Start

In this part, we describe standards and regulations that should inform your green thinking and suggest how to get a running start, such as assessing your current energy use and needs and putting together a plan.

Part III: Greening the Data Center

In many organizations, data centers are the largest consumers of energy. We discuss ways to make data centers more efficient, which often produce dramatic savings. We cover topics from ways to save energy in cooling your server, to reducing their number through virtualization, to improving storage and network management techniques.

Part IV: Greening the Office

IT presence in the office is both ubiquitous and diffuse. Here are lots of savings and resource use reductions to be had, such as using greener computers and monitors, reducing desktop energy waste, using less paper, and evaluating your green gadgetry.

Part V: Greening the Organization

IT can do more than reduce the environmental footprint of your operations. IT can help shrink the entire organization's carbon footprint and even help green the organization's business partners. In this part, we explain how you can do so by greening your facility, retiring electronics the green way, and establishing a virtual presence.

Part VI: The Part of Tens

If you've read other *For Dummies* books, you're no doubt familiar with The Part of Tens, which contains helpful lists with roughly ten useful suggestions. This part includes lists of organizations that can help you reach your green objectives, tips for computer recycling, and tips for a green home office.

Appendix

We've included a bunch of useful reference material, such as an appendix of consumption and savings worksheets, which can help you complete specific tasks in this book.

Icons Used in This Book

The Tip icon marks green suggestions that you can implement directly, such as "Turn out lights when rooms aren't in use."

Remember icons mark information that's especially important to know. To siphon the most important information in each chapter, skim through these icons. For example, "Computer room air conditioning can consume more power than all the electronics in your data center."

The Technical Stuff icon marks information of a highly technical nature that you can normally skip over, such as "Dew point isn't the same as wet bulb temperature."

The Warning icon tells you to watch out! It marks important information that may save you headaches. For example, "Check building and electrical codes before making major wiring changes."

Where to Go From Here

Where you land first in the book depends on your specific interest and involvement with green IT. If you're exploring its implications for your business so that you can plead the case to management, jump into Part I. But you might just need to understand the effects of greening IT on the data center you have to manage; if so, check out Part II. If you're responsible for the data center, take a look at Part III. If you make buying decisions around anything from computers to paper or are in charge of disposing of electronic equipment, Part IV can help. To read about creating a greener way to do business, see Part V.

Write to us and tell us about your "greening" experiences at `greenIT4d@ yahoo.com`. We want to keep growing and sharing what we find. We hope you'll help and wish you all the best on your journey.

Carol, Jeff, Arnold, and Jhana

Part I
Understanding the World of Green IT

The 5th Wave   By Rich Tennant

GREEN IT GAME PLAN

©RICHTENNANT

"Well, I suppose we should plan on getting rid of those coal burning servers."

In this part . . .

Green IT is getting a lot of attention. In this part, we tell you just what green IT is and why it's so important. We give you lots of reasons and ways to get started as well as lots of examples of real-world organizations that have already boldly embraced tangible green strategies and are already realizing the benefits.

Chapter 1

Win-Win Winning with Green IT

*G*reening IT won't be as painful as you might think. The information technology community has many straightforward opportunities to help solve problems affecting our environment just by doing what you do best — making informed choices and sound investments and using them to deploy quality solutions. These green choices and investments can save your organization money in the long run, and often in the short run as well.

You may have heard that meeting green needs in business requires sacrifice, belt tightening, and lost profits. These conditions may result when greening other business practices, but greening IT is different for two reasons:

✔ **IT suffers from inefficient practices:** We've been bad. In the rush to deploy the amazing advances in computing and communication, IT departments have adopted very inefficient practices. Simply put, they tend to throw hardware at every problem. The IBM Corporation estimates that for every 100 kilowatt-hours of electricity supplied by the power company to a typical data center, as few as 3 kilowatt-hours are actually doing productive work. The remaining energy is consumed by first powering and then cooling underused hardware.

Greening IT means finding better ways of storing and processing data, that recover much of that wasted energy. Cutting energy consumption, or at least slowing its growth, benefits the environment in many ways. And in many organizations, IT is the biggest single consumer of energy. So savings on the energy used in IT can have a big impact.

✔ **IT practices reach beyond department boundaries:** IT has the power to do more than simply green its own house. The influence of the technology that IT commands can help organizations find better ways to do business — reduce commuting and travel expenses, run buildings more efficiently, minimize the waste stream, and upgrade the supply chain.

Sustainability, corporate responsibility, and greening business practices have jumped from social movement to business imperative. Green IT is a dynamic, strategic, and ethical framework of practice for all IT. Green IT is about doing what it takes to be innovative, agile, efficient, responsive, profitable, and responsible all at the same time. Our goal is to help you bridge the gap between good green intentions and sustainable IT excellence.

In this chapter, we give you a big-picture look at going for green IT. In particular, we explain what we mean by the green IT ecosystem and show you all the areas that greening IT can positively impact — from energy and cost savings to better relationships with customers, business partners, and your organization's staff. You also find out quick ways to start green practices and basic green IT concepts that help you identify how to help your organization go green.

We're Talking to You

We admit it. The whole issue of green can be polarizing. But regardless of your views on environmental issues and global climate change, we know this book has something to offer you. Find yourself in the following list — or discover that your views fit with more than one depiction. In either case, find out that the topic of this book has aspects that are important to you whether you're

✔ **An environmental activist:** You're rearing to go. You want to make a difference. Feel free to skip the rest of this chapter and dive into the meatier parts, where we tell you good places to get started with your green IT initiatives. Or review the issues here to arm yourself for the inevitable discussion with less-committed colleagues.

✔ **An open-minded skeptic:** This chapter is especially informative for you. We try to make clear why global climate change and other environmental concerns are among the most pressing challenges of our time and why you — as an IT professional — are in an ideal place to help meet them.

✔ **A total disbeliever:** You're sure global climate change is a lot of tree-hugger baloney and no yellow-and-black *For Dummies* book is going to convince you otherwise. You're in business to make money, period. That's the only bottom line that matters. You might want to skip the rest of this chapter, too; it may only raise your blood pressure.

> *But consider this before you go:* Ignoring the ideas in the book will cost you money. Pretty much everything we talk about reduces expenses.

And like it or not, additional environmental regulations are coming. You can spend a lot of money at the last minute to meet them or you can get ahead of the curve by investing in green IT initiatives now. Do so, and your business will be ready — when the regulations come — to comply with minimal added expense. Let your competitors waste their time and money later, scrambling to comply. Green is good business.

Recognizing the Basic Green Concepts

Before you go too far, make sure you understand what we mean by green. Green is commonly used as shorthand for a group of related concerns:

✔ **Environmental responsibility:** The need to consider the well-being of the environment and protect the health, balance, and diversity of human and natural resources.

✔ **Global climate change:** A specific concern that human activity is contributing to a buildup of greenhouse gases in Earth's atmosphere that is slowly increasing the average temperature near Earth's surface.

✔ **Sustainable development:** Defined by the United Nations' Brundtland Commission as "development that meets the needs of the present without compromising the ability of future generations to meet their own needs." Much of the material and energy used to make things (you know, books, bikes, bags, boats, and billiard balls) comes from limited supplies of natural resources (such as paper from trees, aluminum and steel from ores, plastic from petroleum, and so on).

✔ **Corporate Responsibility (CR):** How businesses extend their sense of responsibility to consider the well-being of society and the environment with an understanding that global societal, environmental, and economic challenges are interrelated and that everyone depends upon one another for not only success but also survival.

Awareness of and worry over climate change, energy crises, rising energy costs, and the dangers of hazardous materials in society are growing. These issues have people, governments, and organizations of all types talking, and many are having a difficult time trying to figure out what to do about them.

With the advent of blogs, wikis, and social networks, organizations are increasingly under the eyes of (and subject to) the opinion of a world that's watching to make sure they're doing the *correct thing*. Remarkably few opinions can have a remarkably large impact when it comes to creating buzz — both positive and negative. So in a world where everyone's watching, you can't assume no one cares how your business comports itself.

Green and IT — A Good Fit

Information Technology — IT — is the central nervous system not only of our businesses, but also of our governmental and social infrastructure. In fact, IT connects the globe. Records are computerized, traffic is controlled, and paychecks are issued, all courtesy of IT. In many parts of the world, completing daily activities (such as writing e-mail for work or doing research) and conducting daily business (such as running a retail store) depend entirely on IT. IT depends on electricity, and available electricity is finite. As IT continues to grow, we depend more on it. Its unchecked consumption of power is threatening the financial resources of the organizations it serves, and, quite literally, is putting an ultimately unsustainable burden on the earth.

We must find a way to green IT. Industry leaders recognize this fact — look at IBM, Cisco, Sun Microsystems, APC, HP, Dell, and EMC. These companies are continuously examining and improving their own practices to make themselves green. They create products that are more environmentally friendly and energy efficient for their customers, as well as work collaboratively with organizations like The Green Grid, which focuses on helping the IT industry address energy use. (See the sidebar "Meet The Green Grid," later in this chapter.) But you can't throw a switch and suddenly be green. *Going green* is indeed a process and just the beginning of the efforts required for true sustainability. Still, going green may also be the shortest route to economic savings and the overall health of an organization.

While the greening of IT is being driven by a demand for energy conservation as well as an increased awareness of conservation's impact on the planet, going green is often complicated by real business circumstances. That is, organizations' green efforts are commonly challenged by inefficient legacy business practices, ever-tightening budgets, and no process for measuring or tracking performance.

At the end of the day — ready or not — clients, customers, peers, employees, bosses, governments, watchdog organizations, and your own facilities and operations management will be demanding that IT go green. And here's the good news: Several factors put IT in an excellent position to contribute:

✔ **IT uses a lot of resources.** In many organizations, IT is the biggest consumer of electricity. Efficiency improvements have a real impact.

✔ **IT turns over its equipment every 3-5 years.** Capital equipment in other departments lasts much longer, so greening new investment can require decades to take hold. Not so in IT.

✔ **Technology is IT's second name.** IT folks know how to navigate complex technical criteria and make informed decisions. Green is just one more factor to consider.

✔ **What IT *does* is inherently green.** Data is nonpolluting, in and of itself. Virtual travel — and the accompanying virtual meetings, virtual client visits, and so on — takes relatively little energy. The right-of-way for an information superhighway is a very narrow trench that can be covered back over with grass. Along the way, however, we need to remember the enormous energy being consumed by IT — on a par with the airline industry. Studies being done to measure the weight of Internet searches and the impact of sending data back and forth will show that IT is not carbon neutral.

We address green data storage in Chapter 11, later in this book

As IT professionals, your responsibilities and opportunities grow under green. Your networks are in the right place at the right time. IT does more than just deliver YouTube videos and Facebook profiles around the office. IT can sense temperature, humidity, and air flow, and use that data to tune the building's mechanical systems for optimal performance. IT can open and close shades to take advantage of passive solar heating. IT can adjust non-critical power demands to follow the output variation of alternative power sources such as wind and *photovoltaics* (what most folks think of as solar energy).

Embracing Trendy Hooey

For a long time, green considerations have been categorized as faddish and not having real business merit. Much of what we talk about in this book has direct, budget-stretching benefits. But going green affects more than your company's financial statement. For most organizations — including for-profit, not-for-profit, and government — few things are more important than public perception, trust, and reputation — summed up as *brand value.*

Instituting and promoting a credible green program enhances your brand and can help heal brand damage caused by past environmental neglect.

Looking beyond cost savings

Just looking at the economics of going green — saving a lot of money by being more energy efficient, increasing efficiency in your business processes, and improving people- and IT-assets management — would never be called hooey.

In addition to reducing costs, good green IT practice can also do such things as

- Reduce and optimize energy use
- Increase efficiency, performance, and lifespan of hardware, applications, and other assets
- Reduce the amount of hardware needed
- Increase workforce efficiency and performance
- Reduce floor space in the data center
- Reduce air conditioning needs
- Reduce carbon/greenhouse gas emissions and environmental pollution
- Reduce the need for additional facilities
- Reduce risk and liability
- Reduce exposure to deadly toxins and hazardous materials from e-waste by emphasizing reuse, recycling, and biodegradability
- Deliver technological aids to those who need it through donation and reuse programs
- Enable collaboration and increased productivity
- Inspire and motivate people
- Improve work-life balance

This holistic approach to responsible and highly efficient IT practice is what distinguishes green, sustainability, and corporate responsibility from just plain cost cutting and performance optimization. Green IT-focused organizations define value and success through a greener, cleaner lens that considers its impact on society and the Earth in addition to its positive impact on profit and organizational productivity.

Getting the good will of partners, customers, and employees

Jhana, Jeff, and Carol work for a research firm. We have evidence from the research we've done that consumers (and businesses) would prefer to spend their money with companies doing their part to address green matters, and that employees prefer to work for such companies. All constituencies contribute positively to the organization's brand:

- **Business partners:** Responsible companies are looking to partner with other responsible companies in creating their own *green value chain* — choosing green suppliers and business partners interested in creating a sustainable world.

- **Customers:** Brand preference is all about giving buyers *reasons* to buy from you. Establishing your business's green efforts and creating an environment of transparency can be one of those reasons.

- **Employees:** For organizations interested in recruiting and retaining top talent, the commitment to corporate responsibility is proving a big draw. Your organization's future depends on its ability to attract new talent to its workforce. Young people today are keenly aware of environmental challenges. Surveys show that the best college graduates prefer to work for firms where they can contribute to green action or at least be part of a team that is moving in the green direction. One survey found that college grads would accept a $13,000 lower starting salary to work in such an organization. The recruiting potential of a strong green program is a real competitive advantage.

Focusing on the triple bottom line

More and more, governments are looking at ways to reduce carbon emissions and energy usage. The ability to reduce energy consumption with its rising costs while simultaneously increasing efficiency is music to the ears of any organization.

Green IT doesn't focus only on *the* bottom line. Instead, it involves commitment to a *triple bottom line* — a way of measuring organizational success by how positively these initiatives impact *people, profit,* and the *planet.*

You're no doubt familiar with the term *win-win.* Win-win replaced *win-lose* when somebody figured out that you can actually come up with solutions that benefit both sides of a scenario. When it comes to green, we take it one step further. With green you have the possibility of a *win-win-win* scenario where three constituencies, often pitted against one another, can all win.

Too often being green is seen as too costly for business. What people want is thought to be at odds with what's good for the planet. Yet with green IT, all three — people, profit, and the planet — stand to gain, a veritable win for the triple bottom line. The triple bottom line speaks to a win for the business (economic), a win for society (social), and a win for the environment.

Think about how the benefits of greening IT (and your organization as a whole) reflects a culture of corporate responsibility — the triple bottom line — as follows:

- ✔ **We the people:** As organizations become more responsible and efficient, they reap the rewards of better relationships and reputations. Organizations report that they improved their stakeholder, client, and community relations, which in turn, increased the loyalty and satisfaction of clients and employees alike.

  Employees often say that organization-wide communication, collaboration, and innovation have improved as a result of their sustainability initiatives. Every time we talk to folks within organizations whose jobs focus on green, they tell us how great they feel about what they're doing and how important it is.

- ✔ **Planet Earth:** Greening IT helps reduce emissions and pollution levels with the reduction of energy consumption and a shift to cleaner renewable energy. In addition, greener IT also contributes to a reduction in toxic landfill waste by encouraging recycle and reuse programs as well as the production of biodegradable components. Green IT's focus on overall efficiency in material use — and a getting away from the planned obsolescence (for which the tech world is famous) — further supports a responsible approach to IT by reducing environmental impact.

- ✔ **Greener profit:** Not only are organizations able to dramatically lower their energy costs, boost overall efficiency, avoid major disruptions, and optimize the longevity and functioning of costly assets, but they also become preferred tech providers, develop innovative solutions and services, and increase market share.

  With all the environmental regulations already in place (or coming soon), keeping ahead of changing mandates allows organizations to focus on reducing risk, liability, taxes, and penalties. All of these benefits improve competitive advantage, enhance brand value and reputation, and contribute to an effective collaboration and communication strategy within and outside the organization.

Greening the IT Ecosystem

An *environmental ecosystem* refers to the way living organisms are inter-related and codependent on one another and the entire physical complex of the environment. The IT ecosystem includes networks, the Web, and an interconnected and dynamic relationship map that shows how various components influence and impact other components.

The *green IT ecosystem* represents a way of thinking holistically about what, how, and why IT operates — and about who and what their operations impact. The components of the IT ecosystem include

- **All computer hardware, software, and networks** used inside an organization

- **Management strategy** responsible for purchasing, implementing, running, and disposing of or donating hardware when no longer needed

- **The people and organizational culture** that makes all the infrastructure and activities in the preceding bullets possible

- **The systems and networks** that connect with the organization's suppliers, customers, and partners

IT's conspicuous consumption

In case you're not convinced of the green concerns around IT, consider these facts:

- Current data-center energy bills total more than $7 billion a year and are rising sharply.

- Information Technology energy demand is growing 12 times faster than the overall demand for energy.

- In typical data centers, each 100 units of energy production drives (on average) only 3 units of productive computing.

- Data centers consumed 180 billion kWh in 2007 and will double in the next three years or so.

- Data centers emit over 150 metric tons of CO_2 per year, and the volume is increasing rapidly. (As a point of reference, a car produces 18 pounds of CO_2 for every gallon of gasoline it uses.)

- Governments worldwide are moving to enact legislation to track and limit carbon emissions.

- According to the United Nations Environment Programme (UNEP — www.unep.org), humans discard 20 to 50 million metric tons of computer-related equipment — e-waste — worldwide each year, which represents 5 percent of all municipal solid waste.

- Additional toxins, hazardous materials, and e-waste are generated to make IT products.

- By 2010, there's the potential for one billion computers worth of e-waste.

You need to figure out how to look at the IT ecosystem through those rather snazzy green glasses because IT has a big impact on the environment, your organization's profitability, and society (including you). The goal of this book is to help you figure out how you can make effective changes to your organization's IT both for your organization's own goals and to do your part in helping to lead the IT industry into a greener, healthier, and more efficient world.

A Perfect Storm: Why Green IT Now

Many pressures drive the greening of the IT ecosystem but the main elements can be boiled down to the political, economic, and societal. Organizations and individuals decide to be more responsible, sustainable, or green for different reasons. Instead of getting caught up in the deeper motivations, we simply explain why creating a green IT ecosystem offers a path that creates a win-win-win situation for organizations, society, and the environment.

As organizations focus more on understanding their challenges in going green, IT managers will likely be required to understand the scope of the overall issues and come up with a vision and a strategy to address them.

Knowing the green business drivers

For many organizations, going green is exclusively about the explicit business drivers such as cutting costs or reducing power requirements.

- ✔ **Energy costs:** IT gobbles energy and greening IT can dramatically reduce energy costs. According to the Global e-Sustainability Initiative (GeSI — www.gesi.org), the IT industry could save global industry $800 billion dollars in energy costs by 2020.

- ✔ **Energy availability:** In some locations, the borough of Manhattan in New Your City, for example, new power feeds are difficult or impossible to obtain. The efficiencies inherent in Green IT can delay or avoid the need to expand data operations and move them to remote locations.

- ✔ **Equipment costs:** Greening IT optimizes business processes by consolidating servers and storage, which often results in needing less equipment.

- ✔ **Data center costs:** Current trends show data center capacity needing to double every five years. Greener IT can slow the need for expansion as well as reduce the demand for floor and rack space and air conditioning.

✔ **Business process optimization:** Optimizing business processes including supply chain management represents a huge opportunity for managing carbon emissions with such solutions as shipping logistics planning, among others.

✔ **Performance and efficiency:** Many of the steps you take toward green yield a more efficient, better performing IT. Go figure.

Recognizing environmental drivers

Carbon dioxide is one of the major human-generated greenhouse gases that Intergovernmental Panel on Climate Change (IPCC) has concluded is very likely responsible for observed increases in temperature over the last 60 years. Additional temperature increases — with serious consequences for the environment — are projected over the next century if we don't reduce greenhouse gas emissions. The United States is a huge producer of green house gases, and levels of carbon emissions from emerging markets like China and India are accelerating.

In addition, discarded electrical components and electronics (to be distinguished from recyclable units which, properly handled, are considered a commodity) become *e-waste*. You can find the mountains of e-waste that are being disassembled and picked over — at high risk to the pickers — after being dumped in places like China, India, and Nigeria.

IT departments need to take these environmental drivers into account and consider the following when devising green IT strategies:

✔ **Carbon emissions:** In the U.S., coal provides more than 50 percent of our electrical power. A single office desktop computer and display might consume at least 100 watts of power per hour, or 2.4 kW-hours per day, when left on continuously. The coal needed to generate just that much energy 24 hours a day for a year is about 714 pounds. And burning that much coal releases, on average, 5 pounds of sulfur dioxide, 5.1 pounds of nitrogen oxides, and 1,852 pounds — almost a ton — of carbon dioxide. One little computer.

While IT generates tons of carbon, it can save even more tons. For example, transportation accounts for almost a quarter of human carbon dioxide emissions worldwide, and more than a third of that comes from North America. IT can reduce the need for transportation by replacing business travel and daily commuting with telepresence and telework (see Chapter 20).

✔ **E-Waste:** E-waste is filled with hazardous materials like cadmium, mercury, lead, carcinogenic PCBs (polychlorinated biphenyls), and many elements that are not biodegradable and can leach into water and soil. For more about e-waste and efforts to address it, checkout the Basel Action Network, www.ban.org, a global organization focusing on addressing the horrific impacts of e-waste, including the unscrupulous dumping of toxic waste on the world's poorest peoples. Find out more about dealing with e-waste in Chapter 19.

Feeling the governmental pressures

Government and advocacy groups around the globe are grappling with environmental concerns. Some governments are ahead of others in enacting laws and regulations. But it's one world, after all, and legislation passed on one region impacts others as businesses reach across borders.

Registration, Evaluation, Authorization, and Restriction of Chemicals (REACH)

In December of 2006, the European Union enacted, EC/2006/1907, the Registration, Evaluation, Authorization, and Restriction of Chemicals regulation, which addresses the impact of various chemical substances (including a subcategory called SVHCs, or Substances of Very High Concern) on human health and the environment. In force since 2007, REACH will be implemented in phases through 2017.

Any organization importing certain chemicals or articles containing the chemical substances into the EU in amounts of more than one *tonne* (a metric ton) per year must register them with the European Chemicals Agency. (Check out the ECA's Web site at http://echa.europa.eu/reach_ en.asp for more about REACH.)

Failure to register the restricted imports will result in being closed out of the market (in REACH-speak, "no data, no market"). Continued use or import without authorization is illegal. REACH is considered one of the strictest regulations given its impact on the way that manufacturers, retailers, and IT organizations do business and function day-to-day.

RoHS

The European Directive on the Restriction of the Use of Certain Hazardous Substances in Electrical and Electronic Equipment 2002/95/EC — usually known as the Restriction of Hazardous Substances directive (RoHS, often pronounced: *roh hahs*) — is a subset of WEEE. This European directive, covering Waste Electrical and Electronic Equipment and its disposal, includes restrictions on the use of certain hazardous substances in electrical and electronic equipment.

RoHS focuses on the beginning and middle of the electrical and electronic life-cycle by defining what shouldn't go into the components being made and repaired. Since July 2006, most equipment containing components with these hazardous substances can no longer be sold in Europe. For more on RoHS check out Chapter 4 and `http://www.rohs.eu/english/index.html`.

Cap and Trade Legislation

Cap and Trade, or *emissions trading,* refers to a centralized strategy to control and reduce carbon emissions by limiting or capping the total amount of greenhouse gases that an entity can emit. Entities have credits, which reflect the total amount of carbon they can emit. Low emitters may sell their credits to those who go over their allotted allowance. This method of charging offenders for pollution begins with designating a value per tonne of carbon emitted (tC).

The trade in carbon credits provides financial incentives for organizations to lower emissions while working toward the goal of reducing overall emissions to the capped total. It also induces organizations to improve conditions in the developing world by encouraging investment in projects that earn them credits.

Cap and trade legislation will likely drive up the cost of energy, and carbon-free energy sources such as wind, solar, hydro, and nuclear power will become more attractive. When the single biggest cost of the data center is the electrical bill, you can bet that cap and trade will affect data center operations. When deciding where to build a new data center, IT managers will need to carefully consider the cost and availability of power. Also, if organizations with green initiatives can earn carbon credits, greening IT could prove important in a landscape eager to trade.

Staying the Course: The Do's and One Don't of Going Green

Going green isn't new — some folks have been working at it for decades. In this section, we share some specifics from their efforts with the hope that you can learn from their experience.

Do remember the big picture

Greening IT is about more than data center efficiencies and cost reductions. Greening IT requires a comprehensive look at areas of the organization that typically may not be considered part of IT. For example, you should consider where and how people work (workspace and work hours) as well as the systems they work on.

Organizations need to understand the impact of not only their own behaviors, but also the impact of the behaviors and conditions of their extended network of partners. Consider how the whole ecosystem works together: infrastructure, facilities, applications, networks, processes, employees, partners, suppliers, purchasing, reuse, and end-of-life management. Getting your green vision and strategy right require a holistic, innovative, and responsible approach.

Do have a champion and a team leader

A lot of people will have good ideas about the strategies and processes for going green, but nothing's likely to happen without sanction and direction from above. Your organization's green mandate must be clear. You'll probably work collaboratively — in a cross-department, cross-functional team — to arrive at that mandate, but strive to get your organization's direction clear and empowered to make real change.

Having an executive champion for green initiatives is important, but establishing a cross-functional team that works collaboratively is probably better. Green and sustainability shouldn't be lead from the top, but visible executive support is critical. So give your executive champion the support that teams need to accomplish your organization's goals.

Do measure so you can manage

The success of greening IT depends on being able to quantify and demonstrate improvement. This process, known as *performance management,* not only enables visibility into progress and challenges, but also helps uncover areas of opportunity.

Follow these general steps to set up a system for managing the performance of your green initiatives:

1. **Determine the metrics most meaningful to your green initiative.**

   For example, you may be most interested in energy usage, system uptime, energy cost, miles of business travel, and so on.

2. **Measure your current, pre-green levels to establish a baseline.**

   Taking these baseline measurements helps you understand where you are and serves as a comparison point for monitoring progress.

3. **Set performance goals for your chosen metrics and establish a process for tracking and measuring against the baseline measurements.**

4. **Track and communicate about your progress and further challenges.**

   Use the tracked results to evaluate the success of your green initiatives and make adjustments as needed.

Successful green IT programs require a team effort. Recognize achievements at the department or team level, and, if possible, consider incentives that can work to spur friendly competition and innovation that support the greening process.

Do talk about it!

We can't overemphasize the power and importance of communication. Leverage newsletters, calls, and social networking platforms to catalyze collaboration and communication.

Organizations can create a shared sense of purpose and achievement when there is a regular flow of communication around green agendas. Consider these points when you establish communications processes to use in conjunction with greening IT:

✔ Keep communication positive and productive and remember that good ideas can come from all levels of the organization. Collaboration within and beyond your typical organizational borders will stimulate innovation and creativity.

✔ Discussing progress and challenges with internal stakeholders monthly is a great way to share best practices and maintain momentum for green initiatives.

✔ Communicating regularly with external stakeholders, clients, peers, and others helps generate good ideas, connection, and enthusiasm for the organizational goals. Thought-leading organizations are looked to by their peers and even by those in other sectors for inspiration and best practices.

Do remember the community

Green IT initiatives benefit the environment and the bottom line, but they also should have sustained benefits for the organization's community at large. Encourage connecting the skills, interests, and goals of the organization to the needs, goals, and interests of the local and global community by supporting volunteer and philanthropic activities of your colleagues, company, and partners. Find schools, programs, and nonprofits to which you can donate materials, technology, expertise, funds, and time. If your organization changes computer equipment constantly or can extend connectivity or training, find a project in need and collaborate.

There's a need for philanthropy but there's a greater need for organizations to see that they are, in fact, members of a community and that prosperity and value comes from shared success and genuine, not generous, engagement. Investment in communities near and far is an investment in the long term and sustainable societal *and* business ecosystem.

Green IT is just as much about changing an organization's culture as it is about changing its technology and operational processes. This refocusing on the people who make green IT practices happen means never forgetting that people — not products — are at the center of the IT ecosystem.

Investigate effective and, ideally, fun ways to get your employees engaged, trained, and supported in the effort to go green. Involve them in cross-functional, collaborative exercises that encourage creative, innovative, and proactive problem solving. Once you have a critical mass of your people *thinking* green, adopting greener processes is far easier.

Along with copious communications about your green IT efforts, encourage collaboration internally and externally, with partners, peers, and even with groups from other sectors. Collaboration not only improves visibility of what is happening, but it also allows agility and innovation as it better connects with stakeholders and allies.

Don't tell green lies!

With all the green hype, many people get cynical about green initiatives. With so much pressure to go green and so much confusion about what that even means, it's no surprise that organizations can get demoralized before an initiative even gets started, let alone when it runs into challenges along the way.

Avoid telling green lies:

✓ **Tell the truth about your green commitment:** Communicate that greening the IT ecosystem will be a constantly evolving process that needs to be regularly re-evaluated and adjusted. Remember that going green is an ongoing journey toward the larger journey of sustainability.

✓ **Tell the truth about your methods:** Your organization needs to be *transparent* — not hiding nefarious processes. No organization is perfect. Your organization can best avoid being slapped with a *green washing* label (just pretending to be green) if it makes genuine efforts to increase visibility into and take responsibility for its actions, products, and services.

✔ **Tell the truth about your green results:** Don't overstate successes or downplay challenges and areas that need improvement. Like it or not, what organizations do and don't do is extremely visible to the rest of the world with information on the Web, traditional news outlets, and employees, partners, suppliers, and customers talking.

Work hard at going green, but try not to take yourselves too seriously.

What to Green Now and Later

Although the rising green tide of corporate responsibility is driven by complex factors, the greening of IT happens in ways we expect — increasing energy efficiency in the data center, for example — and in ways we might not expect — reusing and purchasing IT equipment with a mind to safety and recyclability. The greening of IT is an ongoing *process*, an approach, and a mode of operating; it is not a destination. Using this approach, you do the best you can with the resources you have, and you make adjustments as information, budgets, capabilities, and priorities change.

The greening of IT is a *process* that includes educating people, framing your visions and decisions, and adopting a set of practices and technologies, in a way that has *genuine* and *concrete* positive outcomes to your organization, society, and the environment. From data centers and desktops to telecommuting and from Web collaborating to donating old equipment, greener IT will positively impact practically every aspect of your organization, as well as society at large.

The ongoing green process involves continuous learning, adjustment, and improvement. A boat load of low-hanging fruit in IT will quickly get you on your way to being greener. Some things are as simple as increasing awareness and changing little behaviors — adjustments that are pretty easy to implement:

✔ Turning off things such as your monitor and printer.

✔ Weeding out low- or nonperforming components (for example, applications that nobody really uses but are running on servers anyway).

✔ Plugging holes in the data center — such as mixing cold and hot air — that make your cooling units work harder.

✔ Selecting hardware products according to energy-efficient criteria; look for Energy Star ratings, for example, where they apply.

These easy-to-green things are what plain old good IT management should recognize, but they're often missed. This book covers both the easy fixes you can do immediately as well as initiatives that take careful planning and roll out over time. We give you concrete places to start your green IT journey in Chapter 6.

Evaluating your starting point

Getting your green journey under way isn't difficult and doesn't even have to cost a thing before you start seeing great benefits. Going green is about adopting responsible frameworks for the often complex, dynamic practices and objectives for the long haul — not chasing some green myth of perfection.

The easiest way to start doing something green is to increase your awareness of how your current practices *aren't* green and identify ways to decrease the negative impact and wasteful actions. Finding out how businesses, individuals, and groups of committed people can impact the world for the better is an important element to green IT success. If people feel that their non-green situation is too far gone or too overwhelming, they may have difficulty committing to the longer journey.

Communicating a can-do green attitude

Though the green IT story is about more than energy efficiency, it is still a central theme of any organization's green agenda. By getting a handle on your power consumption, you can really pack a wallop on your organization's carbon footprint. The green IT initiative can drive a great number of benefits to the organization as a whole by helping it become less wasteful and more mindful of energy usage. IT can empower its people by educating them on the power of simple changes in attitude and behavior.

Remember to do the following when scoping out your green IT program:

✔ **Make it visionary and clear:** Connect your immediate, measurable goals to the overall values of green, sustainability, and corporate responsibility. Don't treat green initiatives as marketing ploys or philanthropy. Articulate clear goals and standards for the organization.

✔ **Make it comprehensive:** Get beyond the data center to include other key elements of the IT ecosystem, such as applications that support digital information exchange to reduce paper. Take a lifecycle approach to the organization to examine what your organization buys, how you use your IT equipment as well as your building facilities, and how you dispose of waste. Make sure that everyday practices and policies support the transformation into a more sustainability-driven organization. Greening your organization can't be a separate, ad-hoc program.

✔ **Build bridges:** For a successful sustainability agenda to take effect, make sure that separate functions like design, purchasing, IT, finance, and the supply chain start working together and are visible in each other's activities. By basing green success on a foundation of communication and collaboration, organizations are more responsive to changing needs.

✔ **Push for an executive champion**: Adopting sustainability and corporate responsibility is best undertaken with a top-level supporter who can oversee a cross-functional team. An executive champion can ensure the communication, coordination, implementation, and effective performance tracking and sharing of the best practices of your green initiatives.

Greening office culture

People are the central expression and driving force of any complex initiative, and this is especially true of greening your IT. Successful initiatives engage an organization's stakeholders and partners and elicit commitment. The simplest way to get that passion and engagement is by talking to people and getting them talking about what they care about and what they don't care about. Stakeholders may want to go green for diverse reasons:

✔ Worry over the climate and environmental activism

✔ Need to lower costs because their work performance is judged by budget management

✔ Desire to feel good about their workplace and its efforts to lessen its societal impact

✔ The challenge of catalyzing innovation to build competitive advantage

✔ Wish to improve the work experience by focusing on the efficiency of its technology and daily processes

✔ Concern about national security and energy independence

Knowing context, and understanding where people come from, will help you craft your green mission in language that resonates with the passions and goals of your greatest resource: your people.

Plucking the low-hanging fruit

You have the energy and engagement to implement the vision. Now what? Post-prioritizing is a great time to see exactly where you are in the game. It's not very useful to say you're more energy efficient if you have no idea how energy inefficient you were before.

Vague ideas of progress can stymie real progress and so establishing a performance baseline is the first and most important step at the outset of any sustainability initiative.

✔ **Look around at your technology.** Know what equipment and products you have. Read their labels and spec sheets to determine any certifications they may have, such as the EPA's Energy Star. This assessment helps determine an action plan and responsible framework for planned purchases and coming equipment retirements. Energy-efficient choices often exist for most budgets.

✔ **Find out what your energy costs are.** Get as granular as you can to understand how much energy your organization uses and, if possible, by which offices and facilities. Perhaps the utility company or facility managers can help you figure out energy usage patterns? Set up a team to examine power usage habits:

- Do people typically leave computers turned on when they're away for extended periods?

- Are computers at the most energy-efficient settings possible? Are unneeded processes running? Are the screens at maximum brightness; do they really need to be?

- Are power strips left filled with chargers and other unused devices? Can they be turned off?

- How much natural light can you take advantage of? Which offices, rooms, or areas could have the lights turned off until needed?

- Are you using energy-efficient lighting? See Chapter 17 for simple ways to identify lighting types.

If you can't get access to real costs, estimate with the help of online tools — many of them free — to get a rough sense of what x number of servers or computers running x number of hours might be costing in your region. Do any organizations or university research units offer free support to companies trying to be more responsible?

✔ **Find out what you're wasting beyond power.** Look around offices and visit your organization's waste-collection area. What's the situation with recycling, and what percentage of paper is wasted? Speak to people and observe the norm regarding paper, copies, and prints. (How often are printed items not retrieved? How regularly is email unnecessarily printed? Do people print on both sides of the paper? What other items could be recycled?) If your organization pays to carry away trash, see if you can get a sense of the costs and patterns of your waste habits and raise awareness there as well.

✔ **Investigate your company's policies for business travel and daily commuting.** Is all the business travel necessary? Can your company support work from home? Figure out how much energy and productive time could be saved by allowing more virtual meetings and telework initiatives. How much could be saved by more efficient use of office space and resources?

✔ **Consider putting green queries into your RFP/RFI process.** Reach out to your partners and ask them to tell you what their organization is doing to be more responsible. Seek support and best practices from your peers, and even from other industries. A great deal of information is available online and from U.S. government sources like the EPA and Department of Energy. If your organization has a transport or logistics component, consider responsible programs like the EPA's SmartWay.

✔ **Understand which processes can be paperless and explore which documents can be digitized.** One quick way to jumpstart a paperless office is to make any organizational forms and guidelines available online. Get the organization off of junk mail lists. Review your office supply choices. What amount purchased is made of recycled content? Work on improving the ratio. There are great Web sites for greener office products:

`www.thegreenoffice.com`

`www.quill.com`

`www.dolphinblue.com`

Knowing where you stand will help you set real goals and track performance. You make an impact simply by making people aware of their own behavior on energy and waste; that awareness can alter organizational culture. Done right, people will not only shut off lights and equipment as second nature but often start to suggest other innovative ways to save energy, money, and the environment — both at work and at home. Organizations of all types have reported that as work behavior becomes more thoughtful, so does home behavior, reducing costs and increasing efficiency there as well.

Many areas are prime for immediate greening — even with little or no budget to speak of. Make eliminating waste a central tenant of your first green year. See Chapter 6 for details on establishing baseline and an action plan for the next 12 months.

Cultivating green education and communication

Once you've established your baselines and objectives, and cross-functional teams are collaborating across the organization, you need an action plan that individuals at every level can implement. You'll need to spark some serious awareness raising, education, and goal setting with your stakeholders and partners:

✔ Institute education plans about overall vision, goals, and steps for the entire organization as well as role-specific guidelines for excellence.

✔ Set clear standards of where the organization is trying to go and appoint performance standards and metrics for individuals and departments to be measured against.

✔ Create incentives for leadership and innovation in the form of bonuses and recognitions.

✔ Start a company e-newsletter to report progress and challenges on a regular basis. Allow social networking and Web capabilities to help your stakeholders connect and inspire one another. Encourage innovation and creativity perhaps through blogs.

Innovating through the supply chain

Much like IT, the supply chain represents a bounty of quick green wins. What is a supply chain, you ask? A *supply chain* is the network of suppliers (the organizations that supply the things — goods or services or people — that another organization needs) and trading partners with whom an organization works to find raw materials; buy, make, and transport products; or deliver services. It includes all the resources, people, facilities, companies, and distribution hubs involved directly and indirectly in production. Supply chains are often complex, layered, and global, making them more supply *networks*.

Organizations embracing sustainability are looking for more responsible suppliers and partners. The greener supply chain's positive impact on IT assets, infrastructure, efficiency, business processes, opportunities, and costs are exponentially felt across a more integrated, efficient, and collaborative organization. From virtualized servers and desktops, to energy-efficient products and processes and recyclable components, greening the supply chain delivers a bevy of efficiencies and opportunities for the entire organization.

Sustainable supply chains offer many opportunities for increased materials efficiency, which result in:

✔ **Reduced waste:** Moving to paperless processes across the organization facilitates data sharing, integration, and storage; it also reduces an incredible amount of waste going into landfills. It also frees up office space that would otherwise store all that paper.

✔ **Energy savings:** What you do as an organization counts and as a result, more requests for proposals (RFPs) and requests for information (RFIs) include questions on a potential partner's environmental or social performance in addition to its ability to deliver products, solutions, or services in an efficient and cost-effective manner.

✔ **Increased productivity:** Sustainable supply chains positively impact the entire organization because greener choices in the purchasing of materials, services, and products create benefits in every other phase of asset and material implementation, use, management, and retirement. Furthermore, sustainability-driven supply chains are more resilient, less risky, more agile, and more responsive to their clients and partners.

✔ **Improved planning and demand management:** Providing operations management within the supply chain gives more insight and visibility in business processes as they impact the environment, thus allowing you to make more eco-conscious day-to-day decisions. Using carbon trade-off modeling for transportation planning and routing allow you to choose the lowest carbon-emitting mode of travel within the constraints of the service-level agreement.

✔ **More effective collaboration:** An enhanced logistics network can more easily get and distribute materials and products to the right places at the right time and in the right amounts. More efficient planning helps reduce transport costs, and allows for better usage of space.

✔ **Improved storage, handling, and recovery:** Avoiding hazardous materials whenever possible also helps lower:

- Training and handling costs associated with their use

- Costs associated with their storage and disposal

- Specialized materials tracking and reporting requirements

By shifting from hazardous materials purchasing to hazardous materials services, companies can partner with other organizations that can source, deliver, track, and dispose of the materials in an efficient and responsible manner.

Meet The Green Grid

The Green Grid (www.thegreengrid.org) is an organization of some 200 member companies taking a leadership role in helping IT users improve energy efficiency in business computing environments, including but not limited to data centers. The Green Grid is actively creating models and metrics, measurement methods, best practices, and processes to work in conjunction with related developing standards. Continuously working to improve all these areas across the globe, The Green Grid collaborates with government organizations, IT end users, and others to ensure that their recommendations align with policies and real-world environments. Throughout this book, we reference their work. We encourage you check out their work because they can help you enormously as you try to figure out how to contend with your own IT energy concerns.

We spoke with two directors of The Green Grid, John Tuccillo and Roger Tipley. John Tuccillo is a Director of The Green Grid and serves as Vice

(continued)

(continued)

President of Global Industry and Legislative Initiatives at American Power Conversion Corp. (APC). He's responsible for building collaborative technology and business alliances with key industry leaders as well as with policy and standards bodies. Roger is a director of The Green Grid and is an engineering strategist in HP's Enterprise Storage and Servers business unit where he has spent the last several years working on technologies to manage power consumption and improve energy efficiency. Their company loyalties on the back burner, they shared their experiences of their involvement with The Green Grid.

Carol: When and how did The Green Grid get started?

John: The Green Grid's official start was on January 16, 2007, but its founders had been working for six or eight months before then to draft bylaws, formalize the varied processes we work within, and structure the organization. With a focus on improving energy efficiency in data centers, we recognize that there are regional aspects that come into play, such as various power transmission architectures, different climates, different geographies, and different geopolitical regulations. We're working to incorporate these nuances through our expansions in EMEA (Europe, the Middle East, and Africa) and Japan.

The Green Grid formed an advisory council made up exclusively of members from the end-user community. Its objective is to stay true to the mission to improve energy efficiency for the end user. They offer feedback and contribute to validating what we're seeing.

We're always accepting new members, especially folks who want to focus on the committee work. We don't have an aggressive market program. One of the benefits of membership is that you get the fruits of our work sooner than the general public. We give everything we do away, but members get an advance view and an opportunity to comment as they see the work in progress.

Carol: How did you get involved? Why is this important to you?

Roger: Well, it was about the time one of my customers complained that I'd just sold him a $10 million server because he didn't have room for one more server and that one more server meant building a new data center.

As an industry, we had a problem. We had no standardization on how things were being measured. About 4 years ago, my research team could no longer fill racks. We couldn't cool them. Our growth depended on figuring out a compelling solution. We had to figure out cooling solutions, and we had to understand how to handle IT load even as more energy was needed.

John: Part of our charter is to promote, essentially giving away the work of The Green Grid. We recognized the need to create a lexicon and a series of metrics around energy efficiency so we have a common way to measure and understand what energy efficiency is and how to make improvements. The intention wasn't so much to create competition among folks measuring for PUE (power usage effectiveness) or DCiE (Data Center infrastructure Efficiency) but to create a method for self-improvement and general industry awareness. Over the last 18 months, things have started to accelerate. Giving people tools is an important first step. Although there's certainly been no shortage of entities touting their *greenness,* we've been focused on creating deliverables, which would be useful, measurable, and supported by credible science, which has been vetted across more than 200 member companies. We focused on deliverables — how to help folks identify where to start.

We spent a lot time establishing bylaws and process. Equal parity for every member is built into the process. Everything we publish goes through an extensive process. All our material is vetted and challenged by our membership, inclusive of our end-user community. It's all balloted. We think we're a little more nimble than traditional standards bodies. We work in an accelerated fashion. Every member has one ballot, one vote. The process resembles standards' bodies but is much quicker. We have the tools and methods to track responses. Stakeholders voice opinions. What we come out with isn't necessarily a standard, but a recommended approach. We reach out to other standards organizations and say, "Here are our efforts. Might this not be an appropriate standard of measurement?" for example. Then we're quick to refine. We have to be. We don't have five years to do what needs to be done. Our process was drafted by a broad base of the membership, and we get things finished, approved, and out. Our members have to then go out to create products that meet these recommendations and guidelines.

Roger: The Green Grid works with utilities companies, such as Pacific Gas and Electric. We work with the EPA (United States Environmental Protection Agency), with the European Union standards bodies, and with the Department of Energy. How many more power plants can we build? We have to figure out how to improve inefficiencies across this ecosystem of entities.

Our first order of business is around measurement. You can't improve what you don't measure. We give organizations a way to measure efficiency and waste, which lets them figure out where to focus and where not to focus. The cornerstone is communicating performance so that each stakeholder can understand where and how to measure and then how to translate that measurement into something meaningful. It needs to be meaningful to the Chief Financial Officer (CFO). It needs to be relevant to the folks

managing IT and to the folks architecting IT solutions. It's important to the folks responsible for facilities. We're trying to talk to all these constituencies and make it easy to understand. Making things simple is hard though. Knowing your utility bill is a great first step. How many folks know the utility bill for the data center?

John: We're seeing an important organizational shift. When facilities and IT begin collaboratively working together, IT understands completely its impact on facilities.

IT needs to involve the business process owner. The CFO needs to articulate the business requirements. Both facilities and IT need to know these business requirements and the business plans, including things like acquisitions that have a big impact on both facilities and IT. The organizations benefit greatly if facilities and IT plan collaboratively. IT needs to break down its silos. Too often storage is its own silo, servers another, networks yet another, and all separate from facilities. Organizations need more global management tools to roll up the disparate parts and see what needs to improve and where to virtualize.

Roger: John and I talk a lot about what improvements can be made by changing behavior, breaking down silos, and communicating. Billing models, for example, can be a big deal. If the data center is billed by the rack, that will drive a behavior that drives up density. Too many trends in computing are driven by bad metrics.

Folks can't make good decisions based on small sample sizes. You need a year's worth of data, compiled and generalized. Every day is dynamic. You need to look toward the future. Does what you're doing with storage and power go down with demand and scale up? You want scalable power, even more dynamic — over the day, week, season — a very dynamic load. The infrastructure needs to be dynamic as well.

Chapter 2

Making the Business Case for Green IT

Green needs more than executive endorsement; green needs executive leadership. Few changes happen in a business without some element of compulsion, and greening is no exception. However, going green is ultimately a highly inclusive process and carries with it the potential for taking what is a good idea and leveraging it into invigorating corporate culture, brand differentiation, and stronger appeal to potential employees.

If you're the executive responsible for leading the change, look to this chapter for help with talking points as you develop your strategy. If you're in the position of needing to "sell" the green philosophy to your upper management, use this chapter as a starting point as you develop a pitch tailored to your organization's culture and concerns.

Growing Policies for Change

Effective management relies on effective governance, and governance of all kinds relies on policy. Policy defines acceptable and unacceptable behaviors for all kinds of business practices. Chances are your organization already has a lot of policies in place — policies about absenteeism, security, vacations, attire, and so on. Policies not only establish expected behaviors and sanction unwanted behaviors, but they also set a critical tone in corporate culture.

When it comes to *going green,* initiating flexible, forward-looking policies is key. And because going green is a process, you should expect your green policies to evolve over time. You can start with easily implemented policies and, over time, refine them into practices with more deliberate requirements. But the sooner you get started, the better. For example, a simple policy to turn off laptop and desktop computers overnight will immediately impact your energy usage for the better. However, your IT department may depend on having those computers online at particular overnight hours for updates, and you'll need to amend the simple policy to accommodate the common (and expedient) practice of updating computers outside regular work hours.

Many policies start out as suggestions or recommendations and are ultimately incorporated as policy only after they've evolved. Trying out a recommended green policy can reveal unforeseen results. But don't give up! After the results make themselves known, you can adapt your policy to address them.

Getting to green, and ultimately to sustainability, is a journey, a process, and a profound change in thinking and doing. No business can become green overnight, but all can make important changes now. Effective, adaptable green policies guide the transition.

Profiting from Greener Practices

No reasonable businessperson argues with cutting costs or growing profits. Fortunately, going green carries the potential for saving greenbacks (or whatever color your currency sports) while promoting environmental responsibility. This section describes major areas of avoidable costs to consider in building the business case for green.

Rising cost of electricity

Although energy costs often fluctuate in the short run, many experts expect electricity prices to rise over the next few decades. The price of electricity varies significantly by region and locality, and charges can also vary by season and time of day.

One of the first details you need to know to prepare your business case is how much your organization pays for its power. Retail electricity prices in the U.S. are typically quoted in cents per kilowatt hour, but you'll see wholesale prices in mills per kilowatt hour, where a *mill* is 1/1000 of a dollar.

A number of factors influence the cost of electricity:

✔ **The cost of fuel:** Fuel expense is a major component of the cost of producing electrical power from coal, and it dominates the cost of producing electricity from natural gas. It's a smaller fraction of the cost of nuclear power, and of course, wind, solar, and hydroelectric power have no fuel cost.

✔ **The cost of capital:** The cost of renewable energy is almost entirely capital cost. For example, building a wind farm requires a capital expenditure to erect towers, install wind turbines, and connect them to the electric grid; but after they're in operation, there's no cost for fuel, only ongoing maintenance. Capital is also a major factor in coal plants, especially proposed *clean coal* plants that sequester the carbon dioxide from combustion, as the coal itself is relatively inexpensive.

✔ **The cost of transmission and local distribution:** Getting power from the generating plant to the user is a growing fraction of electricity costs, and renewable plants are typically farther away from urban areas. If you have flexibility in choosing a location for your data center, placing it near sources of renewable electricity can save you money because it's generally cheaper to transmit data long distances than it is to ship electric power the same distance.

✔ **Regulation:** Here's where government agencies get involved. Carbon caps, utility demand management, and renewable generation requirements all push up electricity prices.

   • Carbon caps give power producers a *quota* (a cap) on how much carbon dioxide they can emit. If they need to emit more to meet electrical demand, they must buy credits from other companies.

   • Many U.S. states require the utilities they regulate to adjust their pricing to minimize new demands for power, making bulk purchase discounts less available.

   • Some states, such as California, also insist that utilities get some percentage of the power they sell from renewable sources — a demand that usually drives up costs. (The utilities wouldn't need a regulatory push to do this, otherwise.)

The long-term rising costs associated with energy are foundational to your case for green. Make sure that you understand the regulations and costs associated with producing and distributing electricity, and emphasize their potential impact on your organization's bottom line when you make your case for green.

Lowering energy bills

Use less power = Spend less money

We talk about the specifics of power usage in many chapters in this book, but hold on to the idea that one huge element of green is reducing power usage, and that when you do so, you simultaneously cut costs.

IT is a power hog — pure and simple. It's such a hog that you can't build new data centers in some places because there's not enough power available to support them. Following are some facts to keep in mind as you put together a business case for green IT:

✔ **A data center takes 50 to 100 times as much electricity per square foot — its power density — than typical office space.**

And the really sad fact is that most IT facilities use power very inefficiently. For every 100 kilowatts consumed by a typical data center, only 40 kW actually powers the IT equipment. The rest goes to air conditioning, *uninterruptible power systems (UPS),* and power management. Of the 40 kW supplied to the IT equipment, often less than 10 kW is doing useful computation and communication work. Lightly loaded servers waste a large amount of power. A server running at 10-percent utilization draws 70 to 80 percent of the power it would draw if fully used.

✔ **In many industries, IT has become the largest consumer of electricity in the company, and the data center is where most of it goes.**

Storage requirements are exploding because new applications, such as image processing, generate gigabytes of data daily and regulations demand longer data retention. Storage is the largest single power consumer in the data center — and your storage arrays likely contain many constantly spinning disk drives filled with rarely accessed data.

✔ **Business mergers and consolidations further strain IT resources.**

As a result of mergers and consolidations, IT departments struggle to support disparate software and hardware in an effort to maintain existing systems, often leading to duplication and more inefficiency.

Desktop computers are spread throughout the organization, so their power consumption is less visible; but in total, they often present the largest corporate opportunity for energy savings. Simply setting and enforcing policy on putting desktops into sleep mode overnight can bring big savings. We tell you how in Chapter 15.

A good place to start lowering energy costs associated with IT is by raising the temperature in the data center. Newer guidelines from ASHRAE (see Chapter 4) call for warmer data centers in hot months and cooler data centers in cold months. Reducing the energy needed to cool and heat data centers is a great first step.

Look around for servers that are plugged in but aren't actually being used — you may be surprised to find a lot of energy being used with nothing to show for it.

Showing success in one initiative can win you the credibility and support to take on somewhat more involved steps, such as enabling data compression to reduce storage needs.

Containing IT

Industry trends suggest that typically IT demands double its current resources every five years — that's double the floor space, double the power, double the cooling, double the equipment. Are you broke yet? Left to its own devices (pardon the expression), IT alone could eventually use up the planet's resources.

Although those of us in IT like to think our work is a strategic asset, in reality, most organizations treat IT as a cost center — just an expensive necessity for doing business. Increasingly, IT departments find their budgets capped, while expectations keep rising. More and more business is conducted online. Demand for processing, bandwidth, and data storage are doubling every few years.

Green principles and green practices can help curb IT's potential for unchecked sprawl. Focusing on business optimization can help keep IT in its place by dramatically reducing current utilization and keeping growth in check:

✔ Server and storage utilization and consolidation

✔ Leveraging virtualization (see Chapter 13)

✔ Defining a life cycle for information

✔ Implementing and enforcing policy

You can use even more IT — explicitly software applications — to help in your green journey. Areas you can explore include

✔ Optimizing business process

✔ Optimizing decision support so that you use information you have to make greener decisions

✔ Using data management software to reduce requirements for physical storage, and thereby, reducing energy use and data center space

✔ Using compression technologies so data takes up less storage, which uses less energy and data center space

Reducing paper and ink costs

Good friend and *For Dummies* author John Levine has been quoted as saying, "The paperless office is about as likely as the paperless bathroom." He has a point, but between your organization's current paper consumption and the elusive paperless office lie many trees (and much cost) that you can save by instituting green printing policies. We take a brief look at those here and explore them in more detail in Chapter 16.

Electronic documents (and signatures) to the rescue

Mounds of paper go into creating contracts and transacting business. You can eliminate (or greatly reduce) these mounds by shifting to

- ✔ Electronic documents
- ✔ Electronic document delivery
- ✔ Electronic signatures

This reduction effort not only saves paper and ink, but it also saves costs related to paper storage, the courier service or postage needed to deliver the paper, the hours spent filing and retrieving the paper, and the filters needed to ensure air quality as the paper accumulates dust.

If you want a dramatic example of how businesses are eliminating paper to reduce costs, you need look no further than the banking industry:

- ✔ If you haven't switched to paperless statements already (and we aren't advocating that you do unless you're completely on top of the security implications) chances are your bank is offering to *pay you* to switch — because the bank reaps the cost savings, related to paper, postage, and labor.
- ✔ Not all banks return physical checks anymore. Rather than handle all those pieces of paper, the banks scan the checks and send electronic images instead.

When you're putting together plans for greening IT, chances are you'll find many paper-based processes that you can replace with electronic substitutes. And these substitutions may, in turn, lead to process improvements. It's not always just the paper and ink that are being spared.

Don't print that file

People use a lot of paper and ink by printing documents out of habit, and they could save a fair amount of related costs by learning new methods of working:

✔ Sometimes people print documents that they can't read easily onscreen, but they might be able to read them if they simply enlarge the image.

✔ Printing two-sided documents or reusing single-sided copies for works in progress can diminish the use of new paper.

✔ Buying recycled paper or paper with recycled content can save as well.

Note it electronically

Many people carry notepads into meetings. And this practice may be more appropriate than sitting across from a stranger madly typing on your laptop. However, if you're on the phone (especially when using headphones), you may find that you type faster than you write and can capture notes better electronically. And if you're careful in your naming conventions, you'll even be able to find them again.

For those who must take notes on paper during face-to-face meetings, we recommend this paper-conscious process:

1. **Take your notes on pads made from the paper you're planning to recycle anyway.**

2. **Transcribe your notes soon after your meeting (so you can still decipher what they mean).**

3. **Save your transcribed notes (using your careful naming conventions) electronically so you can later find and search them.**

4. **Continue with your original good intentions by recycling the pads of already reused paper.**

When you address any kind of paper-and-ink-saving processes in your green IT business plans, make sure that you recognize that different people have different styles of working and don't antagonize colleagues over minor paper-use issues.

Cutting down on travel expenses

Cutting travel expense for both the organization and the employee helps everyone benefit from going green. Widely distributed organizations are finding that they can leverage alternatives:

✔ Conference calls

✔ Web presentations

✔ Telepresence

> ✔ Instant messaging
>
> ✔ Social networking environments

We tell you all about these communications tools in Chapter 20.

Also, establishing policies that encourage employees to work from home can minimize commuting costs and grow employee loyalty. If larger segments work from home more of the time, or work in satellite commuting offices, businesses can reduce the need for high-end office space and create additional cost savings. In Chapter 20, we also expand on the economic benefits telecommuting offers. And, of course, economic benefits are an essential component of any business case.

Collaborating over the Web

We expand on this subject at length in Chapter 20, but for now, think about the advantages of collaboration between employees, and with business partners, suppliers, and customers. The Web enables all these kinds of collaboration, and the tools to support collaboration over the Web are growing.

Add to your business case these advantages associated with using Web collaboration for business communications:

✔ Savings on travel costs (see the preceding section) as well as time-savings associated with travel

✔ Savings on the cost of creating and shipping presentation materials, including documents or physical media such as tapes, CDs, and DVDs

✔ Reducing the cost of facilities for hosting events that can take place online instead

✔ Reducing the cost of customer acquisition

✔ Reducing the cost of business partnership enablement

✔ Optimizing relationships with suppliers

Optimizing business processes — such as how you conduct communications — to make them more environmentally friendly usually translates to more efficient processes and cost savings across the board. In the name of green, organizations are finding better ways of organizing themselves and reaping green benefits of all kinds.

Embracing Less Tangible (But Very Real) Benefits

When you make your case for greening IT, you need to understand the bigger picture: What can going green mean for your organization? Our research shows that real live companies are already enjoying extraordinary effects — such as improved customer loyalty — as ancillary results of going green. These effects weren't the direct goals of the companies' green initiatives, but instead are unanticipated benefits.

Many organizations have sustainability goals that are driven by a wide variety of pressures, including the need to reduce operating costs, enter new markets, or mitigate risk. Perhaps the organization has run out of power, wants to calculate its carbon emissions, or has to comply with European Union (EU) regulations on toxic substances. Green initiatives give a wide variety of positive benefits that address all these issues and many more.

Sustainability and green initiatives are proving to have a powerfully positive impact on the value and reputation of brands. This is true across the board for both service and product-focused organizations, large, small, and mid-sized organizations, in all regions around the globe, and in all industries. No kidding.

If you view green as an environmental, tree-hugging issue that involves IT (at best) as far as energy costs go, you've missed the point. IT is often a necessary and not overly appreciated cost center. Why not go from zero to hero by helping the organization see how IT can add value to the entire company? Construct your business case to show that going green offers IT an opportunity to frame strategy in a meaningful way. It allows the benefit of green IT to infuse the organization with the great energy of innovation, customer-centricity, and eco-friendly success.

The reality is that green carries with it a vision of a better world wrapped around a whole host of concrete actions and outcomes that also better the organization on multiple levels. Sustainability agendas are opportunities for organizations to envision and create a shared system of values internally and externally. These values align highly efficient and inclusive models of innovation with new business opportunities.

Our research has turned up, among others, the following positive ancillary effects.

Closer integration of business divisions

Right now, most organizations aren't particularly well integrated — their various divisions and departments operate autonomously. A facilities department pays the electric bill, and the IT department usually has no idea or little interest in the energy costs or savings. IT keeps the organization operational, meeting service-level agreements and keeping everyone connected. Likewise, the rest of the organization has no idea what's involved in the complex dynamics of IT. As long as the network is up, why wonder? IT organizations, as fairly conservative entities, need to connect with the rest of the organization and global community to understand the cataclysmic shift in the expectations and needs of the organizations it serves. IT managers are being increasingly required to adjust to the deeply cultural changes in the very nature of work and business in a complex global environment.

IT organizations are constantly asked to do more with less, and rising energy costs are cutting into IT budgets. Green provides a roadmap to optimize performance in ways that better connect IT into the overall success of the organization. Sustainability initiatives allow internal stakeholders to understand that overall success depends on not only working together but also on understanding in which ways disparate areas of the organization share key goals and opportunities.

Green IT offers businesses the opportunity to function in new and innovative ways that push better results to the top line, to the bottom line, and to the organization as a whole. The key to this is no longer viewing IT (nor any area of the organization) as a separate entity. Instead, companies must start to look across all departments and functions to reduce costs, boost operational performance, meet and exceed customer and client expectations, and find new opportunities for growth and success.

Optimized performance and cost effectiveness

From a holistic and integrated approach to overall organizational development, the benefits to greening the IT ecosystem become obvious. Internally, greener IT enables improved performance overall — not only in the data center but also in the operation of all applications and technologies that support every corner of the company. More efficient work processes supported by a greener IT can enable people to be more productive and dramatically reduce the cost of business operations.

Sustainability as a corporate philosophy, value, and goal, does the following:

✔ Energizes and inspires organizations

✔ Elicits new ways of working cross-functionally

✔ Supports the integration and sharing of data

✔ Stimulates communication and innovation

✔ Helps employees measure and track progress

✔ More effectively connects departments and catalyzes the sharing of best practices

Organizations with well-organized and implemented sustainability initiatives perform and satisfy better than ever.

Enhanced employee attraction and retention

Connected, efficient organizations are better able to attract top talent and have higher rates of employee satisfaction. They're better able to unify employees' efforts by promoting a shared vision that extends throughout and beyond the organization. Unified organizations get better visibility of their own processes, get better control of costs and risks, and more effectively engage employees and management alike.

The result is that greener organizations are more attractive to potential employees. Current employees feel empowered and motivated, and feel better about their jobs. We heard this from folks at Cisco, IBM, and Aberdeen Group. We hear prospective employees are clamoring to work on green research.

The upshot is this: When you're doing your job and you know you're making a difference in the world and in people's lives — well, it doesn't get any better than that.

All these goals lead to improved brand reputation and increased competitive advantage. A well-enacted green IT initiative allows the entire organization to see the value that IT drives.

Greater appeal to customers and business partners

Green initiatives also produce great results in customer- and client-facing arenas. They improve internal dynamics around processes, communication, and innovation, as well as external relationships with customers, peers, trade partners, and the community at large.

Protecting the planet and its people

In a broader sense, protecting the planet as a whole from environmental disaster makes good business sense. All business depends on customers' ability to buy. If customers are facing higher food bills due to climate change, they have less money to buy other products. The energy and cost-saving benefits of green IT can help support a global effort to save the planet by

✔ **Staving off a power crisis:** The Earth's storage of fossil fuel is finite. Although experts disagree about *when* those reserves will run out, they will run out sooner or later. The more plentiful fossil fuel reserves that remain are the most difficult to exploit, both in terms of cost and environmental damage. Sensible reductions in energy buy society time to develop more sustainable alternatives.

✔ **Reducing carbon emissions and other greenhouse gases:** Reduced energy use directly cuts emissions of carbon dioxide, a major greenhouse gas. Even in areas where large amounts of carbon-free power are available, the marginal demand for electricity often is supplied from plants burning coal or natural gas, which themselves emit carbon and other greenhouse gases.

When organizations can communicate their goals related to positively impacting Triple Bottom Line performance by demonstrating a real commitment to the success of people, planet, and profits, new customer acquisition, retention, and satisfaction improve. Not only do prospective employees want to work for responsible companies, but also trade partners want to work with those organizations, and customers and clients want to do business with them. A green IT ecosystem can actually drive not only employee but also customer loyalty in ways that few other initiatives can.

Conserving Natural Resources

When making your business case for greening IT, be sure to address the entire scope of natural resource consumption. IT equipment production and operation depletes reserves of natural materials besides fossil fuels. Steel, aluminum, copper, tin, gold, and rare earth metals all go into making computers and displays. All are refined from ores that must be mined, often at considerable environmental and human cost. Using equipment more efficiently and taking extra effort to insure that it is recycled (as far as practicality allows) can help conserve these limited resources and reduce the attendant environmental damage from their production.

Shrinking landfills

Much of what humans use ends up in landfills. Poorly designed and managed landfills are a major environmental problem and a significant source of methane, a greenhouse gas two dozen times more potent than carbon dioxide. Such landfills can also allow hazardous materials — such as lead, chromium, and mercury — to leach into drinking water.

Environmental contamination from landfills is a particular problem in poorer countries where much electronic waste ends up (thanks, of course, to unscrupulous dumping). We talk more about the landfill problems in Chapter 19.

Controlling or avoiding landfills

Newer landfills in the United States and Europe must meet strict environmental standards that include measures to prevent ground water contamination and caps to collect most of the methane they produce. This methane can even be used as fuel.

However, space for landfills near urban areas is filling up and, as a result, municipal and industrial waste often has to be transported long distances to more remote sites. This added transportation uses fossil fuels and increases carbon emissions. Once again, the twin measures of more efficient use and recycling of IT equipment has a big payoff in reduced need for landfill space and transportation.

Balancing Your Consumption with Carbon Offsets

Although reducing energy use, or at least slowing its growth, is the best way to achieve a reduction in carbon emissions, another way is for the organization to purchase *carbon offsets*. These are certificates, similar to stocks and bonds, that represent the payment for some activity that reduces greenhouse gas emissions. The activity must be something that wouldn't have occurred otherwise, a concept known as *additionality*.

Elaborate mechanisms validate and trade carbon offsets, but they remain controversial, for example:

✔ Some offset activities are criticized as having undesirable side effects, such as allowing organizations to continue bad behavior and "wash their sins away" by buying carbon offsets.

✔ Use of carbon offsets by companies is sometimes cited as a form of *greenwashing* — trying to appear green rather than actually being green.

On the other hand, the possibility also exists that some of your organization's green initiatives could qualify for carbon offset payment. And so, you should be aware of this feature of green planning and address it as appropriate in your business case.

Getting Ahead of the Regulations

In the world of business, and especially the aspect of technology, it seems we're always playing catch-up. One of the changes you can count on is the changing regulatory environment. Europe is ahead of the U.S in starting to define its regulations, but in this global, more collaborative world, organizations and regulatory bodies are trying hard to work together for consistent standards and regulations.

You can look at what Europe and California are already doing and get a sense of what's coming on a broader level. For example, California has a ban on throwing away electronic waste. You can find out about this and other green regulations at www.dtsc.ca.gov.

To a great extent, the regulations apply to technology vendors, but more regulations about the use of technology and certainly the disposal of technology are coming. Take a good look at Chapter 4 to get a better sense of the regulatory environment and how it can support your case for green.

Chapter 3

Green Journeys in Action

● ●

● ●

*I*n this book, we tell you about all kinds of things you can do to green your IT. Although general green IT principles are fine, we think it really helps to hear what others have done — to see where real people have made real changes. This chapter introduces some examples of taking green action.

Green is not a destination; if anything is evident in these stories, what's evident is the ongoing process and the growing involvement and commitment of the folks who are on the journey. We find the stories inspiring and hope you do, too. If you have one of your own or are beginning one and want us to help you chronicle it, please write to us at greenIT4d@yahoo.com.

Big Blue Goes Green

Some companies have been taking an active hand in guiding how their business affects the surrounding environment, both natural and civic. This approach, known as *corporate responsibility* or *corporate citizenship,* started early in the green movement (then known as *the ecology movement*) with policies that set green goals for business practices. The IBM Corporation — the original IT giant — has been involved in green IT for decades, so its experience is worth a closer look.

Establishing the track record

IBM sounded the keynote for green IT when it published its first environmental-protection goals in 1971. Tom Watson, Jr.'s corporate policy statement called for IBM to

> . . . *be continuously on guard against adversely affecting the environment. This effort must include constant attention not only to the waste incident to producing the product but also to the consequences of the processes established during product development.*

IBM then developed a comprehensive global environmental management system:

- ✔ Between 1990 and 2007, IBM saved 4.6 billion kWh of electricity consumption, avoided nearly 3.1 million metric tons of CO_2 emissions (equal to 45 percent of the company's 1990 CO_2 emissions), and saved over $310 million through its annual energy conservation actions.

- ✔ IBM's procurement of renewable energy and renewable energy certificates (RECs) increased from 11 million kWh in 2001 to 455 million kWh in 2007 and accounted for 8.5 percent of IBM's total 2007 global electricity purchases.

- ✔ IBM's second-generation goal to reduce carbon dioxide emissions associated with IBM's energy use by 12 percent between 2005 and 2012.

- ✔ IBM has reduced its nearly 200 data centers to fewer than ten.

In IBM's 1994 Annual Environment Report, then-CEO Lou Gerstner renewed the commitment:

> *In the past two years, we in IBM have had to rethink much about the way we do business. In the process, it has become clear that there are certain things that should not change. One of them is our responsibility to run a business mindful of the world in which that business operates. When it comes to the environmental well-being of that world, this responsibility takes on added weight for a company such as ours: a multinational organization whose technology represents a powerful engine of change.*

That last sentence also serves as an answer to the question, "Why green IT?" And here's a short answer to the same question: *Because information technology is a powerful engine of change, and responsible change is needed.* When you think about how much attention is finally being paid to the environment today, it's heartening to think that some businesses have been acting responsibly for a long time.

Keeping the commitment

Today IBM's environmental and energy commitments are part of its larger commitment to corporate citizenship and social responsibility. IBM continues to walk the green walk in a range of important areas:

✔ **Maintaining environmental awareness:** IBM has published an annual environmental report since 1990; at the end of 1997, it became the first major multinational to earn a single global registration to ISO 14001, covering all its manufacturing and hardware development operations around the world — which it's maintained ever since.

ISO 14001 is the international standard for implementing an environmental management system (EMS), which gives organizations a framework for measuring and managing the environmental consequences of their operations.

The International Organization for Standardization originated this standard and certifies those companies that comply with it.

✔ **Working smarter to save energy:** IBM saved $250 million in energy costs between 1990 and 2005. In 2007, in its efforts to green itself, IBM saved $97 million in travel costs by using online collaboration instead of physical travel — saving itself considerable expense that would have shown up as more carbon in the atmosphere otherwise.

✔ **Mandating responsible product design:** In 1992, IBM established its Product Stewardship program, which focuses on corporate environmental affairs — including the development of products whose design and performance are environmentally friendly. The Product Stewardship program also helps the various development groups within IBM apply environmental considerations to the entire product lifecycle, from initial concept through the end of life. Some ambitious concerns dominate:

- *Extending the life of products.*

- *Designing products with reuse and recylability in mind.*

- *Minimizing environmental impact by choosing more environmentally friendly materials:* IBM's Worldwide Distribution organization first developed Environmental Packaging Guidelines in 1990. These guidelines promote the use of reusable, recyclable packaging, minimizing the use of toxic elements and minimizing waste.

- *Recycling existing equipment:* IBM GARS (Global Asset Recovery Services) works to recover, reuse, and responsibly dispose of electronic equipment.

✔ **Maintaining consistent environmental effort:** In IBM's case, this means not only establishing a track record but also planning for future improvements:

- Between 1990 and 2007, IBM avoided energy-use-CO_2 emissions equivalent to 45 percent of the company's own 1990 energy use.

- Since 1987, IBM has decreased its generation of hazardous waste by 94.7 percent.

- Since 1995, IBM has reduced its PFC emissions from chip manufacturing by 32.7 percent.

- From 2007 to 2010, IBM expects to double the computing capacity of its IT centers without increasing energy use — and is providing its IT capabilities to boost research on climate change and water management.

✓ **Embracing transparency:** IBM is one of a few small numbers of manufacturing companies to report its greenhouse gas (GHG) emissions under the U.S. Department of Energy voluntary reporting program since the inception of the program in 1995, and has reported through the Carbon Disclosure Project (CDP) since that program's inception in 2003.

Across the board, end to end, IBM is actively looking at how to not only green *itself* but also at how to help its customers go green. To this end, they've created a framework (as shown in Figure 3-1) that identifies starting points for organizations that are ready to begin their green journeys.

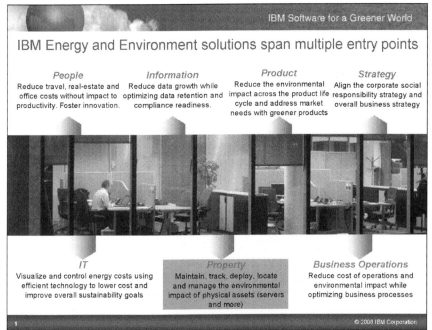

Figure 3-1: IBM's Energy and Environmental framework.

From every corner of the organization, IBM applies green thinking to eliminate waste, conserve energy, and optimize business processes. Its standard procedures include

- ✔ Incorporating virtualization of applications, storage, and servers. (Read all about virtualization in Chapter 13.)

- ✔ Improving facilities management including heating, cooling, lighting, and power consumption.

- ✔ Using more online collaboration and reducing travel.

Result: Doing business in a more environmentally responsible way.

Twenty-Five Percent by 2012: Cisco Takes the Challenge

The Environmental Leader (www.environmentalleader.com) in 2008 proclaimed the bold goal set by Cisco Systems: to reduce "greenhouse gas emissions from its worldwide operations by 25 percent over the next four years, reaching its goal in absolute terms by 2012."

Believing that IT must take the lead in greening organizations, Sean Worthington, Vice President for IT Business Services, leads the Cisco IT green effort. "As part of the coordinated company approach, our focus is to use Cisco IT's technology, knowledge, and employee goodwill to improve Cisco's environmental performance while we share our learning with our customers and partners," he says.

The Environmental Leader reports that Cisco "worked with the EPA's Climate Leaders program as well as other parties, such as the Environmental Defense Fund and sustainability consulting firm Domani to assess its worldwide GHG footprint and set goals." According to the article, Cisco's gross GHG footprint was 832,000 metric tons of CO_2 equivalents (CO_2e) for 2007.

Here's some of what Cisco's doing:

- ✔ **Using telepresence to conduct meetings, which translates to far less travel and far less carbon.**

- ✔ **Encouraging a mobile workforce that allows employees to work from home using collaboration technologies.**

✔ **Using its own products to make working green pay off.** By using Cisco Connected Workplace, employees can work at a variety of locations: their desks, conference rooms, and outdoor environments. Cisco workers who use it report higher levels of both job satisfaction and productivity. The new space accommodates up to twice as many employees as a traditional office, and as a result Cisco has

- Reduced the number of per-capita IT-related devices by 22 percent

- Reduced cabling requirements by 54 percent

- Reduced total IT equipment wattage by 44 percent

- Increased the usage of their current office space by 40 percent

- Reduced greenhouse gas emissions

- Helped lower traffic congestion and alleviated the strains of commuting

Cisco points out that the network is central to efficient usage and management of energy. "Because it is ubiquitous, touching every part of the business, the network can create a *multiplier effect*" that greatly extends the benefits of green initiatives. Deploying efficient network architectures, Cisco IT moved services into the network that provides more electrical efficiency than traditional designs. Specifically, Cisco IT made the following changes:

✔ **Reduced overall appliance count by six per logical server group, removing 600 watts per group.** Network service modules provide more efficient architecture than appliance-based ones. (Cisco has approximately 250 server groups × 600 watts each.)

✔ **Drove utilization on 5 petabytes (PB) of storage to approximately 70 percent through network-based storage virtualization.** (See Chapter 11 for details.)

To create an energy-efficient production data center Cisco used a green approach in site construction and used a *Service Oriented Data Center (SODC)* framework, which uses consolidation, virtualization, and automation of data-center resources to reduce power and space needs.

Cisco is purchasing renewable energy. Cisco bought about 460 million kWh of renewable energy worldwide in 2008.

Cisco challenges the CIO with taking responsibility for greening the organization. We highly recommend the article "Why IT Must Take a Lead in Greening the Enterprise" at www.cisco.com/en/US/solutions/ns340/ns414/ns802/ns803/cisco-green-it.html.

RackForce Rents Green Machines

One important part of the change to green IT is getting people used to the idea. That isn't always a matter of badgering your company to go buy a slew of greener machines. *RackForce,* a fast-growing hosting-service provider, has a different approach: It rents servers wholesale to e-businesses, application providers, and hosting resellers. RackForce's larger green strategy involves rethinking business process and coming up with innovative ways to save energy while doing green-savvy IT.

RackForce started its green journey about seven years ago; VP Brian Fry puts it this way:

> "We didn't start out with a full understanding of green or green strategy. In 2001, we understood that we were very inefficient with our servers, adding 20 servers a day, with low utilization on every server. We also understood that if everything from one customer is linked to one server, failure could be catastrophic."

RackForce decided to look at virtualization to see whether they could do more with what they had. They needed to use less power — power is a big expense. They adopted a virtualization strategy to address not only server consolidation, but also overall efficiencies of the data center, the ability to make changes on the fly, the ability to move things when they need moving, maximizing utilization.

They began to innovate from within. They switched to hardware that was more power efficient. When they added space to the data center to create a major data center (150,000 square feet), they had to learn all about data center efficiencies.

They didn't understand the power cabling design or the impact of moving from one part of the data center to another. They learned about uninterruptible power supply (UPS) inefficiencies and where they were losing power. They learned the importance of containing cold air and not allowing it to mix with warm.

They learned you can double your efficiency with that air and that experimenting really paid off. They simply put up plastic curtains, which had an enormous impact — they improved efficiency by 50 percent. Eventually they created total air separation; that warm air gets used for heating homes and businesses.

Today's chilling systems below 50°F can use cool air without using a chiller at all. Because chillers are very energy expensive, RackForce chose to locate where cooling is part of the environment, which was part of making the decision on where to site the new facilities — Kelowna, British Columbia. Because IT can be located anywhere — you can outsource it — they chose to locate it where it made the most sense from an energy perspective. RackForce connects to everything with Cisco lossless network. If something goes wrong, the forward error correcting fixes it.

RackForce used a modular design for the data center, which is a big part of their efficiency. They use water to cool. Water cooling is many times more effective than air cooling, but if you don't have enough water, you can't do it.

"The carbon impact from IT is getting to be as bad as the airline industry and soon it'll be worse," warns Brian, "People just need to understand. Is your data center running on coal? Data centers need to be put in places that have the least impact on the environment. Put data centers in colder locations. With hydropower, the only carbon footprint comes from the dam itself."

Hydropower is very, very clean compared to coal. Think about how close you can locate to those dams. Using the right engineering and power source is equivalent to reducing 100,000 cars to 1,000 for a 150,000 square foot data center. "Your job gets a lot easier and exciting when you know it can make a difference," says Brian, "You can reduce power consumption up to 100 times. It's a lot easier to ship packets than power."

RackForce points out that you no longer need to have all your IT in one place. Keeping a server in a really bad location is no longer necessary. IT can shift faster than other industries. If you can move from the small to the large, you can gain great efficiencies. Moving that server could mean a 3X improvement. With virtualization, you can replace 20 servers with one. Overall, RackForce got a 300-percent performance and reliability increase and a 30-percent power-consumption reduction by implementing IBM System x3550 servers.

Being Green On Line in Brazil

Despite global economic woes and collapsing currency, one company in Sao Paolo, Brazil, is growing. *On Line do Brasil,* forced to look at alternatives because of space and energy costs, looked not only for current needs but for their anticipated growth over the next five years. On Line do Brasil provides IT and services for both small and midsize companies.

A service and hosting provider, On Line do Brasil rents space within a larger data center and populates it with *blade servers* — slim, compact servers on individual circuit boards, a design that first hit the market in 2001. Switching from racks to blades has helped On Line do Brasil reduce the space and energy each server consumes. When you think about 1,000 servers, the difference between racks and blades is huge (see Chapter 10 for more information). Certainly it works for On Line do Brasil; they were on the point of running out of both room and energy allotment — now they have room to grow.

On Line do Brasil's aggressive growth plans made good operational efficiency a necessity. The company approached this need in several ways:

- They developed a good knowledge of virtualization and used VMware with their blades.

- They engaged IBM to consolidate its existing systems onto three IBM BladeCenter HS21 XM servers, housed in an IBM BladeCenter E chassis.

- IBM implemented an IBM System x3550 server to manage the new environment. The System x platform lowers power consumption and increases performance.

On Line do Brasil reduced their energy and space requirements and has gone from an organization of 23 employees with revenues of $1 million to an organization of 33 employees, revenues of $4 million, and host contracts for 120 customers. Going green for them has clearly translated into a triple bottom-line win — they're better able to serve their customers, they're making a better profit, and they're reducing their energy consumption.

Part II
Getting a Running Start

The 5th Wave   By Rich Tennant

"Of course, according to green technology best practices, we'll replace that old broken washin' machine with a more energy efficient one that doesn't work."

In this part . . .

To help you go green, this part equips you with the various regulations that may already affect you or will affect you soon. This part also covers how to understand, measure, and monitor energy use and ways you can get started right away.

Chapter 4

Getting to Know the Standards and Metrics

*S*tandards play a central role in modern information technology. Since the introduction of the American Standard Code for Information Interchange (ASCII) in 1963, use of widely accepted industry standards has made IT growth even faster: Such standards allow users to mix the best solutions from multiple sources, instead of locking them into proprietary products from a single vendor.

Standards development and application can produce broad, long-lasting effects:

✔ **Timely, well-crafted standards often create major new markets.** The Internet Engineering Task Force RFC series was key to the Internet's explosive growth.

✔ **Standards often find application in areas their creators never dreamt of.** The ubiquitous 19-inch racks that fill your data center — all built to the EIA-310-D standard — trace their ancestry to the early days of railroad signaling, when 19-inch racks held electromechanical relays that controlled the safe movement of trains.

Standards related to green IT are in early development.

✔ The most mature standards — mostly those applying to consumer and desktop computing — rate IT equipment in terms of green concerns, such as energy consumption, the use of hazardous material, and eventual disposal.

✔ Standards for larger equipment, such as servers, are still in development.

✔ Further out are *smart grid* standards that centralize power management over the network; they also let power companies request that a company adjust its power use (based on fluctuations in the availability of energy sources, such as wind or solar power).

This chapter tells you about established and emerging standards, both of which affect your efforts to green IT. For example, you see how the EPA's voluntary Energy Star standards (no doubt familiar if you've recently bought a home appliance) relate to energy use in end-user computer equipment. Also, you find out how various standards — such as Energy Star, WEEE, RoHS, and ASHRAE — affect the production, powering, cooling, and disposal of data center equipment.

Melding Emerging Standards with IT Practices

Most people think IT adopts technology early. IT organizations as a whole tend to be conservative about deploying new technology. Why? The answer seems to depend on business size:

✔ Small businesses may not have the in-house IT expertise to make sure that a new technology works before deploying it and certainly can't afford the downtime connected with deployment.

✔ Most large companies test both hardware and software applications before they're deployed and put into production. This practice is wise because not every new component will work with existing components, nor is every software release without issues. Then there's the matter of deployment — in very large organizations, for example, a software patch might be deployed to 40,000 users! Clearly, IT needs to be really sure that everything works as advertised.

✔ IT organizations are also driven by cost — most budget for capital expenditures and for operating costs. Because companies expect IT to live within those budgets, IT is often reluctant to adopt new technologies unless they're proven to work.

Before blindly adopting new equipment or practices — just because they're green — IT departments must verify, test, and work the changes into the budget. But where do the standards come in? Standards — and products that meet those standards — provide tested solutions that conservative IT organizations can adopt quickly, relying on the work of the standard-setting and certifying organizations.

The regulations pendulum

The past 25 years have seen a move to deregulate many industrial sectors, especially in the U.S. Industries that used to be heavily regulated, such as communications and financial services, have operated with less oversight than ever before. Recent events in the global economy — rising energy prices and a global recession — have raised questions about whether some regulation is desirable. This pendulum is likely to swing between regulation and deregulation in much the same way it has for centralized and decentralized IT.

Voluntary today; mandated tomorrow

We need to understand that green isn't going away. The costs of running several data centers guarantees the need to make informed infrastructure-management decisions.

Many current standards for green IT are voluntary — they're guidelines that a company can choose to implement, or choose not to implement. Even so, concerns about power consumption and energy conservation — as well as climate change and energy security — have caused governmental agencies around the world to scrutinize energy use and propose guidelines that will eventually become mandates.

- ✔ Several cities in the U.S. and Europe are limiting new data center construction — there simply isn't a cost-effective way to bring additional power into bigger cities. And, of course, building and maintaining a larger power infrastructure is wasteful.

- ✔ Manufacturers of data center components (such as servers, storage, racks, electrical, and HVAC equipment) are under increasing pressure from stakeholders, government regulation, industry best practices, and competitive necessity to adopt design and manufacturing principles that recognize sustainability.

Taking continuous measurement

It might seem simplistic to say that if you can't measure it, you can't control it, but this idea ought to be a governing IT principal. Manufacturing companies know that quality control depends on continuous measurement of processes to ensure standards compliance.

There's that word again: *standards*. During the 1990s most everyone thought IT was immune from the application of the principles of zero defects and similar programs that measure processes to improve them; but in fact IT *does* benefit from process management, except the output isn't widgets. Instead, it's

- ✔ Improved performance on service-level agreements

- ✔ Reduced downtime

- ✔ Increased delivery of computing work for each unit of applied resources such as energy, administrative support, and hardware use

To understand how well a particular IT infrastructure — for example, a data center with its individual components and processes — is performing, you must have a way to measure it. IT people often look at the specifications of components (the speeds and feeds) — without seeing the larger picture. Of course, tracking the access time of a particular disk array is important, but so is measuring the amount of electricity consumed when the array is idle.

Before you can draw any conclusions about overall energy consumption, you must understand the baseline consumption for each component in the data center or other IT infrastructure.

Published specifications are a good starting point, but increased concern about controlling consumption led to the development of three important aids for determining baseline consumption:

- ✔ **Software applications** can perform measurements at specified intervals or continually, and are available for various components in the infrastructure. For example, you can easily get network throughput, a measure of network performance, by using software from vendors, such as Cisco.

- ✔ **Hardware with built-in measurement capabilities** allows IT administrators to build a composite picture of data center power usage based on the aggregation of individual components' measures.

- ✔ **Dashboards** roll up the power consumption of individual components into a simple set of meters that let you monitor key system metrics at a glance. IT administrators can customize the dashboard controls and metrics to suit the company's requirements.

Of course, standalone tools such as power monitors have been available for many years. These devices plug into electrical outlets and range from simple voltage monitoring to more sophisticated devices that feed output into a computer for analysis. The real innovation that's occurring is the integration of measurement capabilities into the IT system hardware and software to minimize cost and simplify data collection and presentation.

Reviewing Established and Emerging Standards

Standards that address issues relating to green practices or sustainability are relatively recent. A number of standards are in place or under development to help guide your green decision making.

Leading the way with the EPA Energy Star

The Environmental Protection Agency (EPA) created Energy Star — a voluntary energy-efficiency certification program of the United States government run jointly by the EPA and the Department of Energy. The program covers a wide variety of electrical devices including home appliances, heating and cooling systems, lighting, and office equipment. The last category covered under this certification includes desktop and laptop computers, monitors, printers, and power adapters.

Energy Star specifications are reviewed periodically and typically strengthened and extended to a broader range of programs within a given category.

The European Union is developing directive Eco-design of energy-using products (2005/32/EC). For IT equipment, this directive is expected to coordinate with the U.S Energy Star program and issue similar requirements.

Current end-user computer specifications

Energy Star standards for computers emphasize *power management* — the ability of processors, disk drives, and monitors to enter a low power mode after a period of inactivity, without losing network connections. Energy Star distinguishes between these modes:

- ✔ **Sleep Mode:** The desktop computer must draw no more than 4 watts; 2 watts for certified laptops. To allow automated overnight updates and maintenance of desktop machines while in sleep mode, the machines must have the capability to *Wake On LAN* (that is, to leave sleep mode when addressed by local area network traffic) to receive the update and then return to low power mode.

- ✔ **Standby:** The desktop computer must draw no more than 2 watts; 1 watt for certified laptops. In this mode, the computer is off but still plugged in.

- ✔ **Idle State maximum power:** The equipment's power use ranges from 50 to 95 watts, depending on its processing power category.

Internal power supplies must have a minimum of 80-percent efficiency when running at 20-, 50-, and 100 percent of rated output, and their *power factor* (a measure of how close they are to an ideal resistive load) must be 0.9 or higher. (1.0 is the maximum possible factor; 0.0 the lowest. Low power factors waste energy in power transmission.) See Chapter 5 for more on power factor.

Upcoming data center specifications

Currently, Energy Star doesn't cover data center servers. However, draft specifications — currently limited to blade servers and rack-and-tower servers that have up to four processor sockets — are in process. These specifications address

- ✔ Minimum power-supply efficiency levels
- ✔ Availability of energy-use information on data sheets
- ✔ Maximum power draw at idle
- ✔ The capability to report remotely on power use and thermal output

The EPA intends to extend the specification to network and storage equipment and integrate workload metrics into the specification immediately following the publication of version 1 of the computer server requirements.

 The intent is to have these standards adopted in other jurisdictions, and the EPA is working hard to keep consensus. The European Union's directive for energy-using products — EuP — doesn't cover computers as this book goes to press. When the Energy Star requirements are complete, they'll likely be included in the EuP directive.

Using Energy Star in your green decision making

Requiring newly purchased equipment to meet the latest Energy Star specifications provides one means for your organization to improve the energy efficiency of your IT operations. And although Energy Star provides an important, standard set of criteria for assessing computer server energy efficiency, you have other points to carefully consider:

- ✔ **Your application needs and new virtualization capabilities:** To drive hardware use to 50 percent or higher — which lets you maximize your investment in equipment and facility space as well as deliver the most workload for the energy used — you may need to buy a system with higher processing power (more or faster CPUs) that has a higher idle power measurement rather than a lightly configured, less-capable server system.

A single, more heavily configured system capable of extensive virtualization is likely to use less power at idle and during operation than several lightly configured systems. Because virtualization technology is a relatively recent innovation, there's no standard measurement specifications for power use and workload delivery efficiency. Buyers must carefully consider both options to optimize energy use in their data center.

✔ **Your energy use versus utilization rates:** Energy Star's current hardware recommendations require that each server come with a data sheet detailing its power and performance attributes. The data sheets allow you to compare idle power for different system configurations and evaluate the trade-offs between a lightly configured system that can run only one application with low utilization rates or a more heavily configured system that can run several applications at a high utilization rate.

✔ **Your need for automated data center management:** A server must be able to measure power use and thermal output in real time and make the data available to the data center operator. These capabilities enable more automated management.

RoHS is rolling away the nasties

The European Union's Regulation of Hazardous Substances (RoHS) directive bars the sale, in the European Union, of electrical and electronic equipment that contains any of the following six hazardous materials:

✔ Lead

✔ Mercury

✔ Cadmium

✔ Hexavalent chromium

✔ Polybrominated biphenyls (PBBs)

✔ Polybrominated biphenyl ethers (PBDEs)

Other jurisdictions around the globe are rolling out similar material restrictions, most often conforming with the RoHS requirements, but sometimes with an additional twist. Most computing equipment manufacturers are likely to comply with RoHS and other similar requirements, lest they be frozen out of the EU and other markets. As a user of IT equipment, you may find prices increase a tad as a result, but these directives ensure that new equipment you buy is likely to be free of these hazardous substances. (There are some exceptions in the directive where no substitute for a restricted material is available.)

At this point, you don't need to rid your facility of non-RoHS compliant equipment. Whatever substances are built into such equipment are already there. The environmental effects of the hazardous materials will be mitigated if you use proper methods for retiring and disposing of the noncompliant equipment; find out more about doing so in Chapter 19.

WEEE wants waste winnowed

The Waste Electrical and Electronic Equipment (WEEE) directive is the European Community directive 2002/96/EC, which details how electronic waste *(e-waste)* is to be handled. It places responsibility for the safe disposal and recycling of such waste with the original producer of the equipment, requiring them to take back discarded machines from the end user. There is no similar standard in the U.S. currently, but we expect many manufactures to be guided by WEEE in their voluntary efforts. Your organization might also consider referencing the WEEE directive in your standard purchasing contract.

ASHRAE CRACs down on overcooling

American Society of Heating, Refrigerating and Air-Conditioning Engineers (ASHRAE) sets standards that affect computer room air conditioner (CRAC) equipment. The 2008 ASHRAE Environmental Guidelines for Datacom Equipment widened the allowable temperature and humidity range in data centers. In particular, ASHRAE raised the maximum allowable temperature to 81° Fahrenheit, stating that the areas can be significantly warmer without damaging the equipment or reducing its reliability. Implementing this new guideline can help your green IT efforts by reducing energy costs to run a data center by several percent. See Chapter 10 for more information on the allowable temperatures and humidity limits (they're a bit complicated).

EPEAT products won't deplete

The Electronic Product Environmental Assessment Tool (EPEAT) is a program developed by the Green Electronics Council that lets manufacturers of electronic equipment report how their products measure up against a set of 51 criteria. These criteria are contained in the IEEE 1680 specification; 23 of them are required and the other 28 are optional.

Under the EPEAT, products receive a rating of bronze, silver, or gold, as outlined in Table 4-1. You can find a summary of the IEEE 1680 criteria, along with ratings of many popular computers, on the EPEAT Web site at www. epeat.net.

Table 4-1	EPEAT Ratings and What They Mean
This Rating	*Means That a Product Meets*
Bronze	All 23 required criteria.
Silver	All 23 required criteria plus at least 50 percent of the optional criteria.
Gold	All 23 required criteria plus at least 75 percent of the optional criteria.

NEC sets the ground rules

Although not a green standard per se, the National Fire Protection Association's National Electrical Code details how power equipment is installed and wired in the United States. Comparable standards exist in most countries, and many localities have their own electrical codes that businesses (along with their IT departments, data centers, and so on) must follow. People with special skills and certifications, such as licensed electricians, are needed to insure that these codes are met when installing new electrical equipment, adding another element of complexity to green projects.

LEED leads to less loss

The U.S. Green Building Council's Leadership in Energy and Environmental Design (LEED) program doesn't affect IT equipment directly. Instead, it rates buildings for green design, assigning points for various environment-friendly features. These features include material types and procurement, water and energy use, and access to alternate commuting options. The program awards certificates at a base level and three advanced levels: silver, gold, and platinum.

From a green IT perspective, LEED is primarily of interest in office environments. Development of a standard for data centers is currently underway as this book goes to press, but the LEED program currently has no such standard.

SpecPower tackles servers

The Standard Performance Evaluation Corporation (SPEC) is familiar to most IT professionals for its series of software benchmarks for evaluating computer system performance. SPEC has added a SPECPower benchmark to evaluate power versus performance characteristics of server-class computers. The first version of their energy benchmark, SpecPower SSJ2008, measures server-side Java performance, by testing the server-side performance of CPUs, caches, memory hierarchy, and shared memory processors. Note that this software benchmark is also sensitive to how well the Java Virtual Machine is implemented in your software environment, a potential source of bias.

The SPECPower benchmark helps you compare the performance of server equipment from different vendors, just as the well-known SPECint and SPECfp ratings help you compare integer and floating-point performance. The current specification is to compare servers with a 1U or 2U form factor (the typical "pizza box" design) and one or two processors.

EU Code of Conduct for Data Centers

The European Union is developing a Code of Conduct for Data Centers. A final draft issued in November 2008 lists 87 best practices for green data centers. Businesses can show their support for these practices as follows:

- ✔ **Data center operators** can participate in the program by establishing a publicly available action plan designed to improve energy efficiency and by reporting on their energy use and progress against the action plan on an annual basis.

- ✔ **Manufacturers of IT equipment and providers of data center energy-efficiency services** can endorse the Code of Conduct by offering energy-efficient products or services to improve data center efficiency and by promoting their use through company-specific initiatives.

EPA and DOE partner for improved efficiency

The EPA and the Department of Energy (DOE) have established the National Data Center Energy Efficiency Information Program (which is actually several programs) to help data center operators improve efficiency.

The DOE, in conjunction with the Lawrence Berkeley National Lab, developed the DC Pro online software tool to help data center operators assess their data center's energy efficiency. The tool offers a high-level assessment and recommends improvements. Additionally, more detailed modules assess chillers and heating, ventilating, air conditioning, and IT equipment, and also assess the potential benefits of using a cogeneration system (an electrical generator whose waste heat is used for other purposes, such as heating buildings; see Chapter 5 for more on cogeneration).

You can download the tool at `www1.eere.energy.gov/industry/saveenergynow/partnering_data_centers.html`.

The Energy Star building program is developing a data center rating program, similar to its current building rating system. The EPA is currently collecting data on energy use at existing data centers and plans to establish its own rating system in the latter half of 2009. Although not available as this book goes to press, look for the update on `www.energystar.gov`.

The Green Grid unites for green

The Green Grid is a worldwide group of corporations pushing for higher energy efficiency in data centers and business computing. Members include hardware and component manufacturers, data center operators, manufacturers of the facility equipment used in data centers, software providers, and other interested parties. These members are developing metrics, measurement methods, processes, and new technologies aimed at reducing the power needed for data processing.

Of particular interest to IT organizations are two metrics developed by the Green Grid — power usage effectiveness (PUE) and Data Center infrastructure Efficiency (DCiE):

```
Total facility power ÷ IT equipment power = PUE
```

and

```
1 ÷ PUE = IT equipment power ÷ Total facility power = DCiE
```

These metrics are useful because they give companies a way to measure their IT infrastructure against industry norms or their peers.

Advocacy Rating Organizations

A number of advocacy groups rate computing equipment and manufacturers. Their goal is to affect the move to greener IT by pushing for adoption of the best available technology. Two well-known advocacy groups have such ratings:

✔ **Greenpeace:** An environmental advocacy organization, Greenpeace rates how well computer companies' current products incorporate green criteria and what roadmap the company plans to follow toward a greener future.

✓ **TCO certification**: The Swedish Confederation of Professional Employees runs a TCO certification program for monitors that includes ergonomics, energy use, and magnetic and electrical fields. The last elements (magnetic and electrical fields) involve controversial criteria, with some advocates claiming that such fields are harmful, but no scientific consensus supports their concerns.

Chapter 5

Assessing Your Current Energy Use and Needs

*I*nformation technology (IT) — computers and related equipment — has grown tremendously and is the largest energy consumer in many organizations. Since generating electricity impacts the environment in a big way, wise power use is IT's biggest green concern and opportunity.

In this chapter we explain why IT needs so much power, where it all comes from, the different ways its use impacts the environment, and some of the ways you can reduce that impact. This chapter also explains how understanding energy and electricity sources can help you make the most of the energy you use and offset its carbon impact. Chapters 7 through 15 tell you how IT can reduce the power it uses.

Understanding Energy Jargon

Talking about energy involves a lot of technical jargon. *Energy* itself is a technical term. I had to work up some energy to write the chapter, and it's probably taking some energy for you to get through it, but psychic energy is not what we are talking about in this book. We're talking physics here, where energy is understood as follows:

✔ *Energy* **is the ability to do work.** It comes in different forms, and some forms of energy are more usable than others. The total amount of energy never changes, but the amount of energy that we can easily use goes down every time it's converted. Electricity is one of the most useful forms of energy.

✔ **Energy often must be** *converted.* For example, thermal energy from burning fossil fuel must be converted to electricity to run computers or mechanical energy to make your car go.

Imagine a sledgehammer poised high over a rock: The sledgehammer has *potential* energy. It got that energy from the muscles of the worker who lifted the hammer, who got it from her corned beef sandwich at lunch. The energy in the beef came from grass the cow ate, which, in turn, got it from sunlight, where thermonuclear fusion is slowly converting hydrogen into helium. When the hammer falls, perhaps speeded by more muscle, its mechanical energy breaks the rock into smaller pieces.

✔ **The waste form of energy is** *heat.* As we use energy, some of it always gets converted to heat. For example, the pieces of broken rock after the hammer fell are a tad warmer, but forget about getting anything useful from that little bit of heat. The long chain of energy conversion starting inside the Sun has come to an end. Of course heat can be useful (perhaps it's February and you're in Minnesota), but going from useful energy to heat and back to useful energy always involves big losses. It's one of the basic laws of physics.

The following sections introduce a few more basic concepts.

Powering up: Watts that all about?

Power is another common word we use a lot in green discussions. Your boss may have the power to tell you when to arrive tomorrow morning, but the power we're talking about has a precise technical meaning. Here's what you need to know:

✔ *Power* **is the rate at which energy is used.** The worker who can lift and drop his sledgehammer 15 times a minute has more power than one who can only do it 10 times a minute.

✔ **Power and energy are closely related.** You calculate energy from power by multiplying the power by the amount of time that power is on. So a high power device, such as a hair dryer, that is only used a few minutes a day consumes less energy than a low power device, such as a laptop computer, that is on all day long.

You can go the other way too. If you know the amount of energy consumed over some time period, the average power will be that energy amount divided by the time.

Checking out common units of measure

Power and energy are measured in a number of different units and that's one of the most confusing aspects of the subject. While there is an International System of Units (abbreviated SI, from its name in French) that specifies what unit of measure to use in any situation, it's only followed carefully in academic papers. This section reveals common electrical units of measure that you will encounter.

- ✔ The standard SI unit of power is the *watt,* but green discussions sometimes use other units. A simple variation, allowed in SI, is to put a prefix in front of the word, such as kilowatt (1,000 watts) or megawatt (1,000,000 watts).

- ✔ **Electrical power is generally measured in watts.** A common type of incandescent light bulb uses 60 watts of power. How much energy it uses depends on how long you leave it on. A *compact fluorescent light bulb (CFL)* that is just as bright might only use 15 watts of power.

Switching incandescent bulbs to CFLs is one of the easiest ways to save energy, but don't leave your CFLs on all day at home while you're at work; that uses more energy than the homeowner who still uses incandescent bulbs but remembers to turn them off.

Another example is all the power bricks used to charge laptops, cell phones, and even Bluetooth headsets. They're usually plugged in all the time. They don't use much power — a couple of watts, maybe — but so many are running all the time that they end up consuming quite a bit of energy.

The energy measurements you need to understand as you look at your facility and IT equipment include the following:

- ✔ **Watt-hour (Wh):** The most common energy measure is the *watt-hour* — one watt running for one hour. That's the amount of energy a 60-watt bulb uses in one minute. It's not a lot.

- ✔ **Kilowatt-hour (kWh):** Your electric company charges you by the kilowatt-hour (kWh), which is 1,000 watt hours. Typical power rates range from 5 to 20 cents per kilowatt-hour, but you should find out exactly what you're paying. See the sidebar, "Reading your electric bill."

- ✔ **Joule (J):** The official SI unit is the *joule (J),* which is one watt-second. A kilowatt-hour is 3.6 megajoules (MJ) (1,000 watts × 60 minutes/hour × 60 seconds/minute). You find this unit used in academic writing on energy topics.

- ✔ **BTU (British thermal unit):** This older unit is used mainly for heat energy. One BTU is the amount of energy needed to heat a pound of water one degree Fahrenheit. It turns out one BTU is a tad more that a kilojoule, or about a third of a kilowatt hour. You find the BTU used often in heating and cooling systems in the U.S.

✔ **Ton:** Perhaps the weirdest power unit you'll see in IT is the *ton,* which measures air-conditioning capacity. One ton is the amount of heat removed by melting a ton of ice over the course of a day.

One ton of air-conditioning capacity is equivalent to 12,000 BTUs per hour, or about 3.5 kilowatts. However, that doesn't mean a one-ton air conditioner requires 3.5 kilowatts of electricity to operate. The same law of physics that says a generator can't covert all heat supplied to it into electricity — that it can't be 100-percent efficient — lets air conditioners move more heat energy than the energy they consume. Efficiencies of 350 percent (the *coefficient of performance*) are common for air conditioners. You'll also find the ton used to talk about carbon emissions. There the ton has its ordinary meaning as a unit of mass. We discuss carbon measurement later in this chapter.

Remember we said you can get power by dividing energy by time? Well, there are two more units of power you'll run into that come from the energy units we just told you about.

✔ **BTU per hour:** Often used to measure heating and air conditioning output.

✔ **Megawatt hours per year:** This is an example of how units of measure get out of hand. The watt is a unit of power. We multiplied by the time that power was running to get energy in megawatt hours. Now we are figuring out how much energy we are using each year, which is again a power measurement. It's all a bit silly but very common. A megawatt hour per year sounds like a lot of power, but it isn't that much. It's about 114 watts, which you get by dividing 1,000,000 watt-hours by 8760 hours/year (365 days/year × 24 hours/day).

Speaking electrical jargon

Here are some more electricity terms you'll run into:

✔ *Voltage* **measures how strong electricity is.** An ordinary AA battery supplies about 1.5 volts. You can touch both ends and never notice a thing. Wall outlets in North America supply 120 volts. Touching one of those live wires will give you a nasty shock at best and could even be fatal. The power mains going into a data center might be 25,000 volts. That's enough to cause certain death and other effects too gross to mention here.

✔ *Current* **measures how much electricity is flowing through a wire.** It's measured in *amperes* (*amps* for short). A typical wall outlet supplies up to 20 amps. A car battery puts out some 200 amps when starting your engine.

Reading your electric bill

Base or customer charge: This is a fixed monthly amount that pays for your connection to the utility (polls, wires, meters, billing, customer service, and so on). It does not vary by the amount of power you use.

Energy charge: You pay for each kilowatt hour of electricity you use. Your bill likely breaks this down into half a dozen or more subcharges, such as for energy generation, transmission, fuel adjustments, taxes, credits, and so on. You want to know the total cost you pay per kilowatt hour. Energy charges in the U.S. typically run in the 5 to 20 cents per kWh range. Some utilities let you pick your energy supplier and their generation charge is broken out on your bill. You can shop for a lower cost conventional supplier or you may be able to pick a green energy supplier, usually at a somewhat higher rate.

Demand charge: You pay per kilowatt for the maximum amount of power you used that month. Your electric reader records and reports the peak power used over a brief period — fifteen minutes or a half hour — that month. Typical demand charges can range from $5 to $15 per kilowatt. Demand charges can be a big portion of your bill. An oversized air conditioning system that cycles on and off can cost you extra demand charges. If you know some short-term activity, such as testing a new bank of servers, will add significant to your power use, you can save money by scheduling that activity when other uses are lower, say after office hours.

Tiered charges: Some utilities charge higher prices if you use more energy.

Seasonal rates: Some utilities charge more in the summer than in the winter.

Time of use charges: Some utilities offer you the option of paying different prices at different times of day to encourage you to shift electrical load to off peak hours. If you have data centers in different time zones, you may be able to move computing loads around to take advantage of off peak electric rates in different time zones.

Reactive power charge: Some utilities charge an extra fee if your power factor is less than one.

Connection charges: If you generate some of your own electricity, your utility may charge you for the extra capacity it needs to provide you electricity when your generator is not working.

Stranded cost charges: Many utilities made large investments in equipment when their rates were regulated by the state. As many states deregulated their energy markets, they allowed utilities to add a "stranded cost" charge to their rates to recover these investments when market rates alone would not be enough to pay for them.

Tariff: Commercial electric billing can get quite complex. Utilities publish their full set of rates in a legal document called a tariff book. The specific set of rates you pay are based on one of these tariffs. You may be able to negotiate for a more favorable tariff, particularly if you are building a new data center.

Your electric utility's Web site likely has additional information on how to read your bill. After you figure out what you pay per kilowatt-hour, write the answer in the margin along with today's date. We expect it will look small compared to what you'll be paying in a few years.

The amount of power in an electrical circuit depends on both the voltage and the current. For DC circuits, power in watts is the product of voltage and current. For AC the relationship's more complex, as we discuss in a bit. But first we'd better tell you what AC and DC mean.

Gigabytes, gigawatts — SI prefixes

The energy business uses all those funny prefixes you encounter when buying computer memory. *Kilo* means a thousand, *mega* means a million, *giga* means a billion, *tera* means a trillion. There are also a couple of bigger ones you may not have seen before: *peta,* which is a thousand trillion (some big data centers have petabytes of data storage) and *exa,* which is a million trillion. For example, the total annual U.S. energy production is about 70 exajoule (EJ). If you're riveted, check out www.eia. doe.gov.

Electricity comes in a couple of flavors:

- ✔ **Direct current (DC)** always flows in one direction. Batteries supply DC.

- ✔ **Alternating current (AC)** keeps changing direction. The electricity coming from your wall outlet, called *mains power,* is AC. In North America, most of South America, and parts of Japan, AC current goes from forward to backward and forward again 60 times a second (60 hertz). In most of the rest of world the power-line frequency is 50 hertz.

An industrial strength, three-wire version of AC, called *three phase* (3ø), is typically supplied to large users such as office buildings and data centers. Three phase is also used for power transmission — look for the three wires the next time you see a power line. With ordinary two-wire AC power, there's a moment around each current direction change when little or no power is being supplied. Those few milliseconds don't matter to a light bulb, but they're an eternity for a computer chip. Every personal-computer AC power supply has large components called *capacitors* that store enough energy to keep the computer running during those direction changes. At least two of the three wires in *three-phase power* are supplying power at all times. Three-phase power supplies for computers don't need as much energy storage and can be more efficient.

Auditing Your Building for Energy Use

Auditing your building is a multistep process that involves not only IT but also your facilities and accounting departments, if your organization is large enough to include all these players. The following sections give you an overview of each step to help you get started.

Starting with your electric bill

A good first step in planning for green is finding out how your organization is billed for electricity. Your power utility tracks your electricity usage every month, so you can easily access this information. And, of course, the bill tells you one important fact: how much you pay for electricity each month. Saving electricity expense is a major way to justify green programs. But the monthly amount has limited value. What you really need to know from the bill is how that monthly cost is broken down, so you can translate expected energy savings from green initiatives into dollars and cents paybacks.

If you have ever tried to read your home electric bills, you know they are not simple. There are often half a dozen different charges that make up your total cost per kilowatt-hour. Commercial electric bills are even more complex than residential bills. In addition to the charge for total energy (kilowatt-hours) used, there is usually a charge for the peak power use. Charges often depend on the time of energy use, with different rates for peak- and non-peak hours. Some electric companies offer reduced rates to large users that can shed load on demand when power is tight. Your electric bill will reveal which of these programs currently apply to your organization. See the sidebar "Reading your electric bill" for details.

Here is the information you should glean from your electric bill

- How much you pay each year for electricity
- How much you pay the electric utility for each kilowatt-hour you use
- How much you pay for each kilowatt of power used during the peak period each month
- Whether you are on any rate incentive plans, such as off peak discounts and load shedding reductions
- Whether there are other special charges that might be avoidable, such as connection fees and reactive power charges

Checking your power meter

Your electric utility places a power meter at the point the electric lines enter your building. These typically have a read out that displays the cumulative amount of energy that has entered the building since the meter was installed. Find out where the power meters are located and learn how to read them. The meter provides an easy way to track your total energy usage.

✔ A reading should include the number displayed on the meter face and the date and time of the reading

✔ One reading is not useful in itself. Two readings, separated in time, will tell you how much energy you used in that time period. For example meter readings about one week apart can tell you how much power you used, on average, over that week.

✔ You will need to subtract the first meter reading from the second reading to get the number of kilowatt-hours used and then compute the number of hours between readings to get the time interval. The power used, in kilowatts, is the number of kilowatt hours divided by the time in hours. See Appendix A for a worksheet that leads you through this calculation.

✔ Meters with mechanical displays are a bit tricky to read. The pointers on half the dials turn clockwise, while every other dial turns counter clockwise. When a meter pointer is between two numbers, be sure to always write down the *smaller* number. Your power company can give you more information on reading your meter. Here is one example of a helpful utility Web site from Delmarva Power: `www.delmarva.com/home/requests/meter`.

✔ If your data center is located in the same building as other corporate activities, there may be only one meter for the entire facility. If so, the readings will, of course, reflect the power used by the entire facility.

Reconciling consumption with devices

After you lay the ground work by understanding your electric bill and power meters and compiling historic data for a year or two, you're ready to attempt to reconcile billed use with the energy consumption of your IT equipment. The following steps give you an overview of how you might approach this task. You'll find a detailed description of the steps involved in Chapter 10, and Appendix A includes worksheets for you to use.

1. First you'll need to know how much power goes to your data center. If the data center has its own electric meter, you can use the power reading discussed earlier in this chapter. If other users are on your power meter, such as office areas or manufacturing areas, you'll need to determine the data center's power usage. There may be current meters built into your switch gear, the grey cabinets in the basement that contain circuit breakers and transformers. Ask your facilities people to show you this equipment. Alternatively, you may need an electrician to take power readings for you.

2. The next step is to determine about how much electricity each device uses. The best way is to take actual measurements. We describe inexpensive test equipment for measuring power in Chapter 17.

3. Next, you add up the power of each device. Again the details are in Chapter 10 along with instructions for using the worksheets in Appendix A.

4. Finally you calculate how much of the electricity you buy goes to powering your IT equipment versus cooling and power distribution overhead. Once you know this, you should adjust the cost of the electricity supplied to IT equipment upwards, to reflect the fact that the heat produced costs money to extract. For example, if you use 1,200 watts of cooling for every 1,000 watts of power that goes to IT equipment, you should multiply the billed cost of power by (1,200 + 1,000) ÷ 1,000 = 2.2 to get a better measure of the true cost of the energy the equipment uses.

Automated equipment can monitor power use on a continuous basis and make that information available through the Web. We give some examples in Chapter 17.

Considering Policy-Based Management

An organization's level of energy use isn't often a conscious management decision. Instead, energy use is determined by hundreds, if not thousands, of small, seemingly unrelated choices during business operations and planning, ranging from which servers to buy to how high to set the office thermostat.

The only way to get control of energy use is to set effective policy that makes sure energy and other green issues are considered in all decision making. One first step is to create an enterprise-wide model of the expected future cost of energy that can be applied to upcoming budget decisions. Such a model would include

✔ Expected rises in energy and fuel prices. Projections are always difficult. Your power company may be able to provide some planning guidance.

✔ The added cost of removing heat generated by equipment (see Chapter 10).

✔ Energy costs associated with construction, maintenance, and disposal of equipment. See "Reducing embedded energy in equipment" later in this chapter.

✔ A multiplier of 20–50 percent (as a cushion in case of unexpected jumps in energy prices).

I'm from the government and I'm here to help

It's hard to compete with fuels that are simply dug up or pumped out of the ground. Renewable power's current small role would be nonexistent if not for government incentives, in the form of direct subsidies, tax credits, and mandates. In the U.S., these incentives vary from state to state and year to year, depending on changes in the political climate. Understanding what deals are available on the federal, state, and local level can make a big difference in your organization's green budget. Finding out what's available to you, can be tricky. One place to start is www.recovery.gov. Your local legislator's office might be able to help as well.

By doing this model, you get more realistic electricity costs to use in planning. These costs will typically be higher than what you see on your current electric bill. The higher cost figures will reduce the time that energy-saving investments pay for themselves and make it easier to justify green projects. And they provide a more holistic look at equipment costs (not just the server, but the long term cost of running and replacing it) when IT departments make purchasing decisions.

Figure the resulting cost into all purchase decisions. For example, say a more efficient server costs $500 more but saves 100 watts in power usage. If you use a power cost of $0.10 per kilowatt hour, the server will save $87.60 per year in electricity charges. At that rate it would take 5.7 years to recoup the added investment. On the other hand, if you use a more realistic cost of $0.30 per kilowatt hour, based on the expected increase in electric rates and the added cost of providing cooling for the sever, the pay back period drops to under 2 years, making the efficient server a very attractive investment.

Looking for Efficiencies

Earlier sections of this chapter help you understand overall energy concepts and measurements as well as big-picture green strategies. This section gives a closer look at your IT equipment, in light of the following:

- ✔ How you can apply an understanding of energy to ensure that equipment is more efficient.
- ✔ How IT can add green power technology and work with power companies to increase overall energy efficiency.

Where's the Emerald City?

With more efficient ways to compute, air condition, and move power, why do so many data centers use less than the best? The answer often lies in the higher initial cost of the better technologies. Using more low-power chips fills more rack space in the data center. Better air-conditioning systems cost more, and getting an optimal design usually involves pricey consultants. *The good news is that doing the green thing also saves money.* Electricity is expensive and the price is sure to go up in the coming years. But convincing senior management to make the up-front investments to reduce environmental impacts is a major challenge, particularly when those last-minute budget cuts get made. Understanding long term trends in energy costs and government regulations can help make the case for green investments. See Chapter 2 for more on making the business case for green.

If you're a senior manager, keeping those energy-saving investments is often the difference between talking green and living green.

Choosing an efficient chip configuration

Computers break down problems into many simple, logical decisions; tiny electronic circuits called *gates* or *logic elements* make these decisions. For example, an *and* gate has two inputs and produces an output signal whenever both of its inputs are on. In other words the output of the *and* gate is on only if input one *and* input two are on. Otherwise the gate's output is off. Each of these decisions requires a minute amount of electrical energy. A modern computer processor chip has hundreds of millions of these gates and each make these decisions billions of times every second. All these minute electrical sips add up to big gulps of energy.

Speed increases energy consumption. You can make the gates in a processor chip switch faster if more power is applied. And the higher-frequency signals generated during a fast computer's operation leak across the thin insulating layers in a chip more easily, using up still more power. All that electrical power going into the chip gets turned into heat. A typical processor chip uses roughly the same amount of power as a medium-size incandescent light bulb — and the chip can get just as hot. Getting heat out of the chip affects how fast processors can go.

By definition, the fastest chips on the market can do the most calculations per second, but they generally don't perform the most calculations per unit of electrical energy. If computations can be spread among more than one processor, and that happens in most data centers, using two or three energy-efficient chips instead of one super-fast chip may get the same work done with less electricity and less waste heat.

When purchasing new servers or when consolidating processing loads to fewer servers, take advantage of servers that do the most computation per kilowatt-hour. If you server's data sheet does not provide information on energy performance, ask your vendor.

The un-cool cost of cooling

All the other chips in a computer use electricity and produce heat too, as do peripheral devices such as disk drives, video displays, printers, scanners, and modems. Even the fans that move hot air away from all that electronics use electricity and add more heat to the room. Computer servers would burn up if all that heat weren't removed by large air conditioners — a major expense in data centers.

Air conditioners pump heat from inside the building to the outside air, but those air conditioners also require lots of electrical power. The shocking fact is that for every 1,000 watts of power used by the computers in many data centers, the air-conditioning needs another 1,000 watts or more.

Because cooling represents such a large fraction of IT energy consumption, improving air conditioner efficiency is one important road to green IT. We tell you more about green air conditioning opportunities in Chapter 10.

Powering the chip

Putting aside the occasional handheld PDA that runs on disposable batteries, all the electricity used by IT comes from electrical generators driven by some other source of energy. The computer is connected to the generators by a series of wires. The wires to distant power plants can run for hundreds of miles.

Moving electricity long distances is more efficient at higher voltage — long power transmission lines operate at hundreds of thousands of volts. The tiny transistors in computer chips want low voltages — 5 volts or less. The high voltages are reduced to low voltages in a series of steps using transformers and AC to DC converters. Each of those power conversion devices uses some of the power they are converting. Some vendors have clever, energy-saving ways to get power the last few inches to those chips. We tell you more in Chapter 8.

Getting all the power you pay for

We introduce *direct current (DC)* and *alternating current (AC)* in "Speaking electrical jargon" earlier in this chapter. And we do so because understanding how current works can help you improve efficiencies in your IT systems. Consider the following:

✓ **For direct current, there's a simple relationship between voltage, current, and power:**

```
volts × amps = watts
```

So if run your laptop off your car's 12-volt battery and the laptop draws 2 amps, the laptop is using 24 watts of power.

✓ **For AC the voltage-current-power relationship is a bit more complicated.** Certain types of electrical loads, such as motors and some computer power supplies, cause the peak current to flow at a slightly different time from when the voltage peaks. Calculating the power in watts must include another variable: the *power factor.* Here's what the equation looks like:

```
volts × amps × power factor = watts
```

The power factor depends on how far apart the voltage and current peaks are. When they happen at the same time, the power factor is one and power is just volts multiplied by amps again. A *low power factor* means voltage and current aren't peaking at the same time; they're *out of phase.*

What does all this mean for you? Power companies typically charge for power based on volts × amp. Therefore, if your power factor is less than one, you pay for power you don't actually get. To correct the problem, you have a few options:

✓ **Add power factor correctors to your IT setup:** These devices fix this problem and make the whole electric system more efficient. Your power utility can help you decide if power factor correction makes sense. They may install the necessary equipment or have you hire an electrical contractor to do the work.

✓ **Check equipment's power factor before you buy:** Specifying a high power factor when buying computers and other electrical equipment, such as compact fluorescent bulbs, can reduce the need for power factor correction. The power factor should be listed as such on the product's spec sheet; if it isn't ask your vendor.

IT equipment creates another special electrical problem. The power supplies in many computers only draw energy during part of each power cycle. Specifying equipment with *reduced harmonic distortion* minimizes these issues.

Electrical matters are regulated by complex *codes,* privately created regulations that are adopted by most state and local governments. (This kind of code is not to be confused with the stuff produced by computer programmers and cryptographers, though it can be just as obscure.) The most common code in the United States is the National Electrical Code, published by the National Fire Protection Association. There are sometimes local codes as well, particularly in large cities like New York and Chicago.

Complying with electrical codes is important for safety and insurance reasons, so it's always best to use a licensed electrician for power wiring.

Tapping into the smart grid

When you look at cleaner (as in carbon-free) energy sources, discussed a little later in this chapter, consider ways to deal with the problems of *intermittency* — a fancy way of saying that the wind doesn't always blow and sun doesn't always shine. The *smart grid* offers a possible cost-effective solution that also maximizes efficiency. And it offers IT opportunities to increase energy efficiency as well.

The smart grid creates markets for the variable component of the power stream. A wind farm sells the extra electricity it produces on a windy day to a buyer who can do something useful with a relatively short burst of energy. The electric companies offer price incentives to customers who can quickly shed electric load on command for, say, a half hour when the wind drops, allowing other power sources to come on line.

IT data centers could take advantage of such preferred rates during peak demand periods by

- Shutting down less-critical servers.
- Shifting processing load to data centers in other areas where electrical demand is not so high.
- Slowing processor clocks.
- Running on backup power generators.

They could even buy power bursts from wind gusts and use them for

- Over-clocking processors for special data analyses.
- Charging UPS batteries.
- Spinning up flywheels in energy storage systems.

The smart grid is still in its infancy. Check with your power company on their smart grid plans and ask to be an early test customer. One Web site that keeps you up to date on this exciting technology is www.smartgrid news.com.

Generating power more efficiently

Green power technologies include *distributed generation* and *cogeneration* or *trigeneration:*

✔ **Distributed generation** is generating power where it's being consumed (as opposed to a power plant distributing power across the grid). Distributed generation offers cleaner power generation and transportation efficiency. See "Moving that green power," later in this chapter for more on the challenges of distributing green power.

Distributed power solutions vary:

- *Rooftop solar panels and wind turbines:* Adding these to your building makes sense if you live in an area with lots of wind or sun. (See later sections in this chapter for more on these energy sources.)

- *Natural-gas–powered microturbines or fuel cells:* This option may be a good fit if you can utilize the waste heat produced by these generation devices, which can also supply backup power. To add a microturbine, you need to work with your power company, which likely has safety concerns about local generation devices that connect to the grid. We discuss the pros and cons of natural gas later in this chapter as well.

- *Conventional diesel generators:* If you're a big data center, you likely already have diesel generators onsite to supply backup power in case your local utility service is interrupted.

✔ **Cogeneration or trigeneration:**

- *Cogeneration* systems use the waste heat from the generators for other purposes, such as heating buildings. Such cogeneration systems can be very efficient if there's a *local* need for the heat.

- *Trigeneration* combines power, heating, and cooling. To create this extra-efficient system, add special systems called *adsorption chillers,* which turn waste heat into cold, reducing air-conditioning power requirements.

  You can find out more about cogeneration options at www. distributedenergy.com.

Measuring other gases

Carbon dioxide is not the only gas that traps heat. Other man-made and natural gases, such as fluorocarbons and methane (CH_4), contribute to the greenhouse effect — many with more potency than CO_2, making comparisons tricky, because different gases stay in the atmosphere for different amounts of time. For example, methane is a couple dozen times more effective at trapping heat than CO_2 but it stays in the atmosphere for a much shorter time.

Peak-shaving to even loads and save money

Peak shaving is another potential use of distributed power. Power companies often offer discounts to users who can *shed load* during peak consumption periods — typically a few hot summer afternoons a year. Your organization may already own large generators that run the data center during power failures. Using these generators to take over some of your data center load during periods when the power company is offering load-shedding incentives can cut your utility bills while testing the generators under realistic conditions.

Talk to your power company about peak shaving opportunities. This can be easy if load switching is possible, but gets very tricky if the generator is connected to the grid.

Power companies are very touchy about having back-up power systems connected to their lines: the backups must be carefully synchronized to power-line frequencies, they can overload local distribution systems, and they can come on unexpectedly, threatening the safety of utility employees who may be working on power lines they believe are de-energized.

Reducing embedded energy

While electrical energy consumption dominates IT's environmental effects, other energy impacts are worth considering. Energy is also consumed as data centers are built and as data-center equipment is made and moved. This embedded energy can be difficult to measure exactly, but is typically a fraction of the overall price converted back to kilowatt-hours at the local rate.

Computing equipment has a short useful life; old machines often have hazardous materials such as lead and mercury. The sheer bulk of computing waste is a problem and much of it is transported to third-world countries where the handling of such waste is often poorly managed.

Specifying easily recycled equipment or manufacturer-maintained recycling can reduce the problem. We discuss disposal and recycling options in detail in Chapter 19.

Managing Energy's Waste: Carbon Reduction Options

You've heard about carbon dioxide (CO_2) emissions. What's it mean? CO_2 is an atmosphere gas that traps heat from the sun; scientists confirm that CO_2 gases contribute to global warming. Different forms of power generation produce different amounts of CO_2 for each kilowatt-hour of energy they produce.

We put all this CO_2 into context in this section. You also find an overview of traditional power sources and how they impact the environment, as well as carbon-free options. And last but not least, you find an introduction to issues about moving green power as well as buying carbon offsets to keep your carbon production in balance (which brings the discussion full circle, because the role of the natural carbon cycle is to keep production in balance with absorption). Read on for details.

Understanding the carbon cycle

Before you can reduce your carbon footprint, you must know how and when you generate carbon dioxide and other greenhouse gases.

Carbon is an element upon which all life on Earth depends. All of the chemicals that we're made of — proteins, sugars, fats, DNA, RNA, vitamins — are built on chains of carbon atoms. The carbon in fossil fuels (like oil) is the remnant of organisms that died millions of years ago and somehow got buried.

Almost all carbon in living organisms ends up in the atmosphere as carbon dioxide (CO_2) as a result of the decay process. That same carbon came from the atmosphere — plants take CO_2 from the atmosphere during photosynthesis. This carbon cycle used to keep everything pretty much in balance.

The hydrogen economy

The energy economy, like the software industry, attracts silver-bullet solutions that promise to solve all problems. Hydrogen has been promoted as the ultimate solution to fossil fuel dependence. It burns cleanly, producing only water vapor. And, in theory, it can power vehicles that use fuel cells. That's the good news. The bad news is that there are no natural sources of hydrogen — it all must be produced artificially and that takes energy — lots more than the energy we get from burning the hydrogen. Hydrogen is not a source of energy; it's merely a way of transmitting it. As a transmission system, hydrogen is very inefficient. One possible role for hydrogen in the IT future is storing energy. Hydrogen can be generated from electricity during off-peak times, stored in tanks, and used to generate electricity in fuel cells at times of peak demand. The same fuel cells could serve as backup power generators.

Human activities such as mining and burning fossil fuel adds net CO_2 to the atmosphere; other activities, such as burying solid wastes in land fills, remove net CO_2 (though, unfortunately, it doesn't remove as much as the fuel burning adds). For the past century, the amount of CO_2 in the atmosphere has been increasing. It's still a small amount — a few hundred parts per million — but CO_2 tends to trap heat much like the glass windows on a greenhouse — sunlight gets through, but longer wavelength infrared radiation from the heated Earth doesn't get back out and is trapped, warming the planet.

The natural carbon cycle is quite complex and not fully understood. There is still controversy about how much of the increase in atmospheric CO_2 is due to human activities versus natural cycles. But there is a scientific consensus that human activities are contributing to warming the atmosphere, reflected in the reports of the Intergovernmental Panel on Climate Change (IPCC). Perhaps a major reason for the remaining controversy is the potentially draconic consequences of greenhouse warming and the resulting need to reduce emissions of carbon dioxide into the atmosphere.

Measuring carbon

In discussion of global warming, carbon and CO_2 are measured in *metric tons* or *tonnes*. A metric ton is 1,000 kilograms or 2,204.6 pounds — almost exactly a customary long ton. We're talking about a lot of carbon, so megatonnes

(MT) and gigatonnes (GT) are discussed. And just to confuse things further, the scientific literature prefers grams. At least there are simple conversion rules: A megatonne is a teragram (Tg).

There is one more conversion rule worth knowing: When you burn one ton of carbon, you get 3.66 tons of CO_2.

Traditional power sources and carbon

The different ways power companies generate electricity illuminate how the energy used by IT affects the environment. Different forms of power generation have different impacts. We give a brief overview of traditional power sources in the sections that follow.

Coal

Almost half of the electricity produced in the United States (49 percent) comes from coal. Coal is also one of the least expensive sources of energy and some 90 percent of the billion tons of coal mined in the U.S. each year is burned to generate electricity.

- ✔ **The good news:** The United States has ample reserves of coal and even exports some.

- ✔ **The bad news:** Coal is one of the dirtiest fuels to burn. It consists largely of carbon and so it produces more CO_2 per kilowatt-hour than any other fuel (about 2 pounds per kWh). Modern *clean coal* power plants minimize other emissions from coal, such as sulfur dioxide and particulates, but these emissions are created in relatively small amounts per ton of coal. Every ton of coal burned creates almost three tons of CO_2. Coal-mining operations are massive and often damage the local environment.

 One proposed solution to the CO_2 problem is carbon *sequestration,* pulling CO_2 from the exhaust of coal-burning plants and burying it underground, in old oil wells and the like. CO_2 is a gas at room temperature and sea level pressure, but it turns into a liquid when compressed. For every ton of coal burnt, almost four tons of CO_2 have to be buried for complete sequestration. As this book goes to press, however, no one has yet built a full-scale power plant that does this and the engineering and economic obstacles are formidable.

Natural gas

Natural gas is the fuel of choice for supplying power during peak demand periods, but has other uses, such as home heating and cooking.

✔ **The good news:** Natural gas is the cleanest fossil fuel. Natural gas consists mostly of methane (CH_4), and much of the energy comes from combining that hydrogen with oxygen in the air to form water (H_2O). As a result, burning natural gas to make electricity only produces about 1.3 pounds of CO_2 per kilowatt-hour. Also, a natural gas power plant costs less to build than other types.

✔ **The bad news:** Natural gas is more expensive than coal or oil.

Oil

Only a small fraction of U.S. electricity comes from oil, but oil does play a role in IT; it's the fuel used by most backup generators, which operate infrequently.

✔ **The good news:** Oil sits between coal and natural gas in price and pollution per kilowatt-hour.

✔ **The bad news:** Oil is in high demand for transportation fuel, making it costly compared to coal. Another downside from a green perspective is safe on-site storage. A leaking oil tank requires very expensive cleanup.

Buying carbon-free electricity

A variety of energy sources — some old, some new — don't increase the carbon in the atmosphere. Each source has its own environmental issues and is responsible for some carbon release during the construction of the needed generating plants and transmission lines. Nevertheless, these carbon-free sources promise a green way forward for IT energy.

In many locations, energy consumers can select the source their power comes from. Buying energy from these carbon-free sources, which generally involves paying more per kilowatt-hour, is one of the best ways for IT to reduce its carbon footprint.

Hydro

Hydroelectric power comes from dams built across rivers. The backed-up water flows down through large turbines to generate electricity. The U.S. Pacific Northwest and the Canadian province of Quebec get much electricity from hydro power. Most rivers suitable for hydro power have already been dammed, limiting major expansion of this power source.

✔ **The good news:** Hydro operations produce no CO_2.

✔ **The bad news:** The dams inundate upstream areas and alter the natural river flow, sometimes interfering with fish migration.

Nuclear

Nuclear power was touted as the ultimate source of clean energy in the 1950s. During the 1970s and 80s, environmental groups campaigned against it, citing numerous problems, from worker radiation exposure to difficulty disposing of nuclear waste. Nuclear power fell into disrepute in the U.S. and much of Europe, with hundreds of planned facilities abandoned. Some countries, such as France, continued active nuclear programs. France now gets 80 percent of its electricity from nuclear power, compared to 20 percent in the United States. No nuclear plants have been built in the United States since the 1970s, but several new facilities have begun licensing for more.

- ✔ **The good news:** Nuclear power produces no CO_2 in operation. France generates much less CO_2 per person annually (6.2 tons) than the United States (20.4) or other European nations (typically around 10).

- ✔ **The bad news:** Although new nuclear plant designs are safer, some of the old issues, such as safe disposal of waste and protection of plants from terrorist attack, have not been fully addressed.

Biomass

Biomass energy is generated by burning agricultural material — either plants grown for the purpose or waste from food production. The big push currently is to use plants to make liquid fuels, such as ethanol, for transportation use. However, not all biomass is suitable for liquid fuel conversion, and electricity generation is a potential alternative use for excess biomass.

- ✔ **The good news:** Biomass adds no CO_2 to the atmosphere. All the energy generated comes from sunlight used by the plants in photosynthesis. While CO_2 is released in the burning process, the plants pull all that carbon from CO_2 in the air, so there is no net change. A similar story applies to energy from burning city trash.

- ✔ **The bad news:** In the case of burning city trash, some of the waste stream, such as plastics that are not recycled, comes from petroleum (oil). Also, agriculture has its own list of environmental sins, including cutting down forests and stream pollution from fertilizer runoff.

Wind

Wind is perhaps the oldest power source for commerce, driving grain mills and sailing ships since ancient times. Modern wind turbines provide 20 percent of Denmark's electricity, but under 2 percent in the U.S., though wind's share is growing rapidly. Modern wind turbines tower over the landscape, as high as a 30-story building with slowly rotating blades, each as long as the wing on a 747 jetliner. Some smaller versions are built to sit on the roofs of commercial buildings. The smaller turbines don't produce as much power as their giant brothers, but they let a data center or office building generate a little green power.

✓ **The good news:** Wind power plants produce no CO_2 or other pollutants in operation, and electricity from wind no longer falls in the category of promising new technology — new wind farms are sprouting like mushrooms in regions with favorable wind patterns. Texas views wind as the next energy boom, replacing its declining oil economy. The wind blows inconsistently, but electric grids deal with variations in demand and can accommodate intermittent wind power as long as only a modest fraction of total power comes from wind — up to10 percent or so. Higher levels of wind utilization generally require additional investment in energy storage systems or smart grid demand management.

✓ **The (not so) bad news:** Although electricity from wind has gotten a head start, solutions to wind's on-again off-again ways will be necessary when more electric power comes from wind. IT may play a role here: Expensive solutions include energy storage and building more transmission lines that tie wind farms in widely separated regions to a common electric grid, and a less expensive solution is the smart grid, introduced in the earlier section, "Tapping into the smart grid."

Figure 5-1 shows where the wind blows in the United States. Figure 5-2 shows a pair of wind turbines in Rio Vista, California.

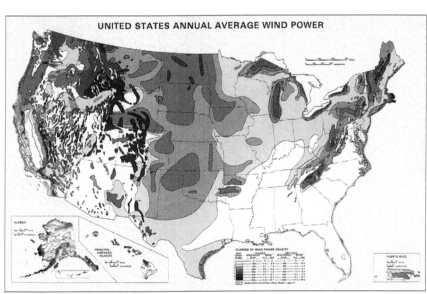

Figure 5-1: A map of the United States shows which areas have the highest wind potential.

Figure 5-2:
A pair of
Vestas
V90 wind
turbines in
Rio Vista
California.
Each turbine
has a
name plate
capacity
(peak output
on a windy
day) of 3
megawatts.

Courtesy of Vestas Wind Systems A/S

Solar

Getting *photovoltaic* electricity — power from the sun — has challenged the imaginations of technologists for decades. Ideas vary from direct conversion in large sheets of semiconductor material, to focusing sunlight on boilers, creating steam to drive turbines, to mimicking photosynthesis.

While wind generators are tall and spread out, solar collectors tend to be flat and must cover large surface areas. One 550-megawatt solar plant being built in California covers some 10 square miles. Here's why: The amount of sunlight power available for conversion is called the *insolation* and is measured in watts per square meter. The peak insolation is about 1 kilowatt per square meter at noon on a clear day. To get the available electricity, you have to know the conversion efficiency, which can range from 15 to 40 per cent, depending on the technology. That insolation figure is for a square meter panel aimed directly at the sun. If the panel is lying flat on a roof, the power output is further reduced, as a function of the angle the sun makes with respect to the panel (the sine of the angle, if you remember your trigonometry). Finally, there is a reduction factor for cloudy days and the fact that the sun doesn't shine at night.

Solar works best in dry climates near the equator.

✔ **The really good news:** The sun provides inexhaustible power. Sunlight falls on the Earth's surface at total power levels that far exceed current and foreseeable human energy needs. Sunlight supplies the energy needed for the food we eat; the wood we build our homes with; the water that we drink, wash, and flush; and the wind that drives those turbines discussed in the previous section.

✔ **More good news:** IT demand is usually highest during the day, which is a good fit with solar energy.

✔ **The bad news:** Solar power currently costs more per kilowatt of generating capacity than most other energy sources, but progress has been steady. Also, solar power availability varies by time of day, season, latitude, and weather. Intermittency solutions for wind power apply to solar as well, although the two sources can complement each other to a limited extent.

Figure 5-3 shows a typical array of solar panels, located in the Nevada desert. The array is expected to produce more than 25 percent of the electric power needed for Nellis Air Force Base.

Figure 5-3:
This solar farm at Nellis Air Force Base, Nevada has some 72,000 solar panels.

U.S. Air Force photo by Master Sgt. Robert Valenca

Balancing consumption with offsets

Carbon offsets are contracts; you provide money and the other party uses that money to reduce the amount of greenhouse gases produced by human activities. These gases can include methane and others, but the credits are typically sold as CO_2 equivalents. This means the CO_2 gas you create isn't eliminated; you pay an organization to do something that counterbalances the gas your organization produces.

The contracts are monitored various ways to ensure the following:

✔ Gas production is actually reduced.

✔ The action done isn't something that would have been done anyway, without the funding.

In other words, an organization shouldn't be able to collect carbon offset payments unless it does something additional with the funds to reduce net greenhouse gases. Certifying groups include the U.N.'s Clean Development Mechanism (cdm.unfccc.int) and the Chicago Climate Exchange (www.chicagoclimatex.com).

Carbon offsets are already a multi-billion dollar market, with prices ranging from $4 to $40 per tonne of carbon dioxide equivalent (CO_2 e).

Offsetting activities include

✔ **Building renewable power systems.**

✔ **Planting trees.**

✔ **Capturing and burning methane generated in landfills:** Landfill gas can make electricity using diesel engines or microturbines to drive generators. Doing so is a double whammy — a highly potent greenhouse gas is kept out of the atmosphere and electricity is generated without mining fossil fuel. This works great if the landfill is near potential customers, but often the land fill is too far from civilization to transmit the electricity efficiently and the landfill gas is just burnt *(flared)*.

Buying carbon offsets is one way for your organization to support greenhouse gas reduction. But experts on carbon offsets say you should do what you can to reduce your emissions first. We think money for buying carbon offsets might be better spent on the many ways IT can reduce its energy consumption that we tell you about in this book. Some of your green IT investments, such as alternative energy generation might even qualify as carbon offsets your organization can sell. Visit the Chicago Climate Exchange Web site (www.chicagoclimatex.com) and click on the Register offsets link for more information on what types of projects can qualify as offsets and the steps you need to take to do so.

Moving that green power

The best places to generate carbon-free energy are often located far from the places that need the power. For example, the best solar sites are mostly in the western deserts. The electrical grid in the U.S. is built to move power between nearby cities and thus even out loads and take advantage of time-zone differences. Grids are regulated at the state level and building new lines requires lengthy permitting.

By contrast, fiber-optic data lines are much cheaper and more straightforward to run than high-power transmission lines. In the long run it may be cheaper to locate new data centers near sources of renewable power and move the data to users rather than move the needed electricity to urban data centers. Real estate and labor will cost less too. And while power transmission is relatively efficient, in the 90-percent range, data doesn't get lost during transmission.

Chapter 6

Go Green in 12 Months: Putting Together a Plan

Getting your green journey underway isn't difficult and doesn't even have to cost a thing before you start seeing great benefits. In this chapter, we help you get started by showing you how to get organized for green action and choose a starting point (or points) for the trip. When you begin a new venture, there's always tension between planning and action. Taking action too soon risks bogging you down in minutiae and missing the big picture. But an overly ambitious planning process risks bureaucratic paralysis.

In this chapter, we want to ease the tension and help you strike a balance between planning and action with some practical advice and guidance.

Begin sound planning for a long-term commitment while getting the easier green tasks started.

Because you're going green, make sure that you distribute your planning documents electronically, whenever possible.

Recognizing Your Mandate

The time to start is now. Begin by writing today's date in the margin to the right of this paragraph. (If you're browsing in the bookstore, please pay the cashier first.) You've just marked time zero in your green quest.

And since you're ready to embrace the challenge of bringing green IT to your organization, you need to evaluate where you stand in its hierarchy and what affinity for green activities already exists. To help you with this evaluation, we want you to ask yourself a few questions. The answers to these questions will help determine the tone of your initial communications with the people above and below you in your organization, as well as clarify the challenges you'll face and the language you must use while you green your IT ecosystem. Answering these questions helps you stay alert to the concerns, strengths, and sensitivities in your organization and gives you a realistic foundation to any green plans you develop.

Where do you sit in your organization's power structure?

Do you carry a big stick, a small stick, or is the stick you carry the handle of a broom? Obviously, what you can accomplish quickly depends on where you are in your organization's hierarchy. We assume that you're in a position to influence IT policy yet not at the top of the chain of command (although we also point out green steps that any staff member can take and make suggestions for senior management as well). The goal of sustainability involves everyone in an organization. So you should seek to enable and promote innovation from everyone toward this goal.

If your organization is like many others, green initiatives get very positive reception, build employee satisfaction and loyalty, and help folks feel better about what they're doing and the organization they work for. Find out how this positive employee response can help make the business case for green IT in Chapter 2.

Where does your organization stand on green concerns?

If you're working at a place with a strong ongoing environmental program, consider yourself fortunate. All too often, corporate environmental efforts are minimal and the IT department is on its own. If a strong corporate program does exist where you work, coordination with those activities is necessary.

Your company may have a corporate committee coordinating green efforts, sustainability efforts, or corporate responsibility efforts. If so, uncover the name of the committee's contact person and find out whether someone in your division already sits on one of those committees or task forces. Such a person is a valuable ally and can help plug your green IT ideas into that effort.

Is IT management supportive of your green interests?

Perhaps IT management has tasked you with the problem of taking IT green or has assigned you to a team. In either case, you know that you already have management backing. But if you're acting on your own initiative, you may find that you get the best results (that is, the most management support) if you develop an initial plan based on cost savings alone, rather than beginning your efforts by waving a green flag. Your approach, of course, is very much subject to your own organizational culture and values.

If you know a green message will be well received, by all means, include it. In any case, you may want to include impending regulations (check out Chapter 4) that have bearings on your organization.

Can IT coordinate its green plans with corporate efforts?

If your organization does have a green effort already under way, you have another set of questions you'll use to get the background you need for plugging in to the corporate effort:

- ✔ Where's the interest or need to go green coming from in your organization?

- ✔ Are the pressures — internal or external — practical, legal, ideological, or some combination?

- ✔ Are the stakeholders already informed and engaged, or will the effort first need to focus on raising basic awareness?

- ✔ If you face hostility, do you know where it's coming from and why?

- ✔ Is the desire or need to green IT part of a larger vision in the organization, or is it all about IT?

Find out the answers to these questions and use the information to construct an organizational chart of your organization's green efforts, including the names, positions, and e-mail addresses of the committee or task force members. Setting up a listserve, a wiki, or another collaboration tool to coordinate green activities would help get IT a seat at the table.

Ideally, your IT department will set up a green IT coordinating committee and include members from the facilities and finance departments, as well as IT operations and software development. All committee members will likely have other responsibilities, so you can set a good example of efficient (and green) practices by minimizing in-person meetings (especially if travel is involved) and using the collaboration tools we discuss in Chapter 20.

Establishing a Baseline

As you build a green program, you'll want to measure your progress. And to do so, you need baseline data on the various parameters you will be measuring. (We quote a mantra from The Green Grid — you can't improve what you don't measure.) Measure and monitor because you'll need to establish both your goals and the progress you make toward them. *Note:* Showing progress helps ensure that your green program takes root and continues to grow.

In this section, you find out what data you need to gather to establish your baseline, as well as what changes in that data you're looking for as a result of your green efforts. See Appendix A for a suggested baseline data template that you can fill out.

Figuring facility power usage

Reducing power consumption, or at least controlling its growth, is one major way a green IT initiative can reduce your organization's environmental footprint. The monetary expense reductions that come along with reduced power demand are either a side benefit or the main justification for the green efforts, depending on your organization's level of commitment. In either case, you'll want to be able to quantify savings.

Even a committed organization's green resolve can falter when times get tight and profits nosedive. Pointing out cost savings can keep green on the front burner during difficult times, acquisitions, and senior management changes.

Start figuring your baseline by determining your data center's current total electric power usage. We recognize that not every organization has a big formal data center, and some have data centers the size of a city block (the whole city block — you know, one block long and one block deep). So the suggestions for determining power usage that we have here apply across the board — they make sense whether your data center is also your coat room or is the size of the Macy's store in New York City.

✔ **Find out what the electric bills show as the amount of power used.** If your organization sports a separate data center facility, getting the required information may be as simple as obtaining copies of recent utility bills. Getting past bills can help you identify seasonal trends including warmer weather (applicable for any business), holiday shopping (for retail businesses), matriculation (for education environments), holiday travel (for airlines, car rental, and other travel-related industries), and so on.

When figuring your facility power usage baseline, try to get records for the past 12 months — extra credit if you can get the past 24 months.

✔ **Find the utility meters and know how to read them.**

✔ **Measure daily power usage room by room.** If you have a smaller IT shop with just a computer room (or even a closet), find a way to measure power on some typical days.

This room-level measuring may require enlisting an electrician to take power readings at the breaker box. Make sure the power readings separate air conditioning equipment. (To benchmark your cooling system efficiency, as we describe in Chapter 10, you'll want readings on both the power usage of your IT equipment and the power used by the air conditioning system.)

The bigger your data center, the more you'll want to leverage (and perhaps already are leveraging) systems management tools that can help you assess and monitor power usage automatically and give you real-time power measurements. And the sooner you get baseline data, the more clear-cut the differences that you report will appear.

Measuring IT power and equipment utilization

Quantifying total power consumption for your data center or computer room is relatively easy. Quantifying the useful work that gets done with all that power is much harder. Here are the general steps you'll follow:

1. **Inventory all the equipment in your data center.**

   If you don't have a good asset management system, this may require walking the aisles with a clipboard and writing down each piece of equipment. You'll want to know how many and what kind of blades are in each server. This data helps you estimate how much of the data center power is used by IT equipment versus cooling and other overhead uses. See the sample inventory worksheet in the Appendix.

While you're taking inventory, bring along a digital camera and take a photo of each rack. You probably can't back up far enough in an aisle to get the entire rack in a single frame, so take more than one picture if necessary. (Be careful not to back into any delicate equipment.)

If you do have an asset tracking system that can give you an inventory report covering the data center, you should still take the report to the data center and compare it to reality, even if you just check an aisle or two. For a complete picture of the IT equipment using power, get an inventory of office computers — desktops and laptops — as well.

2. **While you're in the data center, note the temperature and humidity.**

   You can use this data to look for potential savings on the power used to regulate the data center environment. Many computer room air conditioners are equipped with panels that display temperature and humidity, but an independent check is always a good idea. (Chapter 17 tells where to find inexpensive tools for taking these measurements.)

3. **Measure the power being sent to the electronic equipment in your data center, or measure or estimate the power consumption for each type of equipment in your data center inventory.**

   An electrician may be able to make spot measurements and provide you with a figure for power consumption. Ask for a power factor reading (which tells you how close your systems are to an ideal resistive load) as well. If you can't get a reading on the power transmitted, you can compute a power total from your equipment power-consumption estimates.

4. **Get snapshot figures of server and storage utilization.**

   Many popular operating systems log information related to server utilization, and you can also find software to create reports from this data. The equipment inventory you took in Step 1 shows you how much storage your data center includes, so you just need to find out how much of that storage is occupied by data of some sort.

After you gather and record all this data, you have what you need to figure a baseline for power consumption and utilization for the IT equipment in your data center.

When you're figuring equipment power consumption, note that the power consumption figures on most manufacturers' data sheets are maximum

values, intended to help you make sure that the device is supplied with sufficient power. When you take your readings or estimate power consumption,
you want typical power.

Newer servers can report their own power usage. A report by Jonathan G.
Koomey, PhD, of the United States Department of Energy Lawrence Berkeley
National Laboratory, is available at

`enterprise.amd.com/Downloads/svrpwrusecompletefinal.pdf`

and lists typical power consumption for many brands of servers. If you check
out this report, be sure to see Table 2.

Don't forget to include power consumption of equipment besides servers.
Storage arrays can use as much power and more. Also include communications equipment, such as switches, routers, and line terminations.

Data centers consume (and expel) more than power

Figuring out the total power consumed by the data center is important, but
other factors of IT operations also affect your green IT plans:

✔ **Getting a handle on storage:** Knowing how much storage you have and
how much you use is useful, but it doesn't tell the whole story. You'll
want to ask some additional questions and consider the answers as
you devise your plans for greening IT. How much of your stored data
needs to be retained, and how much is duplicated? How much of
that data could you safely compress without affecting reliability and
performance? How much could you store offline? How much could you
consolidate and virtualize? See Chapter 11 for more on data life-cycle
management's potential.

✔ **Getting the big picture of facility operations:** Have your facilities
people give you a tour of your data center power switchgear, UPS
(uninterruptible power supplies), and cooling systems. Make a diagram
of the plant and note the make and model of chillers, pumps, and other
major equipment. Visit your data center on the graveyard and weekend
shifts. Talk to the cleaning crew. Find out who hauls away your trash
and what they do with it. If your organization already collects paper,
cans, and plastics for recycling, find out where that goes.

✔ **Tracking the trees you terminate:** One other bit of data that will prove useful in long-term reporting is the amount and cost of printer paper purchased (and used) by your organization. Your purchasing department may be able to supply this information. Cutting paper usage (which we discuss in Chapters 2 and 16) further reduces your organization's environmental footprint. In addition, note how much space your business allocates to storing paper — you may be able to reassign some of that space for something more useful.

Mapping the land mines

As you probably know all too well, IT operation folks are very conservative. Their goal is 24/7 reliability. They live and die by service-level agreements. Often they never even see power bills. And so, make sure that you embrace a broader perspective when you set your baselines and decide on where to start with your green activities. Consider the following:

✔ **You certainly want operations management represented on your green IT steering committee.** Understanding the operational concerns will keep you from stepping on a corporate land mine. Be sure to review your security, continuity, and disaster recovery plans.

✔ **Gather information on regulatory requirements where compliance is essential.** For example, healthcare organizations in the United States must comply with provisions of the Health Insurance Portability and Accountability Act of 1996 (HIPAA). Any green initiative must take into account the act's stringent privacy provisions when you're developing guidelines for the reuse of IT equipment.

✔ **Understand which applications and outputs are most important for your colleagues' everyday work.** We once worked with an IT manager who would every so often intercept a regular printed report and keep it on his desk. If he got an angry call from its intended recipient, he'd rush the report to him. But if he received no complaint, he'd reduce that report's printed frequency, from daily to weekly or from weekly to monthly. He saved tons of paper that way.

Picking a Direction for Starting

After you collect all that data and devise a baseline for comparing your results, it's time to pick some short-term projects that will produce measurable benefits. Deciding which projects you start with depends on what *greenable* areas your survey discovers and your assessment of what related activities are possible.

Chilling on cooling systems

If you have good data on overall facility power usage and IT equipment usage, divide the first number (overall usage) by the second (IT equipment usage) to get your power usage effectiveness (PUE) score.

Data centers often fall into the *2-to-3 range,* meaning that the air conditioning, UPS, and power distribution systems take two or three times as much power as do the data center electronics. That leaves a lot of room for improving the efficiency of the plant equipment.

Unfortunately, air conditioning systems are major capital investments. Unlike servers, they last for decades. Major changes to these systems involve considerable engineering and capital. But you do have options for cutting cooling costs without rebuilding your basic HVAC systems.

One possibility is to raise the temperature in the data center. New guidelines from the American Society of Heating, Refrigerating and Air-Conditioning Engineers, ASHRAE, have widened the allowable temperature and humidity ranges for data and communications equipment. Most major equipment manufacturers have signed on to these recommendations. You can realize savings in energy consumption simply by adjusting the set-point for the computer room air conditioners, but be sure to get buy-in from those in charge of operations.

Making a series of temperature increases over several months — while you monitor the data center for reliability issues — may be an acceptable conservative approach. Note that lowering the low temperature and humidity recommendations increases the opportunity to use outside air during cooler weather to economize further. See Chapter 10 for more on data center cooling. The new ASHRAE guidelines are available at www.ashrae.org/publications/page/1900.

Another common issue is that entire computer rooms are cooled to address a few hot spots that are caused by things like concentrated workloads or poor airflow. Although running the entire room at a cooler temperature can provide a buffer for these hot spots, a much more efficient approach is to eliminate them altogether so that the temperature can be consistent across the room instead of icy cold in some places and blistering hot in others. We discuss ways to do this in Chapter 10 as well.

The virtue of virtualizing

Virtualization — using servers more effectively by enabling them to support multiple independent applications — is one of the hottest trends in IT. You may already be rolling out this technology. If not, it's time to consider going virtual. If your server or storage utilization is low (and the odds are that it is low — most distributed environments average only about 20-percent utilization), you have huge savings in store for you by adopting this technology. If the hardware utilization can be driven up by virtualizing machines and consolidating them onto fewer physical machines, you can reduce energy demands dramatically — not only for the servers and storage, but for all the associated power distribution and cooling costs. And end users will see benefits as well because virtualization allows for more graceful redeployment of computing hardware to meet ever-changing demands. Chapter 13 digs into those details.

Configuring office desktops for sleep

While you're doing a midnight walkthrough of the data center, take a stroll through your organization's office area. How many of the desktops and displays are on? *Remember:* Screen savers do not save power. Green considerations indicate that computers should be in sleep mode at night along with their users.

A common reason for desktop computers being on is that IT needs to run updates at night. But you have a way to work around this obstacle to green. Windows and most other desktop operating systems have *wake-on-network-activity* options that wake up sleeping desktops when addressed by the local network. To take advantage of the green benefits of sleeping desktop computers, educate users to configure their desktops for sleep or obtain software that lets you manage desktop sleep options remotely. You could go as far as recommending that all equipment not in use be powered off. If you do so, you can arrange for updates to be deployed when machines reboot. See Chapter 15 for more about this practice.

Eliminating unused or grossly underutilized resources

Studies have shown that a significant number of IT resources that are consuming energy at any given moment aren't associated with any useful work. That server that was purchased for a project six years ago that has long since been forgotten by the project team may still be powered up with a spinning disk. Or how about a server that was purchased for testing that's on 24/7, but is utilized only .01 percent of the time? In fact, it's not unusual to find that 10–20 percent of all IT hardware in a given organization falls into this category.

Finding and eliminating energy-wasters provides incredible bang for the buck — because every piece of equipment that can be eliminated also saves the associated space, power, and cooling. Although it's impossible to ascertain the usage of a machine by looking at the outside of the box, there are automated tools that are capable of identifying those with low utilizations or scanning an environment to identify the ones that aren't connected to any useful applications.

Retiring hardware the green way

Electronic waste — *e-waste* — is becoming a major environmental issue. Few types of capital equipment become obsolete as quickly as computers, which means that most organizations retire such equipment on a regular basis.

Some computers, monitors, and so on just sit in storage for years and then end up in the dumpster when the storage space suddenly is needed for other purposes. Retiring computer equipment to the dumpster is a serious non-green practice. Other organizations believe that they're doing the right thing by transferring retired equipment to recycling firms. But not all these firms follow responsible practices either.

Developing a retirement plan for old IT machines is one more possible piece of low-hanging fruit for your 12-month green plan. Here are some initial activities to consider (find more in Chapter 19):

✔ **Find out how your organization disposes of old electronics.** If you use a recycler, ask what they do with the old material and whether they belong to an e-waste certification program. (Don't just take their word for it — make sure they're being certified by a third party.)

- The Basel Action Network, the Electronics TakeBack Coalition, and 32 electronics recyclers in the U.S. and Canada joined to create the e-Stewards program; www.e-stewards.org. e-Steward certification forbids dumping toxic e-waste in developing countries or landfills and incinerators, and forbids the use of prison labor to process e-waste as well as ensuring the data privacy of data on computers that are discarded.

- Many major equipment manufacturers now accept equipment returns and have responsible reuse and recycling programs.

- Many manufacturers and recyclers *buy back* newer used equipment because they can resell or reuse components. The older the equipment, the more costly it is to recycle, so you may want to look at the optimal time to replace your equipment. Responsibly and legally disposing of used equipment is becoming more costly, so you may find you're better off trading in earlier and saving yourself the hassle of disposal.

✔ **Encourage or, better yet, require disk encryption on all computers, particularly laptops.** The security advantages are obvious, of course, but the green benefits may not be. Using disk encryption makes it more acceptable to release for other uses equipment that stored sensitive data. More generally, find out whether your organization has a standard for disk sanitization and help develop one if it doesn't.

✔ **Set up an equipment swap page on the Internet to help members of your organization exchange and reuse older equipment.** Also see Chapter 22 for creative computer recycling tips.

✔ **Set up an electronics recycling program for employees.** If you have a green equipment retirement program in place, adding material that your employees are discarding may have only a small incremental cost and can make a bigger dent in the e-waste problem.

Buying green

Purchasing new equipment is the flip side of equipment retirement. Most of the major equipment manufacturers are trying to meet stricter, greener standards in the new equipment they build. But putting green requirements, such as the U.S. Environmental Protection Agency's Energy Star certification, into your purchasing specs ensures that newer equipment is more efficient, free from hazardous materials, and easier to recycle. See Chapter 4 for more on Energy Star and other standards.

Making them pay — or at least be aware

Sometimes the best way to change behavior is simply to raise awareness. One way to change the culture and behavior related to energy usage in an organization is to increase accountability. Many energy consumers in IT are completely oblivious to the impact of their decisions on energy usage. More often than not, they don't directly bear the financial costs for their energy consumption because it's paid for out of a separate budget. Creating reports that demonstrate which departments or which applications are heavy energy consumers is a great way to get the entire organization focused on this issue. Turning those reports into energy bills that are actually distributed to the energy consumers can make the point even more strongly. Having this financial information is essential to building a business case for green IT investments.

New data center planning

If your organization is planning to construct a new data center, getting green mandates into that planning process should be a high priority.

After all, the operational cost to provide power and cooling to that new data center may ultimately eclipse the capital spent to build it. You can find many opportunities to make a new data center more efficient and lower its environmental footprint, from selecting more efficient cooling systems to selecting an environmentally optimal site.

Spreading the word

Building environmental awareness in an organization can bring many benefits. An educational program can lead to increased cooperation with measures that take a little effort, such as configuring office computers to use sleep mode or participating in office recycling; it can also unearth new ideas for green improvements from employees who are closer to day-to-day business practices. But be careful not to set expectations too high. A large organization can't turn on a dime, and smaller shops have hard budget constraints. Avoid symbolic programs — *greenwashing* — that attempt to appear to be green.

Because this book is a useful tool, you may want to get a few extra copies to circulate in your organization.

Looking at the larger organization

This chapter mostly covers the nitty-gritty ways IT can go green — addressing power, recycling, and education. But IT can impact the larger organization by encouraging greener work practices, such as telecommuting, using collaboration technologies instead of travel, and reducing paper consumption by substituting electronic processes. There's a lot more to be said on these topics, and we say it in Chapter 20.

Looking Beyond the One-Year Time Horizon

You can accomplish the steps outlined in this chapter in 12 months. But significantly greening IT and influencing the larger organization take a longer view and commitment. You must consider *process* — how the various parts of the organization work together on green goals — on par with technological details. But don't forget to measure that one-year's success and to plan for continuing your efforts. Follow these steps:

1. Find the date you wrote in the margin at the beginning of this chapter and mark the same day next year on your calendar.

2. Repeat the measurements we suggest at the beginning of this chapter so you can compare your progress with the baseline.

3. Schedule a meeting of the green team after your plan's first anniversary to review what worked and what didn't — both in terms of technology and process.

4. Set new, more ambitious goals for the next three years.

Depending on the size of your organization and the challenges you face, you might want to get guidance from folks who do green IT for a living. You can leverage others' expertise to assess your environment and recommend changes. Enormous knowledge is available to help you optimize what you already have, save money on power, and potentially help curb new expenditures on equipment and facilities. If you're faced with inadequate power availability or are pushing the boundaries of your data center now, you may want to get help sooner rather than later. You may be able to avoid costly build-outs and improve your overall efficiency at the same time.

Steps for the corner office

If you're the top boss and want to get green IT off the ground, here are three steps you can take quickly to facilitate and track those efforts:

1. Talk about green is cheap. Get green goals into your compensation plan.

2. Find out the lowest-level manager in your organization with budget responsibility for both the IT department and facilities' electric power expense and then make that person responsible for green cost savings.

   If that person is the chief operating officer or at a division or general manager level, consider organizational changes that will push joint responsibility for those two items

further down the org chart and closer to the action, preferably to the level of IT management itself. Having just one neck to wring — one person who has authority to make changes and is held accountable for the effects of those changes — is always sound organizational policy.

3. Insist on tracking green investments separately so they don't end up on the chopping block when final budgets are formulated.

After you take these steps and get the efforts moving, ask for regular reports from the green IT committee and let the members know that you're reading them.

Part III
Greening the Data Center

The 5th Wave   By Rich Tennant

Neither one of us wanted a silo on the new data center, but things like this can happen when you don't clean the coffee rings off your building plans.

In this part . . .

Beyond the initial steps of going green, real green strategy involves understanding all the IT needs of your organization, optimizing their delivery, and finding concrete ways to get a lot more from your current IT assets. We look at optimizing the data center as well as servers and storage, including everything from cooling the data center to virtualization.

Chapter 7

Laying the Foundation for Green Data Management

***

***

*U*nless you're face to face with a brand new organization that's about to purchase IT solutions for the first time, you're living with decisions about purchases and configurations that may have been best practices at the time of their inception, but may not have been made with green criteria in mind. To take what you have and make it greener requires a real strategy. This chapter focuses on the issues you need to consider in creating your green strategy.

Data is the heart and soul of IT. Not all organizations have data centers — in fact, relatively few have the traditional raised floor, air-conditioned sprawls you might think of when you hear "data center." But every organization has data, plenty of it — and the amount of data is growing rapidly. Indeed, the rate of growth of data storage is accelerating as new technologies, such as document imaging and video conferencing, generate data by the gigabyte.

What to do with all that data? How do you know what to keep and what to pitch, and what to have at arm's length all the time versus tucked away for "just in case?" On top of those decisions, you need to figure out *where* to put it all.

Later in this part of the book, we dig deeply into specific storage solutions, but first, in this chapter, we lay out strategies for approaching the challenge of managing your data with green solutions in mind.

Although the cost per gigabyte for storage devices, such as hard drives, may keep falling, we keep adding more and more drives to handle the data explosion. As a result, the cost of powering and cooling storage systems keeps increasing. In this chapter, take a look at ways to better use your existing resources through information lifecycle management and the use of tiered data storage. Outsourcing some or all of a company's data services is another increasingly popular way to move the cost of managing and maintaining the data center into the hands of an expert vendor.

Formalizing Best Practices for Green IT

No organization succeeds, much less thrives, if it relies on a slipshod or confusing approach to managing the information and applications it needs to perform its vital functions. The best practices for any organization that relies on information technology in order to function (and in this era, that's pretty much everyone) include several key components:

- ✔ **Understanding the company's requirements for data retention and availability.** Staff at all levels of your business or organization need a thorough understanding of what types of data you need to keep, both for long-term storage and for backup in case of loss or power failure. You must also determine which applications are critical for conducting operations.

- ✔ **Designing an infrastructure that meets the company's requirements.** *Infrastructure* includes servers, storage, networking, backup, and disaster recovery systems.

- ✔ **Conducting continual strategic planning to meet economic and business conditions and expected demand.** A strategic review should be held at least once a year.

- ✔ **Measuring progress and adjusting strategies based on this information.** Your strategic plan should call for periodic measurements of the amount of data your store, broken down by categories appropriate to your business, along with other important metrics, such as network bandwidth use and customer response time and satisfaction.

- ✔ **Actively managing for successful service delivery and customer (both internal and external) satisfaction.** Like any other aspect of your business, data management involves finding and fixing problems while looking for opportunities to improve performance and cut costs.

Data management is a complicated issue, and your organization needs to first decide what types of data it needs to keep, classify that data according to its pertinence (how readily available it needs to be), and move the data to appropriate types of storage. Here are those three tasks spelled out a bit more:

- ✔ **Identify:** The organization first needs to determine all types of data to be stored, the source of that data, and its long-term value to the organization. For example, because e-mail became a dominant form of communication between companies and their customers and suppliers, companies had to adjust their policies concerning how e-mail is classified and stored. Changes made in 2006 in the Federal Rules for Civil Procedure (FRCP) — the rules governing noncriminal litigation in the U.S. Federal court system — allowed penalties to be assessed against companies that could not produce electronic documents in a timely fashion during the discovery phase of a lawsuit. (Discovery is a step in civil litigation where each side is required to produce all relevant documents requested by the other side.) In several high-profile cases, companies were penalized for failing to produce electronic documents in what became known as *e-discovery* cases.

If your organization is required to keep all incoming e-mail, you may well want to investigate using an e-mail security service that stops spam from ever entering your network. If you filter e-mail for spam after it enters, you may find yourself needing to archive significantly more e-mail. Spam can account for as much as 95 percent of all e-mail. Yikes!

✔ **Classify:** You should categorize or index the various types of data, and as the data loses its currency, move it to appropriately less expensive storage. (See the discussion of tiered storage in the next section.)

✔ **Move:** Where possible, move the data to data archive systems, such as tape, for permanent storage. (Chapter 11 provides more extensive coverage of physical storage media, and Chapter 13 tells you about using virtual storage systems.)

Some data can eventually be destroyed. For example, many companies recycle their retired or obsolete computers — which is, of course, the right thing to do for the environment. Disposal of computer hard drives presents a security issue of particular concern for companies. Even though the data may be deemed disposable, it should never fall into the wrong hands — a competitor, for instance. We suggest ways of safely destroying data in Chapter 19.

Now that you have a sense of why formalizing your IT policies is necessary, read on to find out about the framework many businesses use to help structure those policies clearly.

Understanding Information Lifecycle Management

Information Lifecycle Management, or *ILM,* is a set of concepts at the heart of formulating IT policy at successful companies. ILM provides a framework within which IT organizations can build processes and implement best practices for creating, storing, archiving, and ultimately disposing of data that no longer has any value to the organization. Although generally applied to electronic documents, ILM can encompass non-electronic documents as well. Some firms depend on paper or microfilm records, such as contracts or architectural drawings, which can span many decades.

The ILM model is important to your green strategy because it helps you identify your actual storage needs so that you can plan accurately. Also, this model classifies data according to its value so that you aren't using electricity to power storage devices for information that's not currently needed, and it addresses the need to eliminate obsolete data so that you can reuse storage and avoid buying additional storage (or at least delay doing so).

The ILM model identifies five stages in the lifecycle of data:

- **Creation:** This phase pertains to generating documents in a word processor, filling a spreadsheet with data, or using a Customer Relationship Management (CRM) system to input customer information. New information might also include scanned paper correspondence, drawings created on a computer-aided design (CAD) system, PowerPoint presentations, recordings of a video conferences, and so on.

- **Distribution:** After someone generates a document, it usually needs to go somewhere beyond the computer it's created on. For example, an e-mail message to a co-worker leaves your computer and is distributed to your co-worker's desktop through a company network and a mail server, but you might also send a copy to a customer. The distribution stage encompasses delivery of data both within a company and externally.

- **Use:** After the document, e-mail, presentation, or other type of data arrives at its intended destination, something happens to it. Maybe the presentation is delivered to an outside salesperson for a meeting tomorrow morning, or six people read the document and add their comments, and then some unfortunate, long suffering soul has to integrate all those contentious comments to create a final version in time for some deadline. Whatever the case, the data is used as part of a business activity.

- **Maintenance:** This is the phase in which the data is managed. For example, an e-mail may be kept in an e-mail inbox, which is one form of filing it. It may also be backed up, forwarded, or archived. What happens to data depends in part on its *currency* (how readily available it needs to be) and how valuable the data is considered to be by the organization. The notion of currency takes into account the fact that data can lose its value over time — last year's accounting transactions may be needed quickly in case of a dispute with a vendor or a customer, or the IRS, but at some point that data can and should be archived. From a cost-effective standpoint, the data should be indexed and moved to less expensive storage or even offline as its value fades. If the IRS conducts a tax audit or a lawsuit requires relevant data to be provided during discovery, the data in question again acquires currency and needs to be recovered.

✔ **Disposition:** Some industries, such as health care or financial services, have very strict legal regulations mandated by the federal government as to how long data must be retained. Even individuals are required to keep their tax returns for seven years. Faced with increasing regulatory pressure to keep certain kinds of data, some companies have responded by trying to "keep everything." Such a strategy only creates an indexing nightmare and *storage sprawl* — the continual need to buy more and more storage capacity to respond to unbridled demand. Companies that have analyzed their data use and storage needs — that is, companies that are using some form of data lifecycle management — can better determine which data needs to be retained and for how long.

Now that you have a sense of how to organize the types of data your organization uses, how do you know what storage methods are best for each type? And, of course, what storage methods are the greenest? The following section gets you started in answering these questions.

Using Tiered Storage Architecture

To grasp the idea of tiered storage, think of data descending a staircase along its lifecycle, with each tier reflecting how the data is currently being used (or not used) and how accessible it needs to be. In other words, each tier represents the data's currency.

The number of tiers necessary can depend on what kind of data the organization is managing, but most companies recognize five tiers. The following list describes those tiers and tells you the green implications for each tier.

✔ **Tier 1 — mission-critical data:** Highly transactional data that needs to be accessed frequently. For this reason, Tier 1 data is stored on high-performance, highly accessible storage — what storage manufacturers like to call *big iron,* in part because of its size in the data center and in part because it's the most expensive storage to buy and maintain. Examples of Tier 1 storage include customer-facing Web servers (the ones that support the Web site your customers see), accounting databases, and in larger organizations, e-mail servers.

   The green way to go: Tier 1 data is the most expensive to store, both in monetary and environmental costs. This data occupies space on spinning disk drives and may be duplicated on user machines, particularly laptops, as access may be needed even when the network is not available. If you have the option, store this data at data centers that are powered by renewable sources.

✔ **Tier 2 — high value but not mission critical:** This data needs to be accessed less frequently, so performance is less of an issue than it is with Tier 1 data. This storage is therefore less expensive to purchase. An example of Tier 2 data might be documents stored on a collaboration server, databases that are accessed infrequently, or a departmental Web server.

The green way to go: Data de-duplication can ensure that Tier 2 data is stored only once. See Chapter 11.

✔ **Tier 3 — transitional storage:** This data is valuable but needs to be accessed infrequently — this is sometimes called *persistent storage.* Examples might include an indexed e-mail or document repository, or older database instances.

The green way to go: Tier 3 data is a candidate for *MAID (massive arrays of idle disk)* storage. Such systems, which are discussed in more detail in Chapter 11, save energy at the expense of slightly longer access times, by keeping disk drives powered down until the data on them is needed.

✔ **Tier 4 — disaster recovery:** This tier serves as a repository for applications and data that need to be available to restore continuity of operations in the event of a business interruption, such as a power outage. Business continuity and disaster recovery is discussed in greater detail in Chapter 13. Disaster recovery systems have specific requirements for data availability and data currency that are different than Tier 1 systems, as they act as "snapshots" of the business process at a particular moment in time to enact a smooth recovery of business operations.

The green way to go: Disaster recovery systems can often be powered down or kept in standby for much of the time. Update or periodic testing can be scheduled at a time when power is more available, keeping load off less efficient "peaking" generators.

✔ **Tier 5 — archive:** The repository of data that needs to be retained but doesn't need to be online.

The green way to go: Some companies choose to use tape libraries for this purpose, or they may use a third-party vaulting provider to keep the archive off-site in a secure, protected location. Any data can be put into an archive, but it's most likely data that the company intends to keep for a long period of time. You might have also guessed that Tier 5 storage is the most efficient in its use of power because it's offline most of the time!

Figure 7-1 shows where categories of data fit into the five storage tiers.

As you can see, using storage tiers also forms a framework for managing data from creation to archive and thus embodies the spirit of ILM. You can move data from one tier to another as its current value to the organization changes — that is, as the data *ages.*

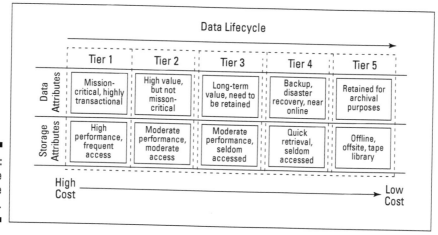

Data Lifecycle

	Tier 1	Tier 2	Tier 3	Tier 4	Tier 5
Data Attributes	Mission-critical, highly transactional	High value, but not misson-critical	Long-term value, need to be retained	Backup, disaster recovery, near online	Retained for archival purposes
Storage Attributes	High performance, frequent access	Moderate performance, moderate access	Moderate performance, seldom accessed	Quick retrieval, seldom accessed	Offline, offsite, tape library

High Cost ————————————————————————→ Low Cost

Figure 7-1:
The five
storage
tiers.

The use of storage tiers also encourages companies to think in terms of storage efficiency, recognizing that the purposeful, automated movement of data from one tier to the next uses progressively less energy and thus supports a green data strategy. The next section tells you more about the efficient use of server and storage capacity.

SOA you wanna green

Service Oriented Architecture (SOA) — a business model with the idea of reuse built in — is hot today. SOA can play a helpful role in developing green enterprise solutions because it combines environmentally friendly concepts with good business sense. One of SOA's key benefits is making it easier to adapt IT to changing business conditions — increased agility. The challenge of transforming business processes and operations to include environmental consideration is simply another business requirement that can be defined as a business policy to implement and sustain through the use of technology.

As an example, take the concept of managing the carbon footprint of an enterprise. Some calculations occur repetitively, such as estimating carbon emissions or assessing carbon trade-offs based on current carbon offset market conditions. With the SOA approach, when you create such new software services, you can reuse them in other business applications across your enterprise, perhaps adding green calculations to accounting systems, travel expense systems, supply chain management, and so on. For more on SOA, get a copy of *Service Oriented Architecture For Dummies,* 2nd Edition, by Judith Hurwitz, Robin Bloor, Marcia Kaufman, Fern Halper (Wiley Publishing).

Outsourcing: Going Greener with Hosted Data Center Services

Your company has a choice when it comes to building your data infrastructure: You can build a physical infrastructure that you staff and maintain, or you can outsource these services. You can still categorize your data according to the tiered storage architecture that we describe earlier in this chapter — the only difference is that you store your data for some or all tiers with an off-premises provider. Here are several reasons to consider using a hosted data center provider:

- **It's greener:** Dedicated data centers consolidate the operations of many organizations and gain economies of scale, thereby reducing the amount of power and equipment that all those organizations would gobble up individually.

- **It's cheaper for you:** The cost of acquiring and maintaining data center equipment, providing management services, and powering and cooling the infrastructure are quite high, and hosted services provide a cheaper alternative to running all these systems in-house. Also costly are the salaries and benefits you have to pay for the knowledge and dedication of an IT staff.

- **Physical plant:** Data centers occupy physical space and should be located in buildings designed for this purpose. Data centers require not only physical space but also sources of power and cooling. In addition, some cities have begun to restrict the amount of power available for powering data centers. As a result, many data centers are being relocated to areas where there is less demand for resources and less chance of business disruption by natural or human-made causes. New data centers are being created near cheaper, cleaner power and cooling. (We tell you a bit more about location considerations in Chapter 8.)

Storage for long-term (Tier 5) data

We talked about the use of archiving and vaulting in the section on tiered storage, but many companies choose to outsource their archiving infrastructure to a third-party service provider. They might do this for several reasons:

- An infrastructure needs to be built for archiving, and to be effective, it should be replicated at an additional location so that if the primary archive site is disabled for any reason, the secondary site can take its place. Many companies can't afford to build the necessary infrastructure.

✔ Many companies don't have in-house expertise to implement and manage an archive infrastructure.

✔ Some companies prefer to use the services of a provider that has specific expertise in archiving. In this way, the company using the service can set expected service levels and manage according to service-level agreements (SLA).

Disaster recovery and business continuity (Tier 4) applications and data

Another part of the data infrastructure that's frequently outsourced is the disaster recovery infrastructure. Disaster recovery systems are designed to hold a "snapshot" of all critical applications and data that a company needs in the event of a business interruption. The disaster recovery system is only one part of the disaster recovery system, however. Ideally, a disaster recovery infrastructure includes the following components:

✔ **A system that provides quick recovery of computer applications and data that's critical to operations.** Such data might include accounting and customer-facing applications and accompanying databases, e-mail infrastructure, and the company's Web server, especially if the company depends on Web transactions as part of its business operations.

✔ **Critical business systems that are available for employees to conduct operations.** If the interruption is severe or lengthy, the company needs to provide an alternative location for operations or allow remote access to systems.

✔ **A method for keeping employees informed.** Employees need to be notified about the nature of the business interruption and how they can participate in the business recovery. We tell you more about emergency notification services in the next section.

✔ **A formal disaster recovery plan for business operations to resume quickly and smoothly.** Companies of all sizes need to engage in this kind of planning as a regular part of their business strategic planning. (See the upcoming sidebar "No business is too small for disaster planning," especially if you're part of a small business.)

Disaster recovery systems have become less expensive in recent years because of the increasing use of virtual servers to host disaster recovery (Chapter 13 tells you much more about virtualization). Using virtual servers to host disaster recovery is a greener strategy than having redundant physical systems.

No business is too small for disaster planning

Note that small businesses are the least likely to invest in disaster recovery plans or systems. The reasons for this range from the need to invest in other parts of the business — a new truck for customer deliveries trumps a disaster recovery system every time — to the mistaken idea that the business is "too small to need this kind of system."

The fact is that a business interruption may be more catastrophic to a small business than to a large one. Large businesses frequently have more than one location and often back up critical applications and data to these locations as well as to their headquarters. You have only to remember the devastation wrought on the Southeastern coast of the United States by Hurricane Katrina to realize how badly the physical infrastructure of cities and towns can be damaged and how long it can take to bring it back to some semblance of normal.

This said, small and large businesses can benefit from outsourcing their disaster recovery infrastructure. One of the compelling reasons is that the service provider's data centers are *hardened* (built to withstand events such as hurricanes and tornadoes), are located away from big cities and in meteorologically "neutral" areas, and are also *redundant* — that is, the data center is replicated in one or more geographically dispersed locations. Businesses need to weigh the cost of using a hosted service against that of building and maintaining a disaster recovery infrastructure, but regardless of which type of recovery you choose, it should be part of the formal strategic planning of every business.

Data center replication

Replicating the data center involves duplicating the functionality and services of a data center in a different location. Data center replication is done for several reasons, as follows:

- ✔ To serve as a backup for a primary data center. The secondary data center provides the ultimate backup and recovery mechanism in the event of a business interruption.

- ✔ To provide a way of decreasing the load on a primary data center during periods of increased business demand.

- ✔ For companies whose business operations are dispersed through numerous countries, additional data centers are used to bring services closer to the end user of those services.

Replicating data centers is standard practice for data center hosting providers to ensure that they provide uninterrupted service to their customers. For that same reason, many large companies and all U.S. governmental agencies replicate their data centers for data security and redundancy.

Branch offices can also act as redundant backup sites, and many companies replicate their critical data and applications, if not the physical infrastructure itself. Virtualization can lower the cost of replication though the use of virtual images or snapshots of a virtual machine that can be moved over the Internet or on physical media to another location. It just happens to be a greener solution, too.

Emergency notification services

Emergency notification services (ENS) are an often neglected component of business continuity planning. ENS is simply an infrastructure built for the purpose of notifying people in the event of a emergency — the occasional tests of the Emergency Alert System on your car radio is an example of a very large scale notification system.

Applied to business, the purpose of ENS is to warn or notify employees of some kind of event — it doesn't need to be an emergency, by the way — and to give them instructions about what to do. ENS can be operated by the business on its own infrastructure, supplied by an outside service provider on the company's premises, or hosted remotely by a service provider. All three instances of ENS provide notification on one or more of the following devices:

- ✔ Internal or external e-mail
- ✔ Voice notification on telephones located in a building
- ✔ Personal telephone, cell phone, or both
- ✔ SMS or text messaging
- ✔ Loudspeakers or alerts within a building
- ✔ Alerts on computer monitors located in a building

The notifications are generally repeated on all the devices that are selected until the employee responds and acknowledges that the message is received. In most cases, employees have a choice about which method(s) of contact they prefer, although they may have to divulge personal information for their cell phones or e-mail — this can and has raised privacy issues. To allay this issue, some ENS systems allow employees to enter their personal information on a password-protected Web site to which only they have access.

As you might suspect, the infrastructure to support ENS is substantial. Suppose, for example, that you're in a building with 2,000 other people and an emergency arises that requires notifying all these employees. Most telephone systems couldn't handle 2,000 calls per hour, let alone 2,000 calls in a minute! For this reason alone, many companies choose to use an ENS provider to provide these services, with the added benefit that they minimize their carbon footprint and utility costs.

Cloud computing: Relocating the infrastructure

Cloud computing may prove to be a green solution for some organizations. *Cloud computing* is one of the latest buzzwords in the computing industry, and although the idea of cloud computing is still not completely defined, it looks very much like the kinds of data center hosting we present in this chapter, with one important difference.

Cloud computing providers have concentrated on building highly flexible and responsive architectures that can be provisioned quickly according to customer demand and decommissioned when that demand goes away — a significant difference in approach from a traditional data center or hosting provider. Hosted data center providers are in an ideal position to reconfigure their infrastructures for cloud services, and many of them have done so already.

Some examples of how cloud computing might be used include records retention and archiving, development and testing, software distribution, large databases — almost any use to which we currently use computers. The key idea is that of scaling data center services into the *cloud*.

A few issues cloud the horizon, however. Detractors point to security breaches at companies that aren't even working in the cloud and wonder how millions of customers' data will be secured and kept private. There's also the matter of cost: Cloud computing is a pay-as-you-go service and includes network charges, storage charges, and access charges. When all is said and done, the costs have to be in line with delivering the same services in-house.

Who will use cloud computing? Most experts think that the biggest users of cloud computing will be small and midsized businesses, which are the least likely to have built an infrastructure already. Enterprise customers are most likely to have built an infrastructure but may be looking to offload some data center operating expenses or capital costs of upgrading data center components. In any case, cloud computing is supportive of green and sustainability because computing services are delivered by providers who have optimized their data centers. One thing's for sure: We're at only the beginning of cloud computing, so how deeply it will affect the future of computing remains to be seen.

Of course, companies can use ENS for purposes other than emergencies. A last-minute change to a meeting room assignment can be "broadcast" this way and with much greater chance of reaching all the participants. The use of ENS is not confined to the business world — schools and universities have increased their use of ENS, especially after the tragic shootings at Virginia Tech in 2007.

Co-locating data centers

Co-location is a computer industry term that refers to sharing space. Virtualization, which we tell you more about in Chapter 13, is a form of co-location because multiple applications are sharing the same server's resources. Here, though, we're talking about the practice of sharing space and resources in a data center by multiple companies. Each company owns the physical equipment that the data center uses to deliver services to that company.

Companies choose to co-locate their data centers for many of the same reasons that they choose to have data center services hosted by a provider. The chief distinction between co-location and hosting is that the co-location center provider is supplying power, cooling, security, and facilities management while the company continues to manage its own servers and storage. By way of contrast, data center hosting providers also provide the equipment and services.

For small- and medium-sized data centers, co-location provides an alternative to building and managing your own facilities. Many co-location providers offer to lease space for dozens of racks or house as little as a 1U server in a shared rack. Providers generally have excellent Internet connectivity.

Co-location providers charge by the amount of rack space provided, bandwidth used, and power consumed. There are also fees for various levels of management services. Choosing efficient equipment can at least save on the power charges, which can be steep because they include the cost of cooling.

Many companies offer co-location services. The market is highly competitive. Some co-location firms offer green design and power sources as added inducements to potential customers. Selecting one of these, after some due diligence, is an easy green step to take.

Chapter 8

Maximizing Data Center Efficiency

Designing a data center for maximum efficiency is a complex problem requiring input from many disciplines not normally associated with information technology. These include architecture, civil engineering, mechanical engineering, industrial engineering, environmental engineering, physics, legal, political, security, and finance. You need to consider myriad factors along with planning for growth and future technological and economic change.

Data center managers are responsible for some of the most critical infrastructures on the planet. The top three priorities are availability, availability, and availability (of your applications and data). Green concerns may never be at the top of the list, but they most definitely have a place, and in fact, sustainability and availability often go hand in hand. For example, using less power means having backup fuel supplies that can run the center longer when they're needed. Renewable power may be more reliable in the long term than fossil fuel. And taking environmental considerations into account when picking a site for a new data center can save resources and improve reliability — in other words, green siting can be safer siting.

We can't begin to delve into all the complexities of data center design in this book, but you can use this chapter to get pointed in the right direction for steering your data center greenward. In this chapter, you can find tips about location considerations as well as power and space issues. We also suggest some metrics of efficiency for you to measure and track.

Choosing the Right Location

Although many companies still locate their data centers in or adjacent to their corporate offices, others are at remote locations. The low cost of sending data long distances with fiber optic lines has diminished the advantages of keeping data centers with the company they serve. Businesses can place their data centers in areas where they can take advantage of lower real estate, labor, communication, and power costs. Remote data centers can also be put in areas less likely to experience natural and human-made disasters, such as earthquakes, hurricanes, tornados, floods, plane crashes, train derailments, civil unrest, terrorism, and war.

In the following sections, we tell you about green issues that you should add to your list of data center site criteria.

Green power

Organizations planning a new data center already put power cost and availability, preferably from two sources, near the top of the planning criteria. Green thinking suggests some additional issues:

- **The nature of the energy source.** Hydropower is clean and relatively inexpensive, which is why you find data centers for both Google and Amazon in the Pacific Northwest, where hydropower is abundant. Coal-fired power plants currently offer very cheap electricity but are not clean or renewable, and their cost is likely to increase as cap and trade systems or carbon taxes are imposed in the future.

- **Availability of power from renewable sources, such as wind and solar.** Methane from a nearby landfill (landfill gas or LFG) is also an environmentally desirable power source. Federal, state, and local governments may offer financial incentives in the form of tax credits, carbon offsets, or subsidies for using alternative energy sources.

- **Proximity to current or planned long distance transmission lines.** The President's administration, as part of their national energy plan, plans to build new transmission lines to bring alternative power from wind and solar farms to urban markets. Locating data centers near these lines and their substations ensures future energy flexibility.

Free cooling

One way to cut the power consumed by data center cooling equipment is to take advantage of cold outside air when it's available. That suggests locating a data center in a cooler climate. Also, evaporative cooling works best when the relative humidity is low. An ideal location has a cool, dry climate with ample supplies of water. Finding such a location can be problematic, but most sites can benefit from free cooling at least part of the year. See Chapter 10 for much more about efficient cooling techniques.

Water power

Data centers consume large quantities of water for their cooling systems. Evaporative cooling is very energy efficient but requires a lot of water to be added to the system periodically to make up for the water that evaporates into the air. Water is also needed to control impurities. Repeated exposure to evaporation concentrates dissolved minerals and other material in the water that remains. To counteract this accumulatation, you have to *blow down* — a process in which some of the old water is discharged and replaced with new water — your cooling system periodically.

You don't have to obtain cooling water from the local drinking water supply. One possible source is the grey water from waste treatment plants. For example, a Google data center in Belgium is located on a polluted industrial canal. Google included a water purification plant in its data center to filter and treat the water to a level suitable for use in its cooling towers, a level below what would be needed to make the water potable.

Another corporation that takes advantage of water power is IBM, which has several data centers using the Hudson River for cooling. Be aware, though, that using a natural body of water as a cooling reservoir will generally require permits from governments at one or more levels, and you'll need studies to document that the water won't be heated to a level that damages aquatic life. Add a marine biologist to your Rolodex.

District cooling

Data centers in urban areas can sometimes take advantage of district cooling systems. These are commercial firms that operate large chilling plants and sell cold water to nearby businesses. Some of these can be quite efficient and innovative. For example, Toronto runs its drinking water supply, which is pumped from Lake Ontario and is always cold, through water-to-water heat exchangers and sells chilled water to downtown buildings. An efficient district cooling system can remove one source of headache for an urban data center by shifting construction and management of cooling equipment to an outside vendor.

Waste heat recycling

A data center can use several megawatts of electricity. All that power is turned into heat, and that heat may have value to someone else. In general, the hotter the heat is, the more valuable it is. Waste heat from data centers is not very hot, so its value is limited, and it can't be sent far economically. Possible neighbors that might be able to use that waste heat include greenhouses, warehouses, and recreation facilities, such as a swimming pool, a gym, or tennis courts.

IBM has a data center in Uitikon, Switzerland, that heats a town swimming pool. Providing the local community with a year-round heated pool can generate enormous goodwill and might help cut through a lot of red tape and permit hassles. The pool can also serve as an emergency water source in case of supply disruption. (Be sure to bring up that possibility early in your negotiations with the community.) Paradoxically, a data center might be able to use higher-temperature waste heat from a neighboring industry to run absorption coolers. These are refrigeration systems that use heat as their source of energy, instead of electricity.

Energy storage possibilities

Energy storage provides numerous advantages to a data center. We're not talking about diesel fuel stored to run backup generators, but rather ways to store energy when it's plentiful to use when it's not. Energy storage makes intermittent alternative power sources, such as wind and solar, more feasible. Batteries are one solution, but you would need a lot of them. Backup batteries in an uninterruptible power system (UPS) aren't well-suited for this purpose because they typically store only enough power to run the data center for a few minutes while the backup generators are brought online.

One way to store energy is as cold water. Having a large, insulated water storage tank lets chilled water be produced during the night when cooling systems are more efficient and utility power may cost less. A large, chilled water tank can back up the cooling system in case of a chiller failure. It can also facilitate the transition from free cooling to chiller plant operation during the fall and spring when afternoon temperatures are too warm for free cooling but night and mornings are still cool enough.

Microclimate

Weather services tend to collect statistics on a city or county, which you can make use of; however, local climate conditions can differ significantly from one area of a city to another. For example, the average air temperature on the downwind side of a lake or river is cooler than elsewhere in the city. Air downwind of a tall structure is more turbulent, which can affect cooling tower efficiency. A site on the north side of a mountain or tall building will get less sun, which makes that location generally less desirable for office or residential use, but it's a good site for a data center that doesn't need the additional heat load of direct sunlight. If time permits, you may want to make local measurements at a proposed site over the course of a year, say, and compare them to official records.

Altitude can also affect data center efficiency. Thinner air carries less heat per volume. Dell, for example, lowers the operating temperature maximum for its blade servers by 1 degree Fahrenheit for every 550 feet above the 2,950-foot altitude.

Brown field siting

Brown fields are areas that have been polluted by previous users. Even after they're cleaned up, they're still difficult to sell because they carry the stigma of the past. Locating a data center at a brown field site supports green cleanup efforts and may qualify for financial incentives, but be sure you do your environmental and legal homework. Be certain the site is really clean and your liability in case problems arise is either capped or insured.

Global warming effects

We hope, of course, that green initiatives will avert the worst predictions of climate scientists, but you can't decide your data center site based on hope. Climate change is real, and you should consider potential climate change effects, such as rise in sea levels and increase in storm frequency and intensity, in picking a site. You should also take care to locate backup and recovery sites in different geographic locations from your main facility.

Planning Your Data Center for Green Efficiency

Sage Yogi Berra once said that the future is one of the hardest things to predict. What will be in your data center ten years from now is almost impossible to forecast. The stakes are high. If you underdesign, much of the resources that went into building the data center might have to be scrapped early. If you overdesign, resources will be underutilized and less efficient. Air conditioning equipment, for example, generally works most efficiently when you match it to the heat load. Systems with excess capacity often waste power. Luckily for new data center builders, vendors such as IBM and Sun Microsystems provide modular data centers that can be rolled out as needed; (see the upcoming sidebar "Exploring out-of-the-box data centers").

Forget about the details of the electronics that will go into your new data center for the time being and think in terms of infrastructure architecture: mechanical support, thermal density, cooling, power distribution, and cabling. The data center that results from the design decisions you make will outlive several generations of server and storage equipment and architectures.

Raised floors versus solid

A wise person once said, never discuss three topics with strangers: politics, religion, and raised floors versus solid floors in data centers. Passions run particularly strong on the last topic.

Raised floors have been pretty much the norm in computer rooms since the vacuum tube era. In those days, computer cables were as thick as your arm and about as flexible. Computer rooms were located on the first floor and had glass walls so that visitors to the corporate headquarters would admire the blinking lights. Unsightly cables had to be hidden. (Three out of four of the authors of this book witnessed this scenario with our very own eyes.)

Aside from getting cabling out of sight, having a false floor makes distributing cool air around the room easy. First, you set up the computer room air conditioners to pump cold air into the under-floor space. Then you put perforated tiles near the front of the racks, where cold air intakes are typically located. If you move equipment, you rearrange the tiles accordingly.

But the higher power densities that are becoming common make the raised floor approach less compelling. To cope with the heat produced by densely packed servers, you need techniques, such as *in-row cooling* — in which air conditioning units located along the row of racks extract warm air and cool it before discharging it into the room. Or you may have to use water cooling electronics modules. If you have to go to in-row or water-cooling anyway, why bother with a raised floor?

The alternative — solid floors — have long been used by telephone companies and have a number of advantages:

- They cost less.
- They can easily support higher loads. (Those denser racks weigh more, too.)
- You don't need to waste floor space on a ramp or lift to get equipment up to the raised-floor level.

✔ You avoid the risk that poorly placed cables under the floor will obstruct airflow.

✔ Fire suppression systems are simpler, and fire risk is reduced. Raised floors can accumulate dust and paper scraps that present a fire hazard. Many false floors require additional fire suppression equipment under the floor.

A solid floor data center requires careful attention to the design of what goes in the ceiling. It can become a complicated maze of air ducts, cable trays, chilled and return water pipes, and other utilities. You should route power and signal cables separately to prevent electromagnetic interference. Overhead space should be high enough to allow warm air to rise without being forced into cold aisles. Sun Microsystems consolidated its data centers in an existing building in Santa Clara, California. The company opted to use solid floors for most of the facility and ran overhead chilled water and power throughout the facility to support modular rack clusters. The result? Sun Microsystems claims a 77 percent reduction in energy use. You can take a video tour at www.sun.com/aboutsun/environment/green/datacenter.jsp. (See Chapter 10 for more on data center cooling.)

Although most data center decisions can be revisited as technology turns over, it's almost impossible to switch floor types in an operating data center without significant expense and productivity loss.

Variable speed drives

If you were a computer science major in college, you probably never expected to worry about what types of electric motor control to use in a data center's air conditioning systems. But in the real world, the choice a company makes in this area affects efficiency. Fixed-speed motor controls run, as the name implies, at the same speed all the time, even if the heat load on the system doesn't require full power. Variable speed motors and controls are more expensive to purchase, but they can tailor cooling power usage to need, producing substantial savings, and therefore may prove less expensive in the long run. When you estimate your costs, try to project the rising price of power over the expected life of your data center. The green choice is variable speed.

Power distribution

Power distribution encompasses all the equipment and cabling needed to bring electrical power from your building's connection to the utility company's lines to the racks containing your IT equipment. This includes transformers, *switch gear* (the grown-up version of the breaker panel in your home), backup power systems, and the like. In many data centers, 10 to 15 percent of total electrical power is lost in these systems. Best practices can cut those losses by up to half. The only time you can usually upgrade your power distribution is during a major renovation or expansion. Of course, building a new data center presents an opportunity to use the best systems available. If you're involved in planning a major data center project, don't ignore the power distribution design.

Holding up those servers

Mechanical support generally means the ubiquitous 19-inch rack (technically known as the Electronic Industry Association's EIA-310-D standard). The controllers for the future 22nd-century teleportation network will probably mount in 19-inch racks. You have plenty to choose from in the design of those racks, however. Fully integrated systems with built-in cooling, power distribution, and hot aisle/cold aisle separation (see Chapter 10) are available from a number of manufacturers, including the following:

- ✔ **IBM:** www.ibm.com/systems/x/hardware/options
- ✔ **HP:** www.hp.com
- ✔ **American Power Conversion:** www.apc.com

Some manufacturers design the system around a particular server or storage manufacturer's products; others keep it vendor-neutral. As always, you have to consider the trade-off between initial cost and long-term energy expenses. The more efficient designs are generally the greener choice and can often pay for themselves in a few years or less.

Thermal density

The trend in servers is to pack more and more CPUs into a single rack. More CPUs mean more power, and more power means more heat that must be removed from the rack. When power densities get above 200 watts per square foot or so, the traditional approach of blowing cold air through the false floor (if you have one) becomes ineffective because too much air is needed to remove that heat. Alternative approaches, such as enclosed racks with built-in chillers or even water-cooled servers, become the preferred solution. Chapter 10 tells you more about cooling issues in your data center.

Exploring out-of-the-box data centers

Data processing wasn't the only industry to transform itself in the post World War II era. The introduction of standardized, trailer-sized shipping containers revolutionized freight transportation. An entire transportation infrastructure — truck, rail, barge, and ocean — has been built up around these containers, which are 8 feet wide (2.44 m) and come in a few different lengths and heights. Several vendors offer server and storage systems prepackaged in modified shipping containers. One example is Sun Microsystems' Modular Datacenter (www.sun.com/sunmd), formerly called Project Black Box. The Modular Datacenter consists of a box that's 20 feet long by 8 feet wide by 8.5 feet high and looks like a standard shipping container on the outside, complete with the standard lifting and stacking fittings at each corner. Inside are eight 19-inch racks, each 40U high, along with cable management hardware, air conditioning, and power distribution capable of supplying and cooling up to 200 kilowatts of server, data storage, and communications equipment. Sun Microsystems claims the Modular Datacenter cools equipment 40 percent more efficiently than a typical data center. All you need to install a Modular Datacenter is a concrete pad along with power, chilled water, and communications hookups. Rackable's ICE Cube (www.rackable.com) uses a similar approach, as does the Verari FOREST (www.verari.com). The lead time for getting such systems-in-a-box online is much less than the time typically required for new data center construction. You can add capacity incrementally, in contrast to traditional data center buildings, which are typically overbuilt initially to allow future expansion.

Buying performance per watt

Traditionally, server buyers have opted for models that offer the most processing performance per dollar of purchase price. But more and more, people are looking at performance per watt. Given rising electric utility rates and the added cost of cooling and backup power provisions, a server can cost several times its purchase price in energy charges over its lifetime. Processor chips that are more energy efficient, such as those designed for laptops, may have lower peak performance, but their energy use drops faster at lower processing loads — and servers are underused much of the time. Thus, energy-efficient CPUs can deliver the same amount of useful work over the course of their service life with lower overall cost. Because the cost saving comes from lower energy use, you reap related green savings with these CPUs as well.

Another approach is to use fewer, but more powerful, mainframe class servers, with virtualization allowing each to replace dozens of x86 class servers. We talk more about selecting green servers in Chapter 9.

AC versus DC

Several vendors offer power distribution systems that use direct current (DC) instead of the alternating current (AC) that comes out of standard wall outlets. DC power distribution for electronics isn't new — telephone central offices have run on negative 48-volt DC power for generations. To achieve high reliability, telephone systems took their power from battery banks that were kept charged by utility mains. That's why phones keep working during a power failure.

The prime benefit touted by DC advocates is greater efficiency. The guts of servers and storage systems run on DC anyway, and doing a single conversion from AC to DC has some efficiency advantages. For one thing, making DC from three-phase AC is easier than making it from single-phase AC because there's less need for capacitors to store energy between cycles. Also, UPS systems have to convert power to DC to charge their batteries and then convert it back to AC to prevent brief power drops during changeover from mains to standby power. The heat generated in a bulk AC-to-DC converter can be kept separate from the more sensitive electronics and removed more efficiently.

You have more than one approach to opt to use DC in your data center:

- **48-volt DC:** This approach builds on the technology used by telephone companies. Its biggest drawback is that transmitting large amounts of power at that voltage requires high current and, consequently, very thick and expensive cables.

- **High-voltage DC:** A central rectifier station produces DC at a high voltage; 380 volts and 575 volts are two proposed standards. It works like this: The high-voltage power is distributed to racks and then to DC-to-DC power supplies each server, storage unit, or other rack mount device. These power supplies replace the AC-to-DC power supply used in those units. A high-voltage DC system can use cables similar in size to those used in standard AC distributions systems. However, special switches, breakers, and connectors are required, whereas AC uses common industrial electrical hardware. An American Power Conversion (www.apc.com) study found 380 VDC to be the most efficient power distribution system, but the runner-up, an AC distribution approach that's widely used in Europe, was only 1 percent less efficient.

- **DC racks:** In this approach, each rack is supplied with AC power and a single AC-to-DC converter powers all the electronics in the rack. The servers must be equipped with –48 VDC power supplies rather than AC units. Rackable Systems (www.rackable.com), which supplies this type of DC powered rack, cites as an advantage the ability to install DC rack in an AC-powered data center without rewiring. Rackable Systems also offers row-based solutions.

Assessing power supply efficiency

One problem for DC advocates is that AC systems keep getting more efficient and cleaner. Much of the early promise of DC was based on the poor efficiency and power factor of power supplies sold five to ten years ago. Effective July 9, 2009, Energy Star–rated desktop power supplies must apply more stringent limits, 85 percent minimum efficiency at 50 percent output, and 82 percent minimum efficiency at 20 percent and 100 percent output. Rated power supplies must have a power factor greater than 0.9 at 100 percent output.

Dell has introduced power supplies that meet the 80 Plus gold standard, which requires 87 percent efficiency at a 20 percent loading, 92 percent efficiency at 50 percent loading, and 86 percent efficiency at 100 per cent loading. The 80 Plus consortium, managed by electric utilities and Ecos Consulting Inc., operates a certification program to encourage PC power-supply makers to boost efficiency to 80 percent or more, and also gives attention to server power supplies. Major vendors, such as Dell, HP, and IBM, also participate in this effort for monitoring power efficiency. The 80 Plus Web site, www.80plus.org, lists power supply vendors that meet its various rating levels. Although DC-to-DC power supplies can offer still higher efficiencies — Rackable Systems, a vendor of DC-to-DC systems — claims 94.5 percent efficiency and higher reliability — at some point the higher cost and limited vendor choices with DC-to-DC supplies may become a problem.

Although the use of DC has promise, it's not clear DC's advantages will overtake the massive market momentum behind AC. Going with best-of-breed AC systems may yield efficiencies almost as high as DC while allowing you the flexibility of a much broader choice of vendors. However, for large installations, even a small improvement in power efficiency can mean big savings. A handy rule of thumb is that one megawatt of electric power running continuously for one year costs a million dollars at a price of 11.4 cents per kilowatt hour. For a 2.5-megawatt data center, a 5 percent improvement in efficiency can save $125,000 per year at that power price.

If you choose high-efficiency power supplies in all new equipment purchases, you can upgrade your data center effortlessly over a three- to five-year replacement cycle.

Redundancy needs versus efficiency

Dual-redundant hot-swappable power supplies have long been the mark of industrial-strength data center equipment. But keeping two power supplies running all the time requires extra power. Failover and virtualization technology can allow applications to transfer to another physical server in case of power-supply failure. In an installation with a large number of servers, a single-supply approach may yield acceptable reliability while saving energy, cooling, and initial equipment cost.

Consolidating the Physical Infrastructure

One of the most effective ways to improve the power consumption and cooling requirements of the data center — the prime components of cost and consumption in the data center — is by consolidating parts of the physical infrastructure. Reducing the number of physical servers, for example, will almost always result in power savings. In this section, we tell you about the value of consolidating servers and storage, followed by reducing the need for rack space and data center floor space.

Servers and storage

Servers consume much of the data center's power, as does storage. For that reason, servers and storage are logical candidates for consolidation. Reducing the number of physical servers or the number of storage systems will have a profound impact on the amount of power and cooling consumed by the data center and thus improve the overall green profile of the infrastructure. Although nothing involving IT is simple, implementing this strategy is easier than you might think.

Consolidating servers usually means consolidating applications. In traditional server architecture, most servers run just one application to achieve optimum performance. You can therefore consolidate your servers in the following ways:

- ✔ **Use a larger server — a server with faster processors and increased memory capacity — to replace several servers.** Of course, you have to move the applications that are running on the individual servers to the larger server. You can then redeploy the smaller servers for other uses, or retire and dispose of them in a green way (see Chapter 19 for suggestions).

- ✔ **Replace physical servers with virtual servers.** We cover virtual servers in detail in Chapter 13, but the essence of a virtualization strategy is to run applications in their own virtual "machine." You accomplish this by fooling each application into "believing" that it has full use of the server's resources — that is, the processing power, memory, drive, network, and so on are "virtually" dedicated to each application. The virtualization manager takes care of allocating resources to each running application so that performance is maintained.

In either case, existing physical resources are displaced or replaced. The potential benefits of consolidation include

- ✔ Fewer physical resources to manage
- ✔ Reduced rack space for servers
- ✔ Reduced data center space floor space
- ✔ Reduced power consumption
- ✔ Reduced requirement for cooling

Note that we use the word *potential* in the lead-in to our list of benefits. Why? If you replace several physical servers with a type of server called a *blade* server (described in Chapter 9), you may not reduce power or cooling requirements at all because of the concentration of processors and memory within each blade and the potential increased heat from each blade. Computer manufacturers are highly aware of this problem with blade servers and are continuing to improve the overall consumption of their processors even as they increase the density (number of cores, or processors) on a single chip.

Storage presents a different story from servers, for several reasons:

- ✔ Very few companies are buying *less* storage capacity — quite the opposite. The seemingly unending demand for more capacity arises from the way most companies do business — almost every business activity includes using computers, and all this activity requires storage.

- ✔ Storage capacity is often allocated to specific applications, such as databases, which require a certain amount of space to be reserved for tables and indices based on the expected number of data elements. Rather than calculate the amount of storage to be reserved, most IT administrators allocate the largest amount, which results in capacity that can't be used for any other purpose.

Estimates are that only 30 percent of storage capacity is actually being used at any given time, which means that companies should be looking at using more efficiently the capacity they have rather than buying additional storage. Again, this is difficult to do because the unused storage capacity isn't sitting in one storage array; instead, it's spread over hundreds or maybe thousands of drives.

Consolidating storage capacity requires moving data from one system to another, which may be difficult without shutting down production applications and is a tedious process in any case. No wonder that companies find it easier to add capacity than rework existing systems!

Nevertheless, IT organizations are almost always upgrading or revamping the servers and storage that deliver applications — it's a regular part of their job description — and this gives IT the perfect opportunity to consolidate with an eye toward greener equipment:

✔ Storage administrators can replace smaller drives with larger ones and save money in the process because newer drives use less power and require less cooling.

✔ Server administrators can replace obsolete servers with newer servers that are designed to provide substantially more computing power while still using less energy than their predecessors.

It's important to recognize that very few companies have the money or the luxury to start over from scratch, so the movement toward a greener data center is a progression over time. It should be a goal of every IT organization to achieve green results over a reasonable time period, given business conditions and resources. Chances are that regulations are coming that may force you in this direction — so you may as well get started!

Rack space and floor space

As you consolidate physical servers through virtualization, or replace them with increased computing power in a smaller form (such as blade servers), you can reduce the number of racks needed to hold data center components. The increasing capacity of hard drives — 1 terabyte of data is quickly becoming commonplace in the same size case that used to hold 500 gigabytes — will have a similar effect on storage racks: more storage capacity in less space.

It's axiomatic that having fewer racks means that the total floor space that the data center occupies can be reduced and that this reduction in cubic footage has a direct impact on power consumption and cooling.

It was common practice in the past to cool the entire data center — what has been compared to leaving the refrigerator door open to air condition an apartment. Even as the numbers of racks are decreasing, rack technology itself is becoming increasingly sophisticated. For example, cooling is increasingly being applied at the rack instead of to the entire space. Moving the cooling closer to the source of the heat — the servers or drives in the rack — means that the cooling mechanism can be much more efficient.

Reductions in data center floor space not only decrease the requirement for cooling but also allow the space saved to be applied to other purposes. When a company rents the building in which the data center is located, this can also mean a corresponding reduction in the amount of space leased.

Measuring and Maintaining Data Center Efficiency

> Owen Glendower: "I can call spirits from the vasty deep."
>
> Hotspur: "Why so can I, or so can any man, But will they come when you do call for them?"
>
> — Shakespeare, *Henry IV Part I,* Act III, Scene 1.

Vendors and consultants make lots of claims, but benefits accrue only if those claims hold up over the long run. Measurement and management are key to getting what you're paying for when you buy more efficient solutions.

You can't manage what you can't measure. The following sections describe some key metrics you should consider tracking.

Power usage effectiveness (PUE)

PUE is perhaps the best overall test of your cooling and power distribution system effectiveness. PUE requires you to know how much power your data center is using and how much power goes to all the equipment racks. You get the PUE by dividing the first number by the second. Lower PUEs are better. A PUE of around 2 is typical. The EPA says 1.2 is ideal and achievable with the best available technology.

In Chapter 6, we suggest ways to estimate your PUE to get started. But a well-run data center should be instrumented to monitor PUE. Ideally, you should measure power at the building input, cooling equipment, UPS system, and individual racks or rows. Smart power distribution units (PDUs) are available that report over Ethernet, as are power measurement modules for heavy equipment.

A simple way to measure power is to measure the voltage and amperage going into a piece of equipment and multiply each of those numbers. For AC systems, this gives you the amount of volt-amps. You then have to multiply that number by the *power factor* to get the power in watts. Good power instrumentation should provide true power in watts (technically known as *root-mean-square,* or *RMS* power) and also indicate the power factor. See Chapter 17 for information on power measuring equipment, including smart PDUs.

Embracing best practices for building

The U.S. Green Building Council (www.usgbc.org) has developed a Leadership in Energy and Environmental Design (LEED) program to rate how well a building project meets the council's green building and performance measures. Although this agency doesn't have a program for data centers, its checklists for new construction and existing building renovation contain many ideas worth considering in a data center design. Some criteria are easy for a data center to meet, such as banning smoking inside the facility or minimizing light pollution from the facility; others are at cross purposes, such as giving workers control of air temperature. Although some criteria are required, such as minimum standards for indoor air quality, most are optional, with points awarded for compliance.

Data center Infrastructure Efficiency (DCiE)

After you figure the PUE, you can easily calculate the Data Center infrastructure Efficiency (DCiE) — it's just 1/PUE. So, if you divide 1 by a PUE of 2.0, you get a DciE of 50 percent, which is typical; less than that is all too common. A value of 80 percent or more is excellent.

Power cost at the equipment rack

When making choices about how much more to pay for energy efficiency when buying servers and storage systems, you need to calculate what the power that equipment uses over its lifetime will cost. One way to estimate this cost is to multiply your average power cost at the utility meter by the PUE of your data center. A better approach might be to include amortization of the capital tied up in your cooling system, UPS, and backup generation equipment. Your finance department can help you figure these calculations. The more complete cost will reflect the extent to which new equipment uses up data center power distribution and cooling capacity, leading to expensive upgrades or even a need to build a bigger data center. Although your organization may be paying the utility 10 cents per kilowatt hour at the meter, taking all these factors into account may mean you should use a price of 30 or even 40 cents per kilowatt hour in choosing between servers and storage systems with different power needs.

Temperature and humidity

Tracking temperature and moisture in the data center helps tell you whether your cooling system is operating optimally. If the readings are outside acceptable range, that's obviously a problem that needs immediate attention. But if the readings don't vary over the course of a year, it suggests you aren't taking advantage of the increased allowable ranges for these parameters as recommended by ASHRAE. Temperature, relative humidity, and dew point should be recorded, with temperature readings taken at several locations throughout the data center, including cold aisles. Finding and correcting hot spots in your data center is key to running it more efficiently. (Chapter 10 tells you about these issues in much more detail.) Record readings of outdoor temperature and humidity as well.

Free cooling performance

If your data center's cooling system is set up to take advantage of free cooling, often called *economizers* in the HVAC trade, be sure to collect data on when you're using free cooling. Compare this data with outside temperature data to see whether better system tuning could permit wider use of free cooling.

Average system life

Keeping track of the installation data of each unit in your racks can be easier if you simply write the month and year of installation on the back of each module. Of course, if you have a good asset tracking database, this isn't necessary. In any case, getting a periodic report on the age of your data center's systems helps you track the turnover rate and identify systems that may be less efficient. In some cases, you can upgrade a system just by replacing its power supply with a more efficient unit. Or you might use a system as a standby unit for peak load times and keep it off otherwise.

Green certifications

Keep track of the number of systems that enjoy green certifications such as Energy Star of Plus 80. Add a field for certifications to your asset database records. Chart progress toward a goal of 90 percent certification.

Chapter 9

Racking Up Green Servers

Servers are the workhorses of IT, whether the data center serves 10,000 employees or 10, therefore much of an IT administrator's time is spent on the servers' care and feeding. Most computer users are unaware of the role servers play in delivering the applications they use every day — they see only the application's user interface, not the underlying server infrastructure.

Servers are also the largest generators of heat and consumers of power — although, to be fair, storage is also a large contributor to these problems, as we relate in Chapter 11. It's also fair to say that the companies that manufacture servers have been working on these power consumption problems for many years. Today's servers are far more efficient in terms of the amount of power they consume, but because doubling or quadrupling the number of processors adds heat, the savings in power consumption tend to be offset.

In this chapter, we tell you about different server options and how they impact energy use for a given level of performance.

It's Not Easy Being Green: Dissecting a Server's Core

To get to the heart of how to make the servers in your data center greener, it helps to know what you're dealing with — both in terms of your current servers and what you can expect to buy in the near future. This part of the chapter tells you about the main components of a server and what computer manufacturers are doing about greening server systems.

The anatomy of a server

As you may already know, a server can look similar to your own desktop computer — in fact, there's no reason that a desktop computer can't be used as a server, although most servers have more memory and the ability to access large storage systems at high speeds. Dedicated servers are designed for minimal down time and often have components that can be replaced while the server keeps running.

Computation capacity in both PCs and servers is rapidly evolving as computer manufacturers put more and more "cores" into a single processor.

What's a core, you ask? Not so long ago — say, three years ago — if you wanted to put four microprocessors in a server (called a four-way server), you had to put four separate microprocessor chips inside the chassis. Because of continual advances in microprocessor technology, those four separate processors, or cores, can now be built into a single processor, called a quad core, to distinguish it from a two-processor, or dual-core, model. Even more remarkable is the continuing drop in prices of this technology. These days, a quad-core processor can easily be put into a desktop computer that most people can afford. (Two-processor, or dual-core, models have been common since Intel introduced the Core Duo processor in 2006.)

What truly distinguishes a dual-core server from your dual-core desktop computer is the operating system on which applications run. Operating systems such as Microsoft Windows XP, Vista, and Apple OS/X are designed for end-user machines and have features and functionality designed for consumers.

Servers, on the other hand, require operating systems that can provide applications to multiple users — and the applications must be designed to support multiple users as well. Operating systems such as Microsoft Windows Server 2008, Red Hat Linux Release 5, Solaris, or OS-X Server are designed specifically for these types of servers and multiple users. (As you might imagine, they are also priced higher.)

Other differences between your desktop computer and a purpose-built server may include the following:

- Components such as power supplies, chassis, fans, connectors that are designed for long service life.

- Inclusion of multiple fans to remove heat from inside the case so that a single fan failure does not bring the server down.

- The presence of storage controllers — the devices that move data to and from the hard drives — that use higher performance protocols such as SCSI, iSCSI, and Fibre Channel (see Chapter 11 for more on storage systems).

✔ The use of "hot swappable" components — components that can be removed or inserted while the server is running.

By the way, you never want to remove components from inside a computer case unless you're sure the computer is designed to allow hot swapping! You might ruin the computer and could get a nasty shock or start a fire.

✔ A server case designed to fit it in a 19"-wide data center rack — which allows a rack to hold many servers in a single rack, but can create a problem with heat. (We go into much more detail about mounting equipment in racks in later sections of this chapter.)

Most data centers use servers that are designed to be "racked." They carry a higher price tag than a desktop computer and are expected to last a minimum of three to five years — conveniently matching the typical accounting depreciation period for a computer asset.

The search for greener servers

As we note earlier in this chapter, computer manufacturers have been working on making servers more energy efficient for some years, and we can report that servers are getting greener, as measured by processing performance per watt of power. But there are some countervailing developments:

✔ The increase in the density of processors within a single chip has raised power requirements and produced more heat, which means that even though a single processor may be more energy efficient, the larger number of processors means each chip uses as much or more power.

✔ Network and storage controllers use more power to provide faster I/O.

✔ Storage density has increased — for example, a 1TB (terabyte) drive has the same form factor as a 100GB (gigabyte) drive, meaning that they look alike but have dramatically different capabilities. However, as drive prices fall and requirements for data storage rise, data centers are adding more and more drives, boosting power consumption.

✔ Power supplies are more efficient than they were five years ago, but the total amount of wattage required by dual- and quad-core processors has increased.

As the sheer amount of computing power has increased for a given space, so has the power requirement and the amount of heat generated. The good news is that manufacturers are aware of this paradox and are continuing to work on increasing the efficiency of the "whole" server so that the sum of its components can ultimately result in savings in energy and cooling.

The bad news is that servers are relatively inexpensive to purchase and many IT shops solve performance and availability problems by simply buying more and more servers. The explosive growth in the number of servers online more than cancels out the efficiency improvements achieved by server manufacturers.

There are some measures that you can take in the data center that have the net effect of reducing overall consumption. We discuss some of those measures in the following sections. The biggest gains however are in using servers and storage more efficiently. We discuss these measures in the rest of this chapter and this part.

Some Are Greener Than Others: Comparing Server Form Factors

Servers come in several "packages," called *form factors* by mechanical engineers. Server form factors can contribute to or hinder attempts to make data centers more efficient in power consumed or cooling required. The traditional "rack 'em and stack 'em" mentality of packing as much computer power in the data center has contributed to the notorious consumption of data centers. As you discover in this chapter, using a server form factor that encourages both passive and active cooling is a design goal of replacing older servers.

Your desktop computer, which can be used as a server, comes in several form factors. The traditional off-white or dark-gray case hasn't changed all that much in appearance since the original IBM PC debuted in 1983. That's unfortunate, because the insides of most PC cases are stuffed with components that inhibit airflow and make cooling fans run continuously. A change in the PC's form factor would do much to improve power consumption and lengthen the life of components. Laptops or notebooks can also generate excessive heat, leading to performance degradation because the onboard processor has to run slower to cool off.

Computers built to be servers generally come in several form factors:

✔ **Desktop case with server "features"** — server operating system, 4 gigabytes of memory, fast hard drives, and fast Ethernet (with speeds from 1GB to possibly 10GB). This is the form factor favored by small businesses whose data center consists of a small room or even a closet. Figure 9-1 shows a PC that essentially doubles as a server.

✔ **A case that is designed to fit in a rack** — the width of this case is standardized at 19" wide (the rack itself is a few inches wider). The height is usually 2U or 3U high. A "U," or unit, corresponds to 1-$^3/_4$" (44.45 mm), so a 3U case takes up 5$^1/_4$" of vertical space in the rack. Figure 9-2 shows a typical server in a rackable form factor, for contrast, and Figure 9-3 shows a typical large rack used in a data center.

Figure 9-1:
Desktop
server.

Figure 9-2:
Server in a
form factor
suitable for
putting in a
server rack.

Figure 9-3:
Typical rack
for servers
or storage
used in a
data center.

✔ **A rolling case containing a server.** Sun Microsystems made this kind of case popular for its "workgroup" line of servers, which were intended for a small business, a branch office, or a workgroup in a larger company. This form factor was convenient because it was designed to fit under a desk and was a self-contained server package — a rack on wheels. Currently, these rolling racks come in various heights — 48" high, for example — and are standardized on the 19" rack size so that several servers can be placed in the rack. Figure 9-4 shows a rolling rack designed for small business or workgroup use.

Figure 9-4:
A small
rolling rack
for holding
a server.

From a "horsepower" standpoint, any of these form factors is capable of housing a current quad-core processor — all were designed and used to house up to four separate processors.

In green terms, however, it's useful to know the differences between them in terms of their power consumption and ability to deal with heat generated within the case itself. As we mention earlier in this chapter, with processors, you experience a trade-off between performance and consumption — a quad core processor effectively quadruples the processing power of a single processor, but at the cost of additional heat and power.

As an example, if you fill a 42U space rack with 42 1U servers, each with one processor, every one of those separate servers would have separate power supplies, fans, hard disks, network adapters, and so on. You'd have a system generating 42 times the heat of a single server.

Now, if you were to replace the same processing power with quad-core servers, in theory you would need only 11 servers to achieve the same amount of processing power. Note that we are talking only about raw processing power, not about how efficiently or effectively that processing power is being used by the operating system and applications.

But you could also fill all 42U of rack space with quad-core processors, achieving 168 times the processing power of a single processor server. Here's the rub: You're also generating plenty of additional heat and consuming more power. This is the problem that a relatively new technology, blade servers, described in the next section, aims to address.

Serving Up Green Power with BladeServers

Blade servers use a packaging idea borrowed from the minicomputer, a computer system that was popular in the 1970 and 1980 and that put each processor, memory, and even hard drives, on a single card. In blade servers, this card plugs into a "backplane" with a series of connectors for multiple processor cards, called blades. Figure 9-5 shows a blade card, and Figure 9-6 shows a blade system that can have up to 16 blades installed.

Figure 9-5:
A blade
server.

Figure 9-6:
A blade
computer
system
including
power
supply.

AC vs. DC Power in the data center

As manufacturers and IT have looked at ways of reducing power consumption, one of the hottest (excuse the pun) topics has been the use of direct current (DC) in place of alternating current (AC) to distribute power in the data center. This topic has particular currency (oops! another one) in any discussion of reducing power consumption in servers.

The reason to switch to DC power is simple: A traditional server is plugged into AC power, even though the individual electronic components

on the server's motherboard — processor, memory, and so on — run on DC voltages, usually 5V or 12V. The role of the power supply in the server's chassis is to convert the incoming AC voltage to DC. The process of converting from one voltage to another generates heat. DC-to-DC converters are more efficient than AC-to-DC converters. So, supplying DC instead of AC power to the server would automatically reduce the amount of heat generated and power wasted.

Blade servers offer a significant opportunity for green efficiency because the power and cooling provided by a single server's case (see the previous section for more about server cases) is now shared among all the blades plugged into the backplane. Specifically, these common services include:

✔ **A single power supply:** Rather than have individual power supplies for each processor, each of which requires a 120- or 220-volt AC power cable, the blades share a common supply. A larger supply is generally more efficient, so the blade packaging uses less power for the same amount of computation. (See the "AC vs. DC Power in the Data Center" sidebar for more information about power supply efficiency.)

✔ **A shared cooling system:** Rather than having one or more fans in each 1U server chassis, the blade system chassis provides cooling for all the blades. The concentration of blades in one chassis allows the server designers to use fewer but larger and more efficient fans and to engineer the air flow for better effectiveness.

✔ **A shared network interface:** In place of individual network interfaces, which are frequently a sizeable consumer of power because they are seldom turned off, the case provides a common network backplane with a port for each blade server. This is similar in concept to a router, which connects a series of network addresses on one LAN to an external LAN — in this case the LAN outside the case. Chapter 12 provides additional details about green networking concepts.

Because of the concentration of blades within the blade server case, blade server manufacturers often supply software to control the power usage of individual blades or the system as a whole. See the later section, "Power capping to cut waste," for more about controlling power use.

The amount of power savings varies by manufacturer, but the idea of blade servers as a way of combining computing performance with efficient design is very attractive for IT in the effort to use less power and cooling.

Blade servers also save floor space in the data center by packing more processors into a single rack. The greater density puts off the need to lease or build ever-bigger data centers. That saves money and avoids the environmental impact of new construction or renovation.

Replacing multiple 1U "pizza box" servers with blade servers generally saves power and space.

Managing Servers for Energy Efficiency

In addition to implementing efficiency at the hardware level — "in the box" — computer manufacturers provide both software and hardware solutions to help IT manage their servers to increase their efficiency. This section delves into what's available to you right now to increase the green power of your servers.

The complexity of measuring server "greenness"

It's a computer industry axiom that what can't be measured can't be managed. Until recently, many IT departments weren't paying their own power bill, so they had less visibility into their own consumption. As companies have become more aware of how much energy data centers consume, management is making IT accountable. For this reason, companies and IT departments are actively looking at ways to measure, and thus manage, their consumption.

A simple way to estimate a data center's base level consumption is to apply the Green Grid's PUE and DCiE calculations, as described in Chapter 8 (and introduced in Chapter 4).

Yet another way to assess power use would be to assign average consumption per server in watts and count the number of servers. To do so, follow these steps:

1. **Find out how many watts each of your servers operates on and average them.**

Say you have three servers operating at 200, 300, and 400 watts, respectively. Your servers' average is 300 watts.

2. **Determine how many hours in a normal day your servers are in use.**

This is likely to be 24 hours a day.

3. **Multiply the average watts by the hours used and then divide that number by 1,000.**

This gives you the number of kilowatt hours per day, which is how power companies calculate consumption.

So, for example, if the "average" server uses 300 watts and is left on all the time, the power consumed in one day would be

```
300 watts × 24 hours per day = 7,200 watt hours per day
```

And

```
7,200 watt hours per day ÷ 1,000 = 7.2 kilowatt hours per day
```

4. **Multiply the result of the previous step by 7 (the number of days in a week) and then by 52 (the number of weeks in a year) to arrive at the total number kilowatt-hours each one of your servers spends running in a year, as follows:**

```
7.2 kilowatts per day × 7 days × 52 weeks = 2,620 kilowatt-hours per year
```

Remember, that's just one server! Remember, too, that this is only an estimated number based on an average. It doesn't account for your aging servers that almost certainly use more power than new ones on the market today. Nor does this simple formula account for the changing load on each server. Network interfaces tend to run all the time, but servers are subjected to varying loads (and numbers of users) throughout a 24-hour period. How many people are logged in after 6:00 p.m. and before 6:00 a.m.? A precise calculation is needed to account for the server's actual power consumption. The next section points you to ways to calculate consumption more accurately.

Achieving more precise measurement techniques

Fortunately, an increasing number of hardware and software-based solutions help you get and track the energy performance of individual servers. These solutions include

- ✔ **Building measurement into the hardware itself.** The server can "report" on its use by recording the energy consumption of various components, such as power supplies, the processor, and so on.

- ✔ **Using software that monitors the amount of consumption** through the use of sensors.

- ✔ **Using inexpensive power meters,** such as the Kill A Watt described in Chapter 17, to measure the energy consumption of servers and other equipment.

By comparing the relative consumption of each server, you can quickly see which servers are "greener" than others. These kinds of measurements will likely become increasingly common and sophisticated as demand for IT to account for consumption becomes more widespread.

As we noted at the start of this section, when you can monitor, you can begin to manage. Software such as IBM's Tivoli and HP's Power Manager allow you to manage server activity according to policies set by IT or patterns of usage. A clear goal of all these efforts is to cut power consumption by putting servers with no current load into a quiescent state, in much the same way that a notebook computer will go into a lower power state after some period of inactivity.

Another goal is to use servers at their full capacity. Industry experts estimate that as much as 60 percent of all servers are underutilized, which wastes energy. Hence, if application loads were more evenly distributed, the number of servers could be reduced. The average utilization rate of an x86 server is said to be between 10 and 15 percent, and x86 are proliferating. Clearly, this leaves a lot of room for improvement!

To ensure that you're using your servers as efficiently as you can, follow these steps:

1. **Use virtualization to increase server utilization.**

   See Chapter 13 for details.

2. **Update your organization's software development tools.**

   More efficient compilers and interpreters can reduce server loads.

3. **Assign older, less efficient servers to provide peak capacity, based on season or time of day, and power them down when not needed.**

Energy Star criteria for servers are still under development as this book goes to press, but use Energy Star ratings to guide new server purchases when they become available. Check this Web site for the latest developments:

```
www.energystar.gov/index.cfm?c=prod_development.server_
               efficiency
```

MIPs and FLOPs: Understanding performance per watt

Performance per watt is a measure of a computer's energy efficiency — it looks at the amount of computing power delivered on a per-watt basis. The relative performance per watt is derived by applying a similar metric to a group of machines from different manufacturers, or a product line from one manufacturer. The result is a ranking of energy efficiency.

Typical metrics used in computing performance per watt are FLOPS (floating-point operations per second) or MIPS (millions of instructions per second). A computer that runs at 60 FLOPS per watt is more efficient than one that runs at 30 FLOPS per watt — making the latter twice as efficient as the former, according to this measurement.

In case you're growing alarmed about having to compute all these FLOPS and MIPS, you don't need to be. Computer manufacturers conduct these tests all the time and publish the results as part of their marketing effort to differentiate their products from other manufacturers.

There is also a list, called the Green500, which is kept by SuperMicro and updated three times a year. You can take a look at the list at `http://www.green500.org/index.php`.

Power-capping to cut waste

Power-capping refers to the practice of limiting (or "capping") the amount of energy supplied to a server at various times during the server's operation. Power capping is generally implemented in a software management tool such as Verdiem Corporation's Surveyor that uses policies set by IT to limit power consumption when the server in question isn't being heavily loaded. This practice, in essence, allows managers to trade power for performance in determining energy consumption. Verdiem also makes a free, simple-to-use software tool, Edison, which helps manage individual PCs.

As this practice grows in popularity and sophistication, computer manufacturers also are installing hardware sensors to detect power levels and give the management software real-time, accurate information about current load and current consumption.

Chapter 10

Cooling Your Data Center

As you may know, computers in data centers consume large amounts of electrical power. A single server rack can use 10 kilowatts, and some analysts project that the power per rack might climb to 30 kW or more over the next decade. Except for a few watts sent down data lines leaving the building, all that power is converted to heat. That heat must be removed from the data center to keep temperatures from climbing to levels that can cause the electronic equipment to fail. (The people working in the facility won't be too happy, either.)

Cooling accounts for 65 percent of a data center's energy use in many data centers. But the good news is that if you follow best practices, you can reduce that number substantially — to as low as 20 percent. After virtualization, improved cooling represents the biggest opportunity for IT energy savings.

In this chapter, we tell you what the main sources of heat are in your data center. Also in this chapter, you get a crash course in basic air conditioning principles, see how to measure your data center's efficiency, and get a close look at various approaches to getting the hot and cold in the optimal places. Green IT, here we come!

Improving Data Center Cooling Takes Planning

Data center cooling is one of the biggest opportunities for energy saving and environmental improvement in most IT organizations. Realizing those improvements, however, can be a challenge. Data centers are the heart of IT operations, often containing tens of millions of dollars in capital equipment and operating 24 hours a day with mission-critical business functions. Any changes to the data center must be carefully thought out and planned.

Other chapters of this book present software and electronic equipment choices that are well within the training and responsibilities of IT professionals — you upgrade software systems and select new server, storage, and networking hardware all the time. Cooling systems involve quite different expertise and technology. Many decisions require input and approval from other professionals, electricians, HVAC (heating, ventilation, and air conditioning) consultants, and even architects. Electrical and building codes must be followed.

Before addressing data center cooling issues, find out how well your data center stacks up. A few measurements we suggest may require the assistance of an electrician, but they shouldn't interfere with data center operations. Some of the ways to improve data center efficiency we describe are quite simple, such as identifying and sealing air leaks or finding places where cool and warm air mix unnecessarily. Other solutions we describe, such as implementing hot and cold or adding water cooling aisles, require more planning and may have to wait for periodic system upgrades. Still others are best implemented when new data centers are built or old ones undergo major renovations.

It's vital that IT professionals concerned about green issues understand the technologies and advanced approaches to cooling so they can advocate for environmentally superior, but often initially more expensive, solutions when planning takes place.

What Makes Your Data Center Hot?

Electrical power is fed to the individual integrated circuits that do the computing your business depends on. All that power is eventually converted to heat. Many high-power chips, such as CPUs and graphics processors, have heat sinks attached to extract heat more quickly. (*Heat sinks* are blocks of copper or other heat conducting materials that are bonded to the chip package. They generally have many fins to speed the transfer of heat to the air inside the chassis.) Fans speed the heat transfer so that the chips don't get too hot and fail. The fans can be arranged to blow outside air into the chassis, to suck the heated air out of the enclosure, or both. Sometimes an additional fan is incorporated into the chip heat sink itself.

Space is at a premium in data centers, so people prefer servers and ancillary equipment that take up as little rack space as possible. (See Chapter 9 for more details about housing servers on racks.) Cramming more power-consuming chips into a smaller space requires more fans to keep the air moving fast enough to get out all the heat.

Each of those little fans is spun by an electric motor that consumes power. Remember, all that power gets converted into heat — including the power that actually moves the air. All those little fans spinning away use a lot of power, often comparable to the power consumed by the chips themselves.

The racks hold other tiny motors, which are spinning the disk drives in storage arrays. In many data centers, the disk drives are the biggest power hogs. And the disk drives are packed into racks as tightly as they will fit, so they, too, need an army of fans to keep them cool. Those fans also generate yet more heat in the process.

You may detect a theme here: Everything that happens in the data center adds to the heat load that those air conditioners must pull out of the building. Even the human operators produce heat, averaging about 100 watts each.

Understanding the Basics of Cooling Systems

The development of the practical steam engine in the eighteenth century led, of course, to the industrial revolution. But what you may not remember is that it also inspired a revolution in physics: the theory of thermodynamics. The second law of thermodynamics says that the efficiency of a steam engine can never be 100 percent, and the maximum efficiency depends on the difference in temperature between the input steam and the exhaust. The greater the difference, the greater the efficiency.

What's all this got to do with cooling systems? Consider this: Refrigerators and air conditioners are essentially steam engines operating in reverse. Rather than use a difference in temperature to create power, they use power to create a difference in temperature. The same second law of thermodynamics governs their efficiency as well, but with a happy twist — air conditioner efficiencies can be greater than 100 percent. In other words, an air conditioner can move more energy in the form of heat than the electrical energy supplied to the unit.

Figure 10-1 shows a typical air conditioner setup. A liquid refrigerant that boils at low temperature is pumped to an evaporator inside the building. There it boils and absorbs heat from the air in the building. The gas is fed to a compressor outside the building that raises its pressure, heating it in the process. The hot gas goes to a condenser, again outside the building, where it's cooled by the outside air, causing it to condense back into a liquid. That liquid is returned by a pump to the evaporator, completing the cycle.

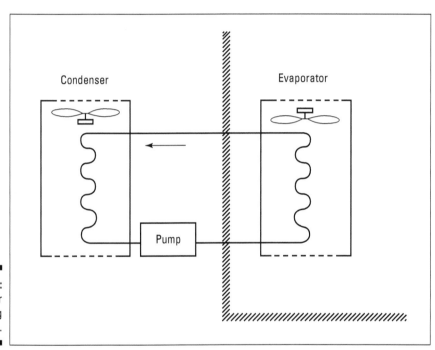

Figure 10-1:
A simple air conditioning system.

The evaporator and condenser are both forms of heat exchangers. These are typically a zigzagging arrangement of pipes in a chamber that allows heat to flow from one fluid to another without the fluids mixing. Often, fins are attached to the pipes to increase the surface area where the heat transfer takes place. Some designs separate the fluids with thin metal plates.

Variations on the condenser/evaporator scheme have been developed that make the process more efficient. Moving cold air long distances is difficult, so in most large building air conditioning systems, the evaporator extracts heat from a flow of water instead of air. The resulting chilled water is pumped to other heat exchangers throughout the building, where it cools air in the building's ventilation system as fans blow the air into the various rooms.

Large air conditioning systems often take the return cooling water, which is now warm because it's carrying the heat from the data center, and spray it inside a cooling tower, starting at the top of the tower. Some of the water evaporates as it cascades down the tower, taking heat with it, and the heated air creates an upward draft that pulls outside air through the tower. Other designs use fans to blow air over the falling water. Figure 10-2 shows a typical data center cooling tower.

TECHNICAL STUFF

Moving heat and cold — the basics

Moving heat around is central to air conditioning your data center. An understanding of the basics can help you follow the many steps involved in getting heat from the electronics to a place outside your building. Here's a quick primer on the four main ways to transfer heat:

✔ **Conduction:** Heat passes between two objects in contact with each other. For example, the heat path from an integrated circuit package to an attached heat sink.

✔ **Radiation:** The warm object emits infrared radiation, which is absorbed by a cooler object. It's what you feel when you stand in front of coals glowing in a fireplace.

✔ **Mass transfer:** The warm object heats a fluid, such as air or water, which then moves and gets replaced by cooler fluid. The air flowing through your servers is a good example of this form of cooling. When the air is moved by the natural effect of hot air rising, this form of mass transfer is *convection cooling*.

✔ **Phase change:** The warm object melts or boils another material. The heat needed to effect this transformation is removed from the object to be cooled. The phase change applies to water spray cooling towers as

well. Evaporating water takes heat from the condenser coils, cooling them to a temperature that's lower than the outside air temperature, thereby improving system efficiency. Technically, the lowest temperature you can reach this way is the wet bulb temperature. A more familiar example is standing outside in front of a fan on a hot summer day. The fan cools your sweaty body even though it's blowing hot air — except on a very humid day. Then the fan is useless. High humidity means the wet bulb temperature is about the same as the air temperature (dry-bulb), so there's no evaporation and no cooling.

Here are a few more basic principles to keep in mind:

✔ Heat flows from hot to cold at a rate proportional to temperature difference.

✔ Warm air rises.

✔ It costs money to create cold air or cold water.

✔ Cold air mixing with warm air before the cold air's been used to cool equipment wastes money.

Figure 10-2:
A typical
data center
cooling
tower.

Remember how the efficiency of a heat engine depends on the difference in temperature between the hot and cold side? Well, water evaporation drops the cold side temperature to near the *dew point,* the temperature at which the air becomes saturated with moisture. Blow on a wet finger to feel the effect. Cooling towers work best when outside air humidity is low.

Benchmarking Your Cooling System's Efficiency

In the U.S., air conditioner cooling capacity is measured in tons. One ton of cooling corresponds to the amount of chill you'd get by melting a ton of ice per day. That's enough ice for a couple thousand martinis. Or, in more useful units to know, one ton of cooling capacity equals 12,000 BTUs per hour, or about 3,517 watts.

As mentioned in the previous section, a heat pump can be more than 100 percent efficient. But rather than talk in terms of efficiency, air conditioning engineers use the term *coefficient of performance* (COP), which is the heat change per unit time at the air conditioner output divided by the input power. So, for example, a COP of 3.5 would correspond to an efficiency of 350 percent.

A measurement, such as COP, is useful for you to know because a higher COP means less electricity is used to cool your facility. However, that measurement reflects only the efficiency of the air conditioning system itself — that is, how much energy, in the form of electricity, is required to remove a certain amount of energy, in the form of heat, from the air. To thoroughly measure a cooling system's energy demands, you have to account for the power consumed by moving that chilled water and air around and providing power to the IT equipment itself.

The Green Grid (see Chapter 4 for more about The Green Grid) has developed two closely related metrics for data center energy efficiency, *power usage effectiveness (PUE)* and *Data Center infrastructure Efficiency (DCiE)*. The PUE is defined as the total power consumed by the data center facility — what the power company bills you for — divided by the power supplied to all the IT equipment inside. So, a PUE of 2.0, a common level in today's data centers, means that for every 2 kilowatt-hours of electricity the data center uses, only one goes to the IT equipment; the other goes to power transformers, switch gear, UPS systems, and air conditioning. A PUE of 3.0 means 1 kilowatt for the IT equipment and 2 kilowatts for everything else.

IT equipment power includes almost everything in the equipment racks except for rack-mounted chillers. It also includes monitors, communication gear, and computers used to control the data center equipment. For more information about PUE and DCiE, see www.thegreengrid.org.

DCiE is 100/PUE, which is the reciprocal of the PUE expressed as a percentage. To translate, a data center with a PUE of 2.0 has a DCiE of 50 percent. The Green Grid folks added the word *infrastructure* and wrote it with the lowercase *i* because efficiency in this case refers only to the power going into the servers and other equipment, not to how well that equipment is being used (which is another big issue in greening the data center). And anyway, lowercase *i*'s are quite trendy these days.

The U.S. Environmental Protection Agency (EPA) estimates that most data centers have a PUE of 2.0 or higher. According to the EPA, implementing best practices can achieve a PUE of 1.3, with 1.2 being state of the art.

The first action for you to take to start improving your data center's cooling efficiency is to collect baseline numbers for your existing power consumption for air conditioning, IT equipment, and overall facility usage. Next, compute your PUE score.

To compute that score, you need two important numbers:

✔ **The total amount of power your data center uses**

✔ **The amount of power used by all the electronic equipment in your data center** — the boxes that store and process all that data

If your data center is a standalone building with its own power meter, getting the first number is relatively simple:

1. **Find your power meter.**

2. **Note the meter reading along with the date and time.**

3. **Wait some period of time, say a week, and then read the meter a second time, noting the date and time.**

   If possible, take the two readings on the same day of the week at about the same time to smooth out daily variations.

4. **Subtract the first meter reading from the second to get the number of kilowatt-hours consumed between the two readings.**

5. **Compute the time difference between the two readings in hours, with time that is less than an hour expressed as a decimal.**

6. **Divide the number of kilowatt-hours by the number of hours to get your average power consumption in kilowatts.**

Appendix A has a worksheet, "Calculating Facility Power from Two Meter Readings," that guides you through the details of this calculation.

If your data center shares a power feed with business offices, you may need to get assistance from your facilities department. Your local power company may also be willing to provide technical assistance.

The second number is a bit trickier to get. Here are two approaches:

✔ **Direct measurement:** You determine the voltage and current flowing into your equipment racks. If measurement equipment isn't already installed, you need an electrician to make one-time readings or to install monitoring equipment. See Chapter 17 for information on relatively inexpensive data logging systems that can collect this information on an ongoing basis.

✔ **Estimation:** You can get a back-of-the-envelope estimate of the data center equipment power consumption by following these steps:

   1. *Take an inventory of the equipment in the data center (or print one if you have an up-to-date inventory in your database).*

   2. *Estimate or measure the power consumption of each type of equipment in the inventory.*

      Chapter 17 describes the inexpensive Kill A Watt meter, which can be used to measure the power consumption of individual units.

   3. *Multiply the power consumption of each unit type by the number of that unit in the inventory to get the power consumption for that type.*

   4. *Add the power used for all types of equipment to get the total equipment power usage.*

Appendix A also has a worksheet, "Estimating IT Power Consumption," that guides you through this calculation.

Knowing where you came from is always a good idea, and if you follow many of the recommendations in the remainder of this chapter, you'll have a lot to brag about.

Green Is Cool: Getting the Most Out of Your Cooling System

After you know how well your data center is performing in the power usage effectiveness (PUE) and Data Center infrastructure Efficiency (DCiE) metrics, consider what improvements are possible. This section describes some of the approaches being used by the best-in-breed data centers to reduce cooling costs and attendant environmental impact. Although a few, such as finding cold air leaks into warm areas, can be done easily, most require careful planning with inputs from professionals with specialized expertise. Here are steps for you to consider:

1. **Assemble a team to review current approaches to data center cooling and to evaluate alternatives.**

   This includes representatives of data center management, your facilities department, and outside consultants for expertise not available in-house.

2. **Identify vendors with promising approaches.**

3. **Develop a proposal and prepare a capital budget request with cost saving estimates, according to your organizations procedures. Include a summary of environmental benefits, such as reduced carbon footprint.**

4. **Develop an implementation plan that allows changes to be made with minimal disruption to data center business functions.**

   For example, rearranging equipment racks into hot aisle/cold aisle configuration might be scheduled on a holiday weekend or in conjunction with other equipment upgrades.

5. **Make sure you've taken baseline measurements that allow you to quantify benefits after the changes have been implemented.**

   See Appendix A for a baseline measurement worksheet with suggested parameters to measure.

Restyling your aisles

Traditional data center layouts had all equipment racks facing in one direction with computer room air conditioners (CRACs) located around the outer perimeter of the room, as shown in Figure 10-3. In this arrangement, the electronic equipment is cooled by ambient air in the room. The air conditioner keeps all the room air within an acceptable range to keep the equipment happy. Placing the cooling at the perimeter of the data center is simple and it works, but it's quite inefficient. The cold air from the air conditioner mixes with the hot air exhausted by the equipment racks, and the lukewarm mixture is then used to cool the racks. Remember, it costs money to make cold air. Any time you mix cold and warm air needlessly, you're wasting money.

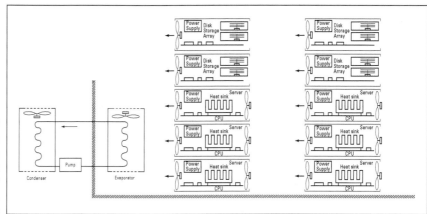

Figure 10-3: A data center with perimeter cooling.

Courtesy of IBM

There's a better way! A more efficient arrangement, *cold aisle/warm aisle cooling,* is shown in Figure 10-4. In this approach, you arrange the racks holding your servers in alternating cold and hot aisles so that the intake side of the equipment always faces a cold aisle and the exhaust side faces a hot aisle. You then feed cold air from the air conditioner to the cold aisle, using your existing false floor. No cold air is allowed to enter the hot aisle.

The cold aisle/hot aisle approach is most suitable for large data centers that have enough racks to organize them in this fashion, but you can apply the principle to smaller centers by ducting the cold air to a location near the intake side of the equipment racks. Figure 10-5 shows one cold aisle in a data center. Note the perforated tiles in the floor that allow cold air to pass from under the false floor into the cold aisle.

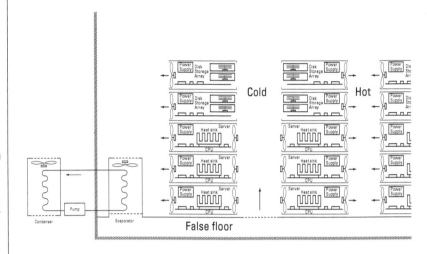

Figure 10-4:
A data center with cold aisle/ warm aisle cooling.

Figure 10-5:
A cold aisle in a data center with perforated floor tiles.

Courtesy of IBM

You can extend the cold aisle/warm aisle principle by segregating the flow of warm air back to the computer room air conditioners (CRACs), as shown in Figure 10-6. You add ducts to the top of the CRACs to ensure that they're taking return air from near the ceiling. A more thorough method connects the CRAC intakes to the plenum formed by the data center's false ceiling. You then install vent panels in the false ceiling above the warm aisle.

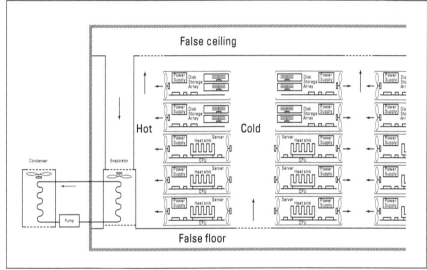

Figure 10-6: A data center with cold aisle/ warm aisle cooling and ceiling plenum return.

Be careful not to overly constrict airflow in the process of modifying airflow patterns. Constrictions reduce airflow rates or cause fans to work harder and can wipe out whatever energy gains you intended the improved airflow to achieve. Although small adjustments to eliminate hot spots can be made by trial and error, work with your facilities department or an HVAC professional in any major airflow redesign.

Adding in-row cooling

You can reduce your energy consumption even more by taking the concept of cold aisle/warm aisle cooling one step further and adding in-row cooling. With this setup, you still go with the alternating warm and cold aisles, but you also box-in the warm aisle with doors and baffels, trapping that heat to keep it from mixing with cold air (which, as we've stated elsewhere, is a needless waste of energy). You also place chillers (essentially smaller CRACs) on or next to the server racks. If they're next to the racks, they use space that would otherwise be used for racks. If you put them in the racks, you need to include one or more chillers per rack. Each rack will also need two plumbing hookups — for chilled water and return — as well as electrical connections.

The chillers extract the heated air inside the boxed-in aisles and chill that air. The chilled air is then discharged into the adjacent cold aisle or the room perimeter.

You can deploy more chillers to sections of the data center that have higher power densities, with an aim toward eliminating hot spots. (In-row chiller vendors can help you determine the correct number and placement of chillers you require.) Downsides include additional cost and plumbing complexity, but you can offset these expenses in new data center designs by eliminating the need for a raised floor because the chillers deliver cold air directly to the racks or cold aisle; the false floor is no longer needed to distribute cold air. Cabling can be run on overhead cable trays, which are easier to access and less expensive than a false floor.

Getting your ducts in a row: Targeting airflow

Remember that you don't want hot and cold air to mix unnecessarily. One way to avoid such mixing is to get the air from the hot aisle to the CRACs via their own path. This can be done by installing a false ceiling to take the heated air from the hot aisles to the air conditioner's intake.

If you don't have a false ceiling in your data center and don't want to install one, you can achieve the same effect by strategically placing new duct work or by modifying existing ducts to change the location of their intakes. A well-thought-out airflow system may have been installed back when the data center was built, but subsequent relocation of equipment racks may have invalidated the original design, possibly now venting cold air into the warm aisle and vice versa. Vents and intakes may even be blocked by newly installed cable ducts and other equipment. When was the last time you toured your data center looking up at the ceiling?

Although some problems may be obvious, such as new equipment blocking a previously functioning vent or intake, a full evaluation of your airflow requires a specialist's knowledge. If your facilities department lacks the necessary expertise, engaging a computer room HVAC consultant may be a good investment.

Plugging leaks

After you've organized your data center into cold and warm aisles or implemented some other strategy to get cold air to equipment intakes before it has a chance to mix with warm air, you can turn your attention to where your system isn't as sealed up as it should be. Keep a pad of paper handy to note what supplies you might need to pick up at a hardware store to plug up or otherwise deal with the leaks you find. Specifically, check the following:

✓ **Equipment racks:** Air should not be allowed to flow out of the front of the racks your equipment sits on. If a rack has empty space in a rack — a rack mounted unit has been removed, for example — you want to fill that the gap with a panel. Depending on the airflow design, it may be worth blocking the gap from the front of the rack to the ceiling.

✓ **Pipes and cables:** Inspect every opening in false floors where cables and plumbing goes in to see whether cold air is leaking around the pipes or cables.

✓ **Floor panels:** Also look for poorly fitting false floor panels. If one of these places is leaking cold air into the cold aisle, that's not a problem. But if it's leaking cold air into the warm aisle or the room perimeter, it should be sealed or blocked.

You can use smoke sticks and smoke generator pens (find them at `meter mall.com/search/smoke.htm`) to trace airflow, although often a wet finger actually works just fine, too. To trace larger circulation patterns, weight a helium-filled toy balloon to neutral buoyancy and then release it in various locations and notice where it goes.

You can seal cracks with tape, silicone caulk, or other products sold for weather proofing. Baffles can be placed to block or divert larger airflows.

Finding your hot spots

Hot spots among your equipment can result from clogged ducts, thick bundles of cables under a false floor, or an aging or poorly designed cooling system. Hot spots pose a serious concern because equipment that takes in air from a hot spot can overheat and fail.

You have two basic ways to deal with hot spots:

✓ Bring more cold air to the area

✓ Rearrange the equipment to put the higher heat producers nearer the cold air supply

Finding the hot spots can be tricky, however.

Remote temperature sensors that report wirelessly or over the network are available, and many servers can take their own temperature and report it. Software packages are available to help monitor the temperature profile in your data center and report on problems.

A number of vendors offer complex software that models and simulates the data center with computational fluid dynamics programs, which were originally invented to design ships, airplanes, and space craft — rocket science comes to the data center. These studies can be expensive, however.

Infrared cameras show the surface temperatures throughout the room in living color.

Or you can just place thermometers at several levels near rack inlets and check them regularly.

See Chapter 17 for descriptions of gadgets that can help find the heat. Inexpensive thermometers may be all that's needed for a small data center, whereas large installations may find the added convenience and thoroughness of constant, automated monitoring a worthwhile investment. Whatever solutions you choose, be sure to remember to check for hot spots periodically, and in particular whenever you make a change in hardware configurations. In fact, even a shift in the placement of furniture can create a change in airflow.

Setting and maintaining the right temperature

Air conditioning systems allow you to specify the air temperature you're trying to achieve, just like the thermostat in your house. The power required to cool your data center depends, in part, on the temperature of the air that you command. The cooler you want the air, the more you'll pay in electric charges.

The American Society of Heating, Refrigerating and Air-Conditioning Engineers (ASHRAE, www.ashrae.org), in consultation with computer manufacturers, recently lowered its recommendations for data center air temperature and computer room humidity. The new recommendations for maintaining IT equipment safely are as follows:

- ✔ **Maximum temperature:** 80.6°F (27°C)
- ✔ **Minimum temperature:** 64.4°F (18°C)

✔ **Maximum relative humidity:** 60 percent (ASHRAE doesn't set a minimum, relying on the minimum dew point instead.)

✔ **Maximum dew point:** 59°F (15°C)

✔ **Minimum dew point:** 41.9°F (5.5°C)

The new maximum temperature is a significant increase over the 2004 ASHRAE maximum, which was 68°F and 55 percent relative humidity. Many data centers still follow the older recommendation, and if yours does, you can see significant energy savings by moving to the new ASHRAE guidelines.

These recommendations don't mean that higher temperatures are optimum for overall energy use — some IT equipment, for example, employs variable speed fans, and these might crank up at higher inlet temperatures. Also, high humidity can cause condensation on CRAC cooling coils, reducing their efficiency.

Why, you might be wondering, does ASHRAE specify the data center humidity in terms of dew point as well as relative humidity? The *dew point,* of course, is the temperature to which the air in the room must be cooled so that water begins to condense. (For example, how cold your drink must be for the glass to begin to sweat.) In contrast to relative humidity, the dew point doesn't depend on the starting temperature of the air. Dew point measures the absolute water content of the air, and ASHRAE has determined that *electrostatic discharge (ESD),* which is a bigger problem in drier air, depends more on the absolute moisture content of the air. ESD is the familiar static zap you get after walking across a carpet and then touching something metal. It's nothing more than a slight shock to you, but it can permanently damage electronics. You get such shocks more often in the winter when the air is dry. Moisture in the air makes the air more electrically conductive, preventing static-charge buildup. The ASHRAE required minimum humidity level was carefully selected to minimize the risk of ESD damage.

ASHRAE also set maximums for moisture content in the air. The upper limit involves both dew point and relative humidity. So to take full advantage of the extended ASHRAE limits, you need to consider both. Figure 10-7 shows a diagram of the recommended temperature, dew point, and humidity limits. The curve on the upper left represents a constant relative humidity of 60 percent. This curve can be approximated by the condition that the dew point should always be at least 14.3°F (8.5°C) below the dry-bulb air temperature.

The temperature and air moisture content in most data centers is controlled by the CRACs, which typically have a set point control for displaying and adjusting these values. The controls are essentially industrial strength versions of the digital thermostats you have in your home.

Some CRACs have settings only for temperature and relative humidity. If that's the case in your data center, the ASHRAE conditions can be met with a minimum relative humidity of 40 percent, although this is more relative humidity than ASHRAE requires at higher temperatures. Check with your CRAC vendor for the availability of controller upgrades that track ASHRAE guidelines more accurately. See Chapter 17 for a tool to measure independently temperature and humidity.

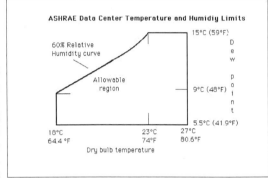

Figure 10-7:
The ASHRAE extended temperature limits.

Figure 10-7 is a simplified version of the psychrometric chart that ASHRAE includes in its *2008 ASHRAE Environmental Guidelines for Datacom Equipment,* which is available from their Web site, www.ashrae.org. (A full psychrometric chart depicts the complex interrelationship between air moisture content, relative humidity, heat energy, and the dry-bulb, wet-bulb, and dewpoint temperature readings. Think graph paper gone wild.)

Free (almost) cooling

Traditional mechanical chillers aren't the only solution to keeping data center equipment from overheating. In most locations, the outside air is below the minimum ASHRAE recommended inlet temperatures described in the previous section, at least for much of the year. Using that outside air when the conditions are right sounds like an obvious solution (after all, it's free!). You still need some electricity for fans, of course, and the air may need to be humidified to meet the ASHRAE minimum dew point. (See the previous section for more details about ASHRAE recommendations.) You might also need some filtration to keep dust out of the data center. Still, all these processes typically take less energy than running traditional chillers. Some computer room air conditioning installations include a feature called an *air side economizer* that makes use of cool outside air when it is available.

Evaporative cooling: Letting water do the work

Google has taken another approach to free cooling. It uses evaporative chillers most of the year. In this approach, warm water that's been used to cool air and equipment in the data center is fed to the top of a cooling tower, where it cascades down. Outside air flowing up through the tower evaporates some of the water, cooling the rest in the process.

This method requires significant amounts of water. Google tries to use water that would otherwise be wasted, such as grey water or local water sources that are not drinkable. The availability of suitable water is one of the factors Google considers in locating data centers. Its Belgium data center is located next to an industrial canal. The data center includes a water treatment plant that improves the quality of the canal water to a level suitable for cooling use but not for drinking. Google claims average PUEs in the 1.1 to 1.3 range for its five newest data centers. These PUEs approach or even exceed what the EPA calls state of the art. For more information, visit www.google.com/corporate/datacenters.

Using available water for cooling is not unique to Google. IBM has several data centers that use Hudson River water for cooling. Toronto is located on the shores of Lake Ontario and takes its drinking water from deep in the lake, where the water is always cold. Before that water is distributed, it passes through heat exchangers that chill cooling water used in downtown office buildings.

Another way to use outside air when it's cold enough is to cool the warm water coming back from the data center's CRACs. Air is blown through a heat exchanger that the return water flows through. This approach is known as a *water-side economizer*. The air has to be colder for a water-side economizer to operate effectively than for the temperature needed for an air-side unit to kick in. Data center designers have been reluctant to make extensive use of outside air due to a variety of concerns, including increased difficulty in controlling humidity and fears of dust and contamination. The new ASHRAE guidelines widen the level of acceptable humidity, and the other concerns may be overstated.

One way to cut the power consumed by data center cooling equipment is to take advantage of cold outside air when it's available. That suggests locating a data center in a cooler climate. Also, evaporative cooling works best when the relative humidity is low. An ideal location has a cool, dry climate with ample supplies of water. Finding such a location can be problematic, but most sites can benefit from free cooling at least part of the year.

Intel did an experiment in which it placed racks of production servers in a modular shelter. One side was cooled the traditional way; the other side was cooled using raw outside air with no treatment at all. The equipment failure rate in the outside air half was only slightly higher than in the traditionally cooled side, but the cost savings were impressive, more than enough to pay for some spare servers.

Tapping into liquid cooling: The pros and cons

Blade servers, which we describe in Chapter 9, have upped the ante in data center cooling. By packing more servers into the same volume, they increase the rack *power density* — the amount of electricity consumed and, therefore, the waste heat generated — in each equipment rack. As the power density approaches 25 kilowatts, air cooling starts to reach a practical limit. Getting enough cold air from the false floor to a rack operating at that power level can require hurricane force winds. Running the fans needed for that kind of airflow takes a lot of power in itself. And some blade designs are pushing to the 50 kW level for a full rack.

It takes a lot less water than air to move a given amount of heat, so one solution is to run chilled water to each rack to extract the heat generated inside. Water cooling can produce significant energy savings. This solution has a back-to-the-future aspect. Large mainframes in the 1960s and 1970s were commonly liquid cooled. IBM is once again a big advocate of water cooling in modern data centers. And Sun Microsystems' new Santa Clara, California, data center runs chilled water and three-phase alternating current (AC) power in lines throughout the computer rooms, allowing modular water-cooled pods to be located directly below.

Water cooling isn't without drawbacks for you to keep in mind as you consider various cooling system designs:

- ✔ Rack mounted chillers are expensive, although some of the cost is offset by a reduced need for computer room air conditioners (CRACs).

- ✔ Running chilled and return water to all those racks is a big plumbing expense that can cost more than the rack chillers themselves. And the installation has to be done right. An air leak is no big deal, but a water leak can be disastrous.

- ✔ Water cooled equipment is more difficult to move around or add to as needs change.

- ✔ Many computer vendors design rack chillers around their own blade server equipment, which can result in vendor lock-in.

Chilling at the heat source

Rack-mounted chillers still require air circulation within the equipment rack. That means a lot of fans whirring away, using up electricity and generating more heat. Why not water cool the hottest chips directly? A number of vendors are starting to offer water-cooled servers that extract heat from the CPU chips by placing them in contact with a water-cooled plate. (Computer hobbyists who run their CPUs at speeds above those recommended by the manufacturer — a practice known as *overclocking* — have been buying water cooled heat sinks for years.) Water flowing to the chip must pass through small-diameter channels, so pipe-clogging corrosion must be avoided. This usually means having a closed system within the server, and using highly distilled water that connects to the data center's chilled water system through a heat exchanger.

The rise of water cooling may lead to different approaches to data center design, depending upon location. In urban settings, where electricity is expensive, real estate is at a premium, and additional power is often unavailable, the space- and energy-saving advantages of water cooling may tip the economic balance in its favor. Even exotic technologies like direct water cooling may take hold. In remote data centers, which are often in locales where energy and real estate are cheaper and plentiful, and possibly where free cooling is available, the lower initial cost and greater flexibility of air cooling might continue to win the day.

Reduce, reuse, recycle: Using waste heat

A data center's carbon footprint can also be reduced by finding a use for all that waste heat it generates. Although this does not directly cut the data center's energy consumption, the user of the waste heat will use less energy, so this practice results in a net savings. IBM has a data center in Switzerland that uses its waste heat to keep a swimming pool warm. Other potential uses for waste heat include supplying heat for greenhouses and for nearby residences. Most large office buildings generate enough waste heat from non-data center operations that they must be cooled the year round, but smaller buildings may be able to use the waste heat in the winter. There's much room for innovation here. If you've found clever uses for waste data center heat, write us at greenit4d@yahoo.com.

Tips for smaller data centers

Many of the cooling improvement ideas presented in this chapter are aimed at large data centers. Although many organizations have smaller operations, when their IT is looked at all together, they still consume large amounts of energy. Concepts, such as hot and cold aisles, don't make sense if you have only a few server racks. Here are some suggestions aimed at smaller data centers:

✔ Get a copy of your air conditioning system's user manuals and check on any periodic maintenance requirements.

✔ Change air conditioner filters and clean coils regularly (at least do it in the spring, before air conditioning season begins).

✔ Inspect refrigerant piping to insure that insulation on the cold leg is intact.

✔ Arrange the CRAC output so it's near server inputs.

✔ Consider using outside air during the cooler times of year.

✔ Use waste heat to heat the rest of the building.

✔ Increase computer room air temperature per ASHRAE 2008 guidelines.

✔ Shade outside air conditioning unit from direct sunlight where feasible without blocking airflow.

✔ Find out if fan motors require periodic lubrication and, if so, make sure this is done on a regular basis.

✔ If you're using tower servers, make sure they're not shoved up against a wall or other obstacle that might limit airflow.

Chapter 11

Building a Green Storage System

Storage systems are among the most conspicuous consumers of power and cooling in the data center. Imagine racks filled with as many as 100 hard drives and you begin to see the problem. To be usable for data storage, drives must be fully powered and running.

Storage manufacturers are working on ways to reduce the amount of power and cooling required by redesigning storage systems and by managing the use of storage capacity more carefully. However, every year "knowledge workers" — you know, the kind of folks who use computers to create documents such as or reports, spreadsheets, or PowerPoint presentations or just sit around sending e-mail — create more stuff that has to get stored. And now in many places there are laws or at least policies requiring that each and every e-mail be "archived" — that is, kept around for posterity or in the event that they're required in a lawsuit. The kinds of files getting created are getting bigger too. Video files, for example, take up huge chunks of storage, and their usage in every day business is growing by leaps and bounds.

Because of the way storage has been used in recent years, there's a lot of room for improvement. Manufacturers and consumers are looking for ways to use available capacity more fully and to apply new storage techniques to reduce overall consumption.

You may notice that we use the word *manage* frequently throughout this book. That's because a successful green strategy goes beyond formal planning and implementation and involves actively managing all the components of the IT infrastructure. Applied to the storage part of the infrastructure, management includes activities such as capacity planning, regularly scheduled maintenance, backup, failover, and business continuity. In this chapter, we present methods for improving the efficiency and utilization of your storage.

Exploring Green Storage Gear

Storage systems are getting greener all the time. Why? In Chapter 4, we tell you all about the EPA's Energy Star program and the EPA's criteria for determining whether a device meets Energy Star definitions. Several causes are driving manufacturers to build storage systems that meet or exceed Energy Star requirements, including:

- ✔ Pressure from customers who want products that use recycled materials when possible and that lower power consumption

- ✔ Competitive pressure (so-called "brand pressure") — which means competition among manufacturers to meet or exceed each others' products in green capabilities

All things being equal, why wouldn't you want to buy a storage system that uses less power and requires less cooling? Actually, there is one big reason — performance. Certain applications, such as customer resource management (CRM), critical databases for logging sales, invoices, or inventory, or high-volume Web servers require high-performance storage to deal with the volume of transactions. Referring to the tiered storage model described in Chapter 7, highly transactional storage belongs in Tier 1. Tier 1 storage systems are the most expensive and consume the most power and cooling — hardly green attributes. The manufacturers of these systems are working on making them greener, however.

Some storage manufacturers advertise the progress in their products' green statistics — they consume less power and require less cooling, for example. Some are actively engaged in helping their customers reap the benefits of green by providing consulting services.

Many companies, including IBM, HP, Dell, and EMC are working hard at green and sustainability in their storage offerings. Also, we find truly exemplary efforts from a storage vendor named 3PAR, Inc. of Fremont, California. 3PAR is committed to green in both their product designs, marketing campaigns, and in their creative use of green to attract and retain customers. 3PAR developed a series of programs around green that include:

- ✔ **3PAR Carbon Neutral Program:** 3PAR purchases carbon credits (described in Chapter 5) to offset every terabyte of disk capacity sold with thin provisioning. (We describe thin provisioning later in this chapter.) To date, 3PAR has purchased credits to offset more than 8,700 metric tons of CO_2 emissions.

- ✔ **3PAR Virtual Technology Incentive Program:** Customers can take advantage of energy rebates for data center storage virtualization and thin provisioning projects from Pacific Gas and Electric (PG&E), a California power utility.

✔ **Energy Conservation and Recycling:** 3PAR is itself actively working at sustainability. Its internal organizational commitments include:

- Recycling (paper, glass, plastics, cans, and so on)
- Collecting and de-processing florescent light bulbs
- Collaborating with Pacific Gas & Electric (PG&E) to design energy-efficient air conditioning
- Compliance with California RoHS standards (see Chapter 4) and participation in CRT collection and de-processing (See Chapter 19).

✔ **Green manufacturing and compliance with standards:** 3PAR's engineering and manufacturing practices and processes include contracting with ISO 14000 certified service providers to sort, reclaim and recycle 3PAR products and components; marking 3PAR products in accordance with European Waste Electrical and Electronic Equipment (WEEE) directives; and product compliance with EU-RoHS and the Japan Green Law.

✔ **Innovative product designs:** 3PAR's products are designed with the corporate philosophy of reducing the negative environmental impact of storage. For example, 3PAR's SANs are among the most energy efficient in the industry. They were early leaders in their commitment to lowering power consumption and cooling requirements without compromising performance.

This impressive list reflects 3PAR's dedication to sustainability and green. As more IT shops look to go green, keep your eye out for suppliers catching on to the demand and offering a wider selection of green storage from environmentally conscious companies — although even the most aggressive attempts to reduce the energy consumption of storage systems won't make them entirely carbon neutral. Unless disks are turned off, they consume electricity and require cooling.

For most companies, making storage greener is a progression along a path: storage systems are retired or redeployed when their capacity becomes too small to support their intended use or when they become defective. The replacement storage system will have more capacity (because component disks have become larger) and consume less power (because continuing advances in technology make arrays more efficient). Newer systems are more likely to have power management features built into the array, instead of added on after the fact.

RAID Arrays: Necessary but not necessarily green

Redundant Array of Independent Disks (RAID) was developed to combat sudden disk failure. Even though most companies also back up data on a scheduled basis, data recovery can take time and (depending on the method used) may present its own problems. The basic principle behind RAID is to write data simultaneously to two or more hard drives at the same time but in such a way that the computer to which the array is attached perceives them as one drive. No matter how many separate drives comprise the RAID array (five are possible, as shown in Figure 11-1), they appear to the computer as one contiguous disk.

Enlisting MAID for power savings

Several technologies have an immediate impact on the amount of power consumed by storage as well as the amount of cooling required. One of these technologies, the Massive Array of Idle Disks (MAID), has been around for several years and is being deployed in large companies as a substitute for more power-hungry, high-performance transactional storage. MAID storage is often used for "persistent" storage, that is, storage for data that you don't need to access frequently. Because the majority of the disks in a MAID array are either shut down or idle at any one time (as opposed to spinning all the time), MAID storage is highly power efficient and requires substantially less cooling than a traditional storage array of the same capacity.

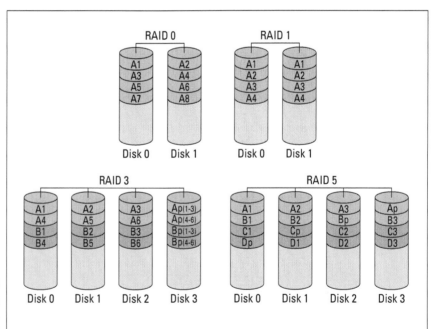

Figure 11-1:
RAID levels.

Spinning drives consume more power than ones that are shut down; they also require cooling, especially when they're kept in a storage array. A typical storage array may have a hundred or more drives, all of which require power and cooling.

A MAID array, on the other hand, is designed to idle most, if not all, of the time, reducing the amount of power being consumed to run and cool them. For this reason, MAID arrays would not be useful in situations where high performance is required, such as might be used with a transactional database. MAID arrays are ideal for storing data that doesn't need to be accessed all the time. In our discussion about storage tiers in Chapter 7, we describe how the third tier is designed for "persistent" data — that is, data that needs to be kept for long periods of time but not accessed frequently. Examples of persistent data include e-mail or document storage.

The MAID array itself is not powered down, but most of the drives in the array are idle at any given moment. Areas of the array, consisting of a group of drives, are designated by the administrator as "active," "idle," or "off," depending on how quickly the data in a particular area needs to be accessed. For example, a completely idle disk might take 30 seconds to start up and reach full speed for access, whereas another group in the array might be running at a slow speed and take 10 seconds to reach full speed. Figure 11-2 illustrates this concept.

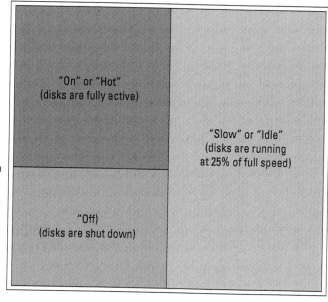

Figure 11-2:
Areas distinguished by access time in a MAID array.

"On" or "Hot"
(disks are fully active)

"Slow" or "Idle"
(disks are running
at 25% of full speed)

"Off)
(disks are shut down)

The efficiencies of AutoMAID storage: A case study

Lenox Hill Radiology provides state-of-the-art imaging services for diagnostic radiology for healthcare practitioners, researchers, universities, hospitals, and individual patients. Its systems ensure excellent patient diagnostics and care; provide cutting-edge data security for reliable and private patient information access; and enable anywhere, on-demand access to Picture Archiving and Communication System (PACS) images. Now, physical prints are replaced with digital images for nearly instantaneous responses to patient and physician needs. As Lenox Hill Radiology grew, the old tape-based archive failed to meet the performance and reliability that doctors and patients demanded. The company's image archive had grown to 14 terabytes, and the time had come for a new solution that would provide the performance, reliability, and operational efficiencies that Lenox Hill needed. IT staff realized that continuous growth in image size and the ever-increasing volume of image files would quickly consume existing data and archive storage resources.

Lenox Hill Radiology turned to the storage experts at Maureen Data Systems. After reviewing all the available options, they selected an innovative approach with Nexsan and its energy-efficient, high-performance storage systems. Lenox Hill selected Nexsan's Assureon, SATABeast, and SASBoy storage products. At the heart of Nexsan's products is its energy-saving technology, AutoMAID, that enables storage systems and the applications they support to have energy efficiency without sacrificing performance. Assureon is a highly scalable, high-performance disk-based archive storage system for PACS images and other fixed-content files. Assureon delivers all the required HIPAA compliance support at speeds that in some applications were 100 times faster than Lenox Hill Radiology's former tape-based system. SATABeast is an energy efficient, high density storage system that delivers up to 42TB in only 4U of rack space. SASBoy is a high-performance storage system that brings together energy efficiency and SAS drives for the first time.

Assureon, SATABeast, and SASBoy storage each deliver high density, energy efficiency, and high reliability. Data center space is expensive in New York City, and the high density storage feature allows Lenox Hill to reduce the number of racks it employs, thereby decreasing its data center footprint. AutoMAID green storage technology reduces the power and cooling required in the data center along with the number of electrical outlets and power distribution units (PDUs) needed. AutoMAID enables Lenox Hill to reduce power consumption by up to 50 percent over its legacy Fibre Channel storage systems at the same operating level and up to 75 percent when using AutoMAID Level 3.

Joe Funaro, Director of Technology at Lenox Hill, had this to say about the success of his company's use of AutoMAID: "We reviewed our operating profile and determined we had six hours a night where our disk storage had little to no activity. Nexsan's AutoMAID feature allowed us to take advantage of this window to lower our power and cooling costs by putting our storage in energy saving mode. The beauty of AutoMAID is that, during those idle periods we can save money while still providing the flexibility to go full speed if a request for information comes in. This combination of energy efficiency, performance, density, reliability, and affordability enabled us to gain tremendous operating efficiencies while extending the life of our storage investment. Moreover, the solution increased our staffs' archive management efficiency by 75 percent, completely eliminating thousands of dollars in annual cost for archive tape media."

In this way, MAID arrays strike a balance between power consumption and performance. The ability to designate how much of the array is dedicated to a particular kind of data also extends the array's usefulness as a repository of many kinds of data.

Most drives implement some form of power conservation — for example, the drives in laptops will slow to idle to conserve battery power after a certain amount of time has passed between use. MAID arrays implement a sophisticated form of power management and offer an excellent opportunity to improve the data center's green capabilities for data that doesn't need to be accessed frequently.

Companies that need the high performance and high accessibility of transactional storage are somewhat stuck with the power consumption of Tier 1 storage systems. The need for speed outweighs the need to be green for critical applications and data. However, a plan for moving data to less expensive, lower performance storage systems can help to alleviate some of the problem.

Tackling Storage Sprawl

Only a few years ago, administrators were worried about "server sprawl." The tendency to dedicate an individual server to a specific application caused servers to proliferate throughout the data center or in the workgroup. Similarly, racks and racks of storage have been purchased and allocated to deal with the increasing flood of e-mails, documents, database records — all the intellectual property of the knowledge worker. Faced with this situation, most companies add capacity on the chance that it'll be needed someday, contributing to mostly unused, but still powered and cooled, sprawling racks of storage devices.

The advent of virtualization (explained in detail in Chapter 13) has helped to tame the monster of server sprawl by allowing companies to consolidate applications and run them on a single server simultaneously, eliminating the need for a dedicated server to attain maximum performance. Dealing with storage sprawl is another story.

Identifying contributors to storage sprawl

The need for additional storage capacity continues unabated. The appetite for storage is fueled by many factors:

✔ **Nearly every person in every organization has a PC — and sometimes more than one.** All those PCs create a veritable blizzard of documents of all kinds: e-mails, letters, drawings, spreadsheets, PDF files, and so on. For most companies, these documents comprise the organization's intellectual property and need to be stored in some fashion against the risk of data loss.

✔ **Many company documents may need to be retained for regulatory reasons.** For example, health care agencies are required to retain patient's medical records for a period of time following treatment. There are also very stringent guidelines about how those records are stored and eventually destroyed. In some government agencies, records of all transactions, including e-mail correspondence, must be kept for 15 years — imagine the storage that requires! Records of deeds and real estate titles need to be kept indefinitely, and as these records move to digitized formats, cities and towns need more storage capacity. Banks, already the keepers of massive amounts of data, now get to store digital images of every check — mmm, mmm, more storage! Digital photography, video, audio, MP3 files — still more storage!

✔ **Paradoxically, virtualization has caused an explosion in the need for storage capacity, even as it has helped retire servers through consolidation.** Storage is what makes virtualization work, so as companies adopt virtualization in their efforts to eliminate servers, their need for storage capacity increases correspondingly. (We tell you about the mechanics for virtualization in Chapter 13.)

The burgeoning need for storage is great for companies that sell storage, but not so good for corporate budgets, power consumption, or the planet in general. Sprawling storage leads to administrative headaches and, of course, the need for increased data center capacity as well as increased power and cooling consumption.

Minimizing storage sprawl

Establish a formal storage plan that takes into account current and new application requirements, the number of users, the number of branch offices — in short, a current picture of your storage infrastructure. After you create a snapshot of your storage infrastructure, you can identify whether the following strategies for minimizing sprawl can help you green your storage system:

✔ **Use existing storage capacity before adding more storage.** Two methods of maximizing your existing storage capacity are through *data deduplication* and *thin provisioning*. We describe each of these approaches in upcoming sections of this chapter.

✔ **Buy storage you'll need for the coming year only.** The formal storage plan suggested earlier should give you guidance about what capacity you need now and what capacity you will need a year from now. It doesn't make sense to buy capacity well into the future because newer technologies inevitably will be better or cheaper or both, and with the focus shifting on making technology more environmentally friendly, waiting to see what's on the market when you need it will likely pay off.

✔ **Use storage management tools to help manage how storage gets allocated and deallocated.** Many storage manufacturers provide software that helps manage storage. These software tools range from simple wizards to migrate data from an old disk to a new one, to very sophisticated tools that manage how applications use available storage capacity. A $100 disk drive from BestBuy will have minimal management software included. A mid-priced storage array ($25,000) will have management software that allows thin provisioning (see the related section later in this chapter), data deduplication, and overall monitoring of the health and status of the component disks that comprise it. Management software can also be purchased from companies like DataCore. The goal of managing capacity remains the same: to increase the efficiency and utilization of storage capacity. These actions cut infrastructure costs, slow the speed at which new capacity needs to be added, and contributes to building a greener infrastructure.

✔ **Consider implementing a tiered storage architecture.** A tiered architecture takes into account the types of data that the company retains and for how long. This is also called Information Lifecycle Management (ILM) and can be an important part of the formal storage plan. We tell you all about tiered storage and ILM in Chapter 7.

✔ **Consider consolidating storage systems.** Most companies still use the hard drive inside their desktop, also known as direct attached storage (DAS), as their basic "unit" of storage. DAS storage is more difficult to manage than some types, unless you use an application specifically built to assist system administrators in managing DAS storage. Network attached storage (NAS) and storage area networks (SAN) are easier than DAS to manage because they are designed to be shared, as well as to be directly accessible and managed from the network. Chapter 13 covers these storage systems in greater detail.

Cutting Fat, Part 1: Data Deduplication

Using data deduplication is one of the approaches we mention in the previous section for maximizing your existing storage capacity. *Deduplication* is a computer industry term for "removing the duplicates," and, as this strange word implies, it's a process that examines a hard drive or storage system to find and remove duplicate files — effectively reducing the amount of storage required for a given set of data. The "reclaimed" storage is then available for additional data. The net effect of deduplication is to increase available capacity and perhaps forestall the need to buy additional capacity. It's clearly a good green measure to take.

Here's a simple example of how deduplication works. Say that you send an e-mail to a customer and to several coworkers, about a delivery that needs to be rescheduled. The customer replies to all the people on the original e-mail and includes the text of your original message. After several iterations of e-mail discussion, your e-mail has to grown to ten pages, as have the copies that went to all the recipients. Now, consider the number of e-mails you receive and reply to every day; then, multiply *that* number by the number of employees in your organization.

You can see how e-mail quickly adds up to a great deal of data, all of which passes through (and is stored on) your company's mail server. Don't forget about your calendar appointments, slide presentations, documents, and so on — most of which get sent to several people for approval or delivery.

All these individual e-mail events don't need to be stored — in fact, even your original e-mail isn't needed. Only one complete version of the chain of responses and attachments needs to be preserved. The process of deduplication is intended to remove all the unnecessary duplicates and thus reclaim the space formerly occupied by those duplicates.

Deduplication is generally performed "offline" — that is, on a storage area that already contains data. Performing deduplication in real time would be a very slow process. Some storage system manufacturers provide deduplication in a single device (or "appliance"); others provide it as part of the software that manages a storage array. In either case, the goal is to free up storage by removing redundant or duplicate information.

Cutting Fat, Part II: Thin Provisioning

Some applications require a certain amount of storage to be reserved, or allocated, when the application is installed. As we mention in Chapter 7, thin provisioning offers a strategy for allocating that storage.

So, how does thin provisioning contribute to green? By helping to increase the overall utilization of storage systems, thin provisioning can forestall the need to add capacity, which means fewer storage disks, less power consumption, less cooling, and less data center capacity required. Putting off the acquisition of additional storage capacity has a nice impact on the IT budget too.

Introducing how thin provisioning works

To understand how thin provisioning works, consider a database application, which typically requires storage to be allocated for tables and indices. How much is allocated is based on an estimation of how many records will eventually be stored in the database. Here are some of the factors that affect allocation:

- ✔ Every record has overhead, which means that it requires a certain amount of storage space based on the number of fields in the record. For example, a car registration record includes fields for the owner of the car (last name, first name, middle initial); the address of the owner (street number, street name, apartment number, city, state, ZIP Code); the manufacturer (make) and model; the year the car was manufactured; its vehicle identification number (VIN); the name and address of the insurance company. (We're up to about 20 fields already.)

- ✔ Every table, index, form, and so on requires a corresponding amount of storage based on the record's overhead.

- ✔ Creating an empty database, one with no records in it yet, also requires some space.

We haven't even included space for the database application itself in this list! When you start writing records to the database, storage gets used up quickly. For this reason, and because not everyone is a good estimator of how much storage will eventually be required, most administrators allocate as much storage as they can during installation. The problem with this approach is that it wastes storage space. The unused part of the allocated space can't be used for anything else.

Thin provisioning — the allocation of just the right amount of storage when you actually need it — helps fix the problem of unused capacity. By allocating storage as it's needed by applications and then using storage management software to adjust it (similarly to how software manages a storage array), all the storage that's actually available can be consumed as it's needed rather than being hoarded and possibly never required.

To properly allocate or provision storage capacity for an application, storage management software uses each application's storage requirements to configure the correct amount of storage capacity.

The benefits of thin provisioning are twofold:

- ✔ Storage is "dynamically" allocated — it can grow or shrink according to application requirements.

- ✔ Storage management software can monitor many applications simultaneously and provision the unused capacity for them all as needed.

Applying thin provisioning to your storage system

Effective use of thin provision starts by taking the following steps:

1. **Identify all the applications used in the company.**

2. **Determine how much storage is allocated to the application (this is the application's data "footprint").**

3. **Use the thin provisioning management software to reallocate storage capacity from the available pool of storage dynamically.**

For many organizations, this may be a sobering exercise. We know of one company that found that ten of the "critical applications" in the data center weren't so critical after all.

Here's an effective, if brute-force, method of determining which applications are truly "critical": When no one can figure out who's using a server or what applications it's running, try turning that server off and see who calls in.

After you compile a list of the applications that use the most storage, you need to enter these requirements into the thin provisioning software, so that storage capacity can be properly allocated for each application. Microsoft SharePoint server software has storage requirements that are different than, say, Microsoft Exchange Server software. Storage management software providers usually supply software specific to a particular application, or management software may be provided as part of a storage hardware solution, such as a storage area network (SAN).

An emerging technology: SSD

Solid-state disk (SSD) is logical evolution of the "memory stick" that has become popular as a way of moving several gigabytes of data from one place to another. SSD storage is very fast, nearly as fast as computer memory, and is inherently efficient because there aren't any moving parts (such parts are the major reason hard drives consume so much power). SSD has two major drawbacks at this time: cost and reliability. Several storage manufacturers are offering SSD arrays, but they are very expensive. Time will cure that problem as the technology gains wider acceptance and manufacturing costs decline. The reliability issue involves the number of times data can be written to the SSD without error, but designers are actively working on a new design that dispenses with this problem. It seems likely that SSD may be a standard storage medium in the future.

A SAN is ideal for thin provisioning because it is literally a network (or pool) of storage that can be assigned to applications by a storage management software. A SAN may consist of a single array of drives in a compact enclosure, or it may be composed of many individual storage systems that are managed as though they were one system, even extending over the Internet. A SAN is often called "virtual storage" because the applications using it don't need to know where the storage is located or how much capacity is available at any given moment; the storage software manages those details. We discuss the use of SANs in the context of a virtual infrastructure in Chapter 13.

The idea of thin provisioning depends on managing capacity dynamically in response to application demands and because a SAN is a storage system whose capacity is managed in a similar way, thin provisioning is often implemented as part of a SAN storage manager. Companies like 3PAR and Compellent provide thin provisioning capabilities as part of their disk arrays, while DataCore's SANMelody software can be used with their storage arrays or separately.

Backing Up More with Less

If you've ever had the sinking feeling when you switch on your computer and it won't start, you'll be familiar with the importance of backing up your work. If you haven't, either you're very, very lucky or you haven't been working with computers for very long.

Being diligent about saving your work is an important first step. You're even better protected if you save or copy your important work to a USB "thumb" drive, memory stick, or even another disk. No other disk handy? In a pinch, e-mail a copy to yourself and your e-mail can act as a backup. We don't recommend this as a regular backup routine, but it's a whole lot smarter than chancing that everything will be there tomorrow when you start your system.

However, saving your work may not always protect your applications, user profile, and other data that you don't think about but are part of your computing environment.

A regular, systematic system of backing up your computer(s) is an important part of managing your computing world. In this following sections, we look at some of the alternatives available for backing up your valuable data. Be sure to include your backup storage needs in your overall storage assessment so that they're included as you green your storage.

The basics of tape

Here are a few of the reasons some organizations continue to use tape:

- ✔ Tape is relatively inexpensive, especially when compared to the cost of losing data.

- ✔ Using tape can be relatively green. If you don't need immediate access to some data, you don't need to keep it powered up on a disk, consuming power and demanding cooling.

- ✔ Most companies already have an investment in tape.

Unfortunately, tape also has some significant problems, the worst of which are the following:

- ✔ Tape can be adversely affected by temperature, humidity, and other physical problems, which can make part or all of a tape unreadable.

- ✔ Tape is a "streaming" media — in contrast to a hard drive — which means that the data is written and read in a sequence from beginning to end. If the file you're trying to recover is at the end of the fourth tape in a backup sequence, you need to read through all four tapes to recover your file.

Alternatives to tape

In spite of the continued use of tape in companies of all sizes, you have plenty of alternatives to physical tape that eliminate some of tape's most notorious flaws. These alternatives include hard drives, network storage, Blu-ray discs, CDs, DVDs, USB drives, flash drives, and optical discs. The following sections explain each of these in more detail.

Hard drive

Using a hard disk avoids both the chance of tape damage and the need for a special tape drive. Drive capacity continues to increase while the cost per gigabyte continues to drop. A 1 terabyte (TB) drive, which holds 1,000 gigabytes, costs about $200. One of the best aspects of using a hard drive is that it contains a file system, so you can locate a specific file on it without having to read the whole thing. Hard drives are easiest to control from a centralized management perspective.

Local network storage or public network (Internet) storage

These days, network speeds and reliability make it possible to use remote resources for backup. An increasing number of companies offer backup at low cost. Some of them, like EMC with its Mozy online storage product, are even well-known manufacturers of "big iron" — the most expensive and highest performing server and storage systems.

The most recent industry buzz involves so-called "cloud computing," which makes computing resources such as servers or storage available on a pay-per-use basis. Cloud computing provides two things that a dedicated data center cannot provide:

✔ A flexible infrastructure that can be built "on-demand" to serve for the duration of a specific project

✔ Infrastructure that requires no capital investment on the part of the person or company using the infrastructure

This infrastructure-for-hire approach also indirectly promotes green as companies shift parts of their dedicated infrastructure to cloud providers who can achieve green economies of scale that an individual company cannot.

Companies like Amazon (with S3 storage) and Google (with Google Apps) offer public computing resources on a per-use basis that are affordable for individuals or small businesses. Enterprise companies can build so-called "internal" clouds, in which the data center is repurposed to provide on-demand infrastructure, applications, and services — often on a charge-back basis. It's still too early to tell if cloud computing will be the next big thing in computers or if the market will fail to adopt it (like its predecessor grid computing). The current economy favors avoiding capital expenditures, so it may well be that the timing is right for cloud computing.

Blu-ray disc

Blu-ray disc — Sony's new CD-sized disc — holds 50GB of data, but both the discs and the writer are still expensive compared to DVDs. Of course, prices will drop quickly as more users adopt this storage media.

CD or DVD

Nearly every computer made today has either a CD or DVD writer installed in its case. The main drawback to CD or DVD is capacity; CDs hold no more than 800MB, and single-layer DVDs hold 4.3GB and dual-layer DVDs hold (surprise!) 8.6GB.

USB drive or flash drive

USB drive or flash drive memory sticks offer ease of use and portability, but their capacity is still limited compared to a hard drive.

As with tape, you can store Blu-rays, CDs, DVDs, and flash drives "cold" — that is, they don't need power and cooling as long as you keep them in a relatively controlled environment.

CDs, DVDs, Blu-rays, and flash drives can be convenient but aren't a good substitute for regular system-wide, automated protection. They also can be problematic when you consider the data that's being backed up to be "sensitive" — that is, access to it is limited to certain people. You need to carefully consider how sensitive data is backed up and who has access to it. Laws and standards govern the handling of all kinds of sensitive data. Regulations and policies that apply to the original data apply to copies of the data as well. If the data you want to back up is sensitive, chances are that the choice of removable media like a flash drive or CD is not a good one.

Optical disc

The optical disc was invented at about the same time as the CD but is larger and thicker than a CD. Another term often used for optical discs is WORM, an acronym for "write once, read many." Optical discs have several attributes that recommend them for long-term, archival storage:

✔ Because a glass barrier surrounds the optical media, optical discs are more impervious to damage than CDs and DVDs.

✔ Unlike streaming media (tape), optical discs store data as files that operating systems such as Windows and Linux can read. This means that your document file is stored as a document file.

Chapter 12

Grooming the Network for Green

. . . .

. . . .

*Y*ou may not often think about the technologies that enable you to get e-mail and the Internet, but the network inside your building can be a substantial contributor to going green. The routers and switches that move network "traffic," even the wiring in the walls, can be part of a green network.

In this chapter, we describe the network and the network devices that connect you to the outside world and make activities, such as e-mailing and surfing, possible. We discuss how always-on devices, such as gateways and routers, consume power at a small, but steady rate and how, in the aggregate, their consumption needs to be greened. We also look at some of technologies that are under development to change the way network devices and even network wiring will help reduce network power consumption in the IT infrastructure.

Power-Hungry Networks

A deep dive into the components used for networking isn't part of our purpose here, but several key concepts, including how to assess the power consumption of your network devices, are important to understanding how the network can be a contributor to making your data center more environmentally friendly.

First, here's a look at some of the main components used in a modern networking scheme:

> ✔ **Router:** Also called a *bridge*, this device routes packets of data from one network to another. The network can be a LAN or a WAN, but in the case of a WAN, the router features may be combined with a firewall.

✔ **Switch:** A device that's used to provide additional ports or connections on the network. A switch generally doesn't have an address on the network, although a managed switch provides the ability to turn ports on and the switch on or off.

✔ **Firewall:** A device that protects a network from outside translation by inspecting incoming packets to make sure they're truly addressed for the network to which the firewall is attached. A firewall is often combined with a router to provide a complete connection between a LAN, or a WAN, and most often the Internet.

✔ **Wireless router:** Provides a wireless connection to the LAN using a number of security schemes, such as the wireless encryption protocol (WEP) or, more recently, the Wi-Fi Protected Access (WPA or WPA-2) protocols, which make it difficult for an outside person to "snoop" on your network.

✔ **Wireless access point:** A device that lets you extend a wireless network without using a wireless router. The wireless access point was quite common five years ago but has become less popular as newer all-in-on devices have become more prevalent.

Nowadays, devices that combine some of the functions described in the preceding list have become very popular for home and small business use. These devices integrate a router, a firewall, a switch, and a wireless router or access point into one device. The differences between professional, data center network devices and consumer devices relate to service life, warranty, and control features. In terms of energy use, a combination device might save as much as 75 percent over the devices it replaces.

Most network devices run 24/7 because network services are typically available all the time. In a small home office, the power consumption of a router/firewall may be relatively small — say, 25 watts per hour, but a larger organization likely uses a mix of numerous devices — lots of routers and switches and probably a few firewalls. You can add to this picture the likelihood that the routers and switches are of different "vintages," and the older devices are inefficient compared to new ones.

So, how much power do all these devices devour? Here's an example of how to calculate the power consumed by a router in a small office or home office. For this example, the router uses 25 watts of power per hour. The formula for calculating consumption is as follows:

```
watts x hours used ÷ 1,000 = Consumption in kilowatts
```

We divided by 1,000 so that we have an answer in kilowatts, which is how the electric company measures consumption.

So, if you leave the router on for 24 hours, the power consumed is

```
25 watts x 24 hours ÷ 1,000 = 0.6 kilowatts
```

Now, for a year's worth of usage, multiply as follows:

```
0.6 kilowatts per day × 7 days × 52 weeks = 218.4 kilowatts
```

Using 218 kilowatts per year isn't so bad for a small office — it's equivalent to leaving a 25-watt incandescent light bulb on continuously for a year. But for large companies, power use grows exponentially. Using the same formula with 300 watts as the consumption number, this time including wireless access points, several switches, and a router, the numbers come out like this:

```
300 watts × 24 hours ÷ 1,000 = 7.2 kilowatts
```

So, here's a year's worth of power use:

```
7.2 kilowatts per day × 7 days × 52 weeks = 2,620 kilowatts
```

As you can see, the number is beginning to become much more noticeable!

In a large, geographically dispersed government agency with, say, 30,000 employees, administration of a network is a huge part of the IT budget. All the remote offices require their own firewalls, routers, and switches. The job of finding and replacing obsolete networking gear alone is staggering, and all this gear is an always-on power consumer.

Greater, Greener Network Efficiency

Fortunately, during the past ten years, network devices, such as routers and gateways, have begun to change, driven mostly by user demand for devices whose capabilities can be upgraded, thus extending the service life of the devices. At the same time, manufacturers have become smarter about the advantages of sustainability — in the manufacturing process, materials used, and power consumed. The result is network devices that have power conservation built into their design, including:

- ✓ **Lower power consumption under varying degrees of network "load" as a design objective.** For example, network switches that don't always supply a network signal to every wire connected to them are being designed to sense when they need to connect a port and when the port can be disconnected or idled.

- ✓ **The ability to reduce power consumption during periods of inactivity by monitoring network traffic with network monitoring software,** such as Tripp Lite's PowerAlert Network Power Management System or Raritan's Power IQ management system. The Cisco Catalyst 6000 line of switches incorporates sensor-based power management into the switches themselves.

✔ **The ability to put equipment into a quiescent, or powered-down, state according to set policies** — for example, network segments can be shut down on weekends and at night when inactivity is most likely.

✔ **Devices, such as switches and routers, that can measure the length of cable plugged into each port and "scale" the amount of power needed for each cable based on these measurements.**

As we show in the router example in the previous section, the amount of power consumed can rapidly grow to a big number, but the aggregate savings from the combination of power saving measures built into current network devices can be substantial, even for a smaller company.

Wandering around with wireless

In addition to network devices, such as routers and switches, a network in a large business can require thousands of feet of cabling. As technology has progressed, however, the idea of running miles of network cable in a new building, or rewiring an existing building to replace an obsolete (that is, slower) network, is beginning to look like a waste of time, materials, and money.

Why? Wireless network speeds have increased dramatically, and although they're still slower than the speed of wired networks, the savings resulting from not running cable and the convenience of being able to move freely about a building and maintain connectivity on a laptop are appealing.

Wireless networks are easier to deploy and maintain than wired networks because they need so much less cable. Even a wireless network does use some wired components, of course. For example, the connection to the external network — the WAN — is wired to the firewall, as are the connections to wireless routers. It's best to have the devices that form the "backbone" of the network wired to maximize throughput and bandwidth.

Concerns about the costs and efficiency of wired networks are even more pronounced for developing countries that need network access but lack an extensive "wired" infrastructure. For those countries, deploying wireless networking and cellular (now digital) technology makes more sense than running thousands of miles of wire — which, by the way, traditionally consists of copper wire, an expensive natural resource. Some alternatives to wiring are under development, and we discuss these emerging technologies a little later in this chapter.

Keeping your network consistent

Our friends at Cisco remind us of the importance of enforcing standards across your network. More consistency in your network means making it easier to monitor. Work to eliminate redundancy.

Doing more with less

Today you can often get the functionality of what used to be many separate devices all in one device, which usually translates to less power consumption. For example, you might find a system that combines a router, wireless LAN, WAN/application optimizer, security applications, and voice applications all in one box. Companies, such as Cisco and Netgear, sell devices that combine these capabilities.

Power over Ethernet (PoE)

Many buildings have been wired for networking, but they're *all* wired for electricity — if you have an alternative way to distribute electricity that doesn't use wires, you'll be a wealthy person soon. So, most buildings have lots of wire, electrical and network related, and chances are that the electrical wiring goes to the same places the network does, so laptops, desktops, and servers can be powered as well as networked.

What if you could use network cable to distribute electrical power as well as networking? That's the basic idea behind *Power over Ethernet, or PoE.* PoE doesn't deliver standard AC (alternating current) electricity at 125 volts (the U.S. standard), but it does deliver up to 48 volts of DC (direct current) power over standard twisted-pair Ethernet cable with no modifications to make to the cable itself.

PoE works like this: Special switches or routers deliver the voltage along with the data. The cable needs a device at each end, to supply the power at one end and then separate it from the data at the other end. You might think that this a revolutionary idea, but in fact telephone systems have been doing exactly the same things for a hundred years or so. That's how telephones used to get their power: from the telephone wire. Only since the advent of wireless phones have masses of people stopped using wired telephones. In fact, during a power outage, most wireless phones won't work because their base stations need power to work, but old-fashioned telephones do work, even when the power is out, because they get their power from the wiring.

Some of the uses for PoE include providing power for

- Network devices, such as routers and switches
- IP telephones (used increasingly in offices and some homes)
- Network cameras

It's exciting to think that servers and desktops can be powered this way, but there are also some limitations on the extent to which PoE can be used. The larger network outside your company's firewall will benefit from technologies, such as the fiber optical cable used by companies like Verizon (under the FiOS brand name) to replace the traditional copper cable that the telephone company used for so long.

Heading Toward a Greener Internet

The larger network — the Internet — is also undergoing some greening. The following sections describe two technologies that are already being used to help make the network greener. Their continued adoption will ensure that the network will be faster and more power efficient.

Optimizing with optical technology

An optical network is the application of *fiber (or fibre) optics* — the ability for glass fibers to carry light over long distances — to networking. Optical cable has the following advantages over traditional copper cabling:

- **Sending a signal down a cable results in some signal loss** — this is true whether the signal is electricity, audio, or data. Fiber optic cable also loses signal, but at a much slower rate than metal cable.

- **Metal cable is susceptible to *electromagnetic interference (EMI)* —** signal disruption or degradation caused by electric motors, like the one in your washing machine — and must be shielded to prevent it from disrupting or degrading signal quality. For example, CAT-5 cable uses twisted pairs of wire to minimize EMI.

- **Because optical cable is fabricated from glass, it doesn't use copper, which is a non-renewable natural material.** Copper is also expensive to mine and turn into cable, which increases the cost to the end customer. Copper is sufficiently valuable so that companies that lay optical cable are removing the old copper cable and selling it to be melted down and reused.

Each optical fiber carries one "stream" of signals at a time, but the cable is composed of a bundle of fibers, which means that optical fiber cable is capable of carrying a high bandwidth of signals.

A good example of an optical fiber network is Verizon's *FiOS* (reputed to stand for *fiber optic service*) network, which is slowly replacing the traditional copper cable in Verizon's network. FiOS can carry telephone, Internet, and video — *broadband* — at higher speeds than was previously possible with regular copper cable.

An environmental benefit to optical fiber cable is that the copper wire used inside traditional cable can be reused. It seems likely that optical fiber will eventually replace the *plain old telephone service (POTS)* that's been the backbone of wired communications for more than a century.

Creating an energy-efficient Ethernet

The premise behind the Energy-Efficient Ethernet standard is that not all devices using an Ethernet network need the full bandwidth of the network available all the time. According to studies conducted by the *Institute for Electrical and Electronics Engineers (IEEE)* — the largest international standards body for electronics — most people don't use their Ethernet connection at full bandwidth more than 5 percent of the time, on average. However, network devices, such as routers and switches, are powered for full bandwidth all the time, which wastes power. An IEEE task force found that in 2005, "all the network-interface controllers in the United States — computers, switches, and routers all have them — burned through 5.3 terawatt-hours of energy, enough to keep 6 million 100-watt light bulbs shining all year."

This finding raises the question, why not create a way to power down or "throttle" a user's connection when a network device senses lower demand? Researchers have proposed such a scheme, *Adaptive Link Rate,* but implementing it turns out to be more difficult than it appears. The problem is that when a network link is established, a maximum connection speed is negotiated and that speed stays the same for the session. For example, if your laptop has a 1 gigabit Ethernet port and you connect it to a network running at 1 gigabit, that speed remains static until you disconnect, even if you're doing nothing more than checking your e-mail occasionally.

To switch from a 1-gigabit connection to a 100-megabit speed requires dropping the connection momentarily and reestablishing it — obviously not a good solution if you're in the middle of surfing or transmitting data at the time. Intel Corporation has proposed an alternative scheme, *low-power idle.* Under this scheme, the Ethernet controller would be put to "sleep" when not in use. The network link never has to disconnect, and this scheme is far easier to implement.

It's not clear yet which scheme would yield greater savings, but with 10-gigabit-per-second Ethernet already in use, we're sure to be using some kind of power-efficient Ethernet in the future — there's too much power to be saved!

Conserving Resources with Networks

Networks now connect virtually everyone everywhere. Or is it that networks now connect everyone everywhere virtually? Whatever the case, the fact that everything and everyone is connected means that some things can be done in a greener way using the network and other things that help with green are enabled by the networks. Here are some ways networks themselves help green:

✔ **Online collaboration:** Using online tools, such as e-mail, telepresence, Web conferencing, and all the things we talk about in Chapter 20, to work with colleagues and others around your country and the world saves time, cost, fuel, and travel wear and tear.

✔ **Send files electronically:** Saving time, money, and physical media by using electronic file transfer is green because not only can you eliminate the need to create the physical media (actual paper, x-rays, tapes, CDs, DVDs, and the like) in the first place, but also you save on the fuel needed to transport the physical objects.

Using a network to transfer information that otherwise would've been mailed or shipped can be a lot faster, cheaper, and ultimately easier. For example, digital images are replacing x-rays; electronic computer-aided designs are eliminating the need to ship hard-copy drawings; full-length feature films are downloaded to users' computers instead of being stored and shipped on DVDs. Banks, of course, have switched to providing customers with electronic images of checks rather than handling the paper originals, thereby saving paper, labor, postage, and storage — and, of course, energy.

✔ **Monitor and control your facility's environment:** You can use the network to collect data from various temperature, moisture, and air quality monitoring systems and can enable either automatic adjustments or remote remediation. Check out Chapter 18 for more on greening your facility.

Chapter 13

Using Virtualization

*O*nce upon a time, most computers came with only one operating system on which to run applications. Then came the magic of virtualization, which uses virtual memory technology to enable a computer to run multiple operating systems or applications — all at the same time. Virtualization has become highly popular for many reasons — a main one being that it's a great way to increase the use of any computer. Companies therefore get more bang for their technology buck, always a happy result for budget-starved IT departments.

Virtualization increases utilization by consolidating applications onto fewer servers, thereby reducing the number of servers needed. This in turn reduces the data center's power consumption and cooling requirements, making virtualization one of the easiest and quickest ways to achieve a greener data center.

In this chapter, we explain how virtualization works, how it can be applied to servers and other parts of the infrastructure, and how virtualization can provide an easy start to greening the IT infrastructure.

Understanding Virtualization

Believe it or not, the idea behind virtualization dates back to the 1960s. Early mainframe computers from companies, such as IBM, had very little random access memory (RAM) in which to run *programs,* the series of instructions that tell the computer which tasks to perform — what we now call *applications.* Computer designers came up with the idea of tricking the mainframe into thinking it had more memory than was actually present on the machine. They did this by moving parts of a program into a special file on the computer's disk — a process known as *swapping*. When a computer needed some part of a program that was stored on disk, that part was loaded from disk into memory just as though it were always there. Think of someone juggling bowling pins and you've got a good image of what the computer was doing. Figure 13-1 illustrates the concept of swapping.

That special file on disk is a *swap file* and is still used in computers today, except that operating systems, such as Windows, Mac OS X, and Linux, manage the swapping process as a matter of course, without the end user's notice.

Are you with us so far? This rather simple scheme became known as *virtual memory* because the amount of memory available for applications to use was limited only by the size of the disk (rather than the amount of actual memory) — meaning that it was essentially unlimited.

Although virtualization has actually been around a long time, it's now a mainstay of contemporary computing and a pillar of Green IT. Virtualization means higher utilization of the equipment you have, which translates into needing less stuff, which in turn translates into less energy and fewer materials that need to be manufactured, less energy consumed in running said stuff, and less stuff to dispose of.

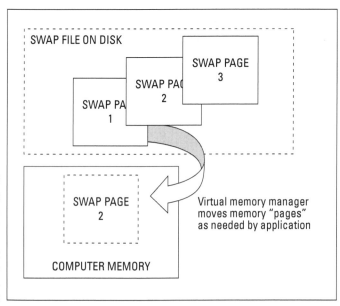

Figure 13-1:
Swapping
parts of an
application
in and out
of the
swap file.

Virtual memory turns into virtualization

The original IBM personal computer had very little RAM and no hard drive, and by today's standards, ran very slowly indeed. As computer technology evolved through the 1980s and 1990s, computer chips became faster, memory became increasingly inexpensive, and hard drives became indispensible for storing applications that we use all the time, such as for word processing or spreadsheets.

In 1999, VMware took the idea of virtual memory one step further and applied it to the PC architecture. VMware's initial product, VMware Workstation, focused on the desktop computer and was rapidly adopted by software developers who wanted to run more than one operating system, such as Windows and Linux, on one machine.

Some applications, such as e-mail, database, or Web servers, typically require all the resources of the server on which they're running in order to provide the best performance for multiple users. VMware's product ran not only multiple operating systems but also multiple applications; it did this by putting each application in its own virtual machine. A separate program — a *hypervisor* — managed the virtual machines and connected them to the underlying computer resources. Figure 13-2 depicts the relationship between the applications running in their own virtual machines and the underlying computer.

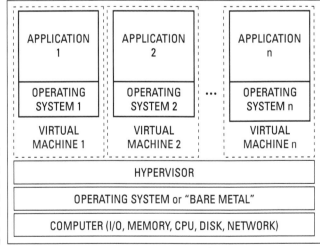

Figure 13-2:
The elements of a virtual server.

IT quickly saw the value of running multiple applications on a server and started using the Workstation product on servers. Now, servers that deliver critical business applications — *production servers* — are expected to run continuously under heavy use and so require industrial-strength operating systems and applications that are optimized for server use. VMware saw the need and developed VMware Server, and more recently, VMware ESX.

Of course, the number of virtual machines that can run on one computer is still dependent on the computer's resources. The performance of the applications running on the virtual machines are also subject to these limitations and may experience slower than expected performance, the inability to support additional users, and so on.

VMware now has plenty of competitors. Operating system developers such as Red Hat (Linux) and more recently, Microsoft (Windows Server 2008) provide virtualization at the operating system level. Companies, such as Oracle and Citrix, provide products that directly compete with VMware. VMware is still the largest supplier of virtualization today, but at last count, at least 25 different companies were supplying some kind of virtualization scheme in software or as part of a hardware device, such as a storage appliance.

Where's the green in virtualization?

We said at the outset of this chapter that using virtualization is one of the easiest paths to green, and here's one of the key reasons. Every time you run more than one application on a server — *application consolidation* — you reduce the number of servers required to support these applications. The reduction in the number of physical servers is *server consolidation*. Fewer servers mean less power consumption and a lower requirement for cooling. If these applications are running in a data center, having fewer servers also translates to less rack space and thus a smaller footprint for the data center.

A more subtle benefit to replacing physical servers with virtual servers is that it reduces the burden of server administration, the care and feeding that servers (and applications) need on a regular basis to provide maximum performance.

Three kinds of virtualization

We've mentioned a major use of virtualization — consolidating applications onto fewer servers. Server virtualization has received the most attention from the computer industry and has been most widely adopted because it's the quickest, and perhaps easiest, way of realizing the virtualization benefits. Server virtualization is also one of the quickest paths to green savings.

But you can also apply virtualization to other areas of the IT infrastructure, namely storage and desktops, as follows:

- ✔ **Virtual storage:** This type of virtualization differs from server virtualization in that individual storage systems, storage area networks (SANs), or even direct-attached storage (DAS), are _pooled_ so that it appears to applications as though all the storage is one large disk. Storage virtualization is often considered to be an essential part of a server virtualization strategy; but storage virtualization works equally well with physical servers as it does with virtual servers.

- ✔ **Desktop virtualization:** End users can take advantage of virtualization by remotely accessing their own computer's resources and applications (their _desktop_), as well as applications, such as word processing, spreadsheet, e-mail, or calendar. Virtualization can even replace the traditional desktop computer with a smaller, less power-hungry device. Desktop virtualization can also be used to extend the life of older equipment.

- ✔ **Application infrastructure virtualization:** Virtualizing the application infrastructure can result in considerable energy savings because it allows applications to be separated from the physical infrastructure on which they run. In a virtualized application infrastructure, you can dynamically allocate or migrate application workloads across a pool of server resources in response to business needs. For example, you can prioritize workloads according to the most critical applications or users, thus optimizing the use of hardware and making the most efficient use of CPU availability. We say more about virtual storage in Chapter 11.

Consolidating applications on virtual servers

We can break the process of consolidating applications into a series of steps:

1. Understanding application requirements.

2. Looking for servers that are underutilized.

3. Building virtual machines on servers.

4. Testing the virtualized applications before putting them into production.

We describe these steps in detail in the following sections.

Building a Virtual Infrastructure

Building a virtual infrastructure, one in which servers, storage, and maybe even desktops use some form of virtual technology to provide services, is surprisingly easy. As with any IT strategy, building a virtual infrastructure requires

- ✔ **A thorough understanding of the current infrastructure's architecture** — what applications run on which servers, end user usage patterns, and so on.

- ✔ **A formal plan to implement virtualization,** including expected costs and expected benefits, a plan to test virtual servers before placing them into production, and making sure that staff is adequately trained to implement and maintain the infrastructure.

Even a small company can benefit from building a formal plan, but in a large company, such a plan is critical to make sure that everybody who's affected (not just IT) understands the goals, timelines, and expected results.

Understanding application requirements

The first step in building a virtual infrastructure is to take a hard look at which applications run on which servers. The traditional IT paradigm of "one application per server" doesn't apply in a virtualized infrastructure, but it's critical to understanding every application's requirements for memory and disk usage.

For example, database applications are highly transactional — that is, they read and write records almost constantly. Applications like these require the fastest server and the fastest storage to maximize application performance.

Contrast a database application's profile with a server that supports file storage and printing. These servers experience bursts of activity followed by periods of inactivity, and although performance is nice to have, it isn't critical to the server's tasks.

Hunting down underused servers

Servers that are only lightly used are another likely target for application consolidation. Some applications require that storage space be allocated in advance — for example, a database might require a *minimum* of 25 gigabytes of disk space to hold its tables and indices. Of course, the wise administrator knows that after an application is installed and configured, it becomes exponentially harder to reallocate more space, so rather than allocate the minimum amount of storage, the administrator does some calculations and allocates 10 times more space than the minimum — 250 gigabytes, which might be the whole disk drive's capacity.

Now, if this database is the only application running on the server — which would be typical for a database application — there's a possibility that the server's storage is being underutilized. Because this storage was allocated ahead of time, this wasted capacity means that the server can't be used for any other purpose. These servers become likely candidates for virtualization because the virtual machine's resources can be dynamically allocated to allow for increasing application requirements.

Building virtual machines on target servers

Actually, this is probably the easiest part of the process. VMware, for example, provides installation wizards that make building a virtual machine a nearly foolproof process. In fact, the process is so easy that administrators have been known to put too many virtual machines on a server, causing *virtual server sprawl.*

In most cases, the administrator needs to supply only information about what resources the application requires for installation and operation — the same information the administrator supplies for installation on a physical server. This information includes

✔ **The amount of "memory" required:** Memory in this case really means the amount of drive space (virtual memory) to allocate to the application.

✔ **The type of network connection:** The administrator needs to determine if the application needs to use the underlying computer's network or can instead use a virtual network connection provided by the virtualization software manager.

After the virtual manager has this information, it builds a virtual machine of the correct size that's optimized for the operating system and the application. This virtual container is empty at first, waiting for the administrator to perform these steps:

1. Install the operating system (for example, Windows XP or Linux) on which the application will run.

2. Install the application itself onto the newly installed operating system.

3. Restart the virtual machine — which is equivalent to rebooting a physical server.

That's it. The virtualized application behaves exactly as it would on a physical server.

Testing the virtualized application

An IT best practice is to test a new application on a physical server before placing it into production, and you should treat virtual applications exactly the same way. Because there are substantial differences among virtualization products, operating systems, applications, and so on, here are some of the steps involved:

- ✔ **Testing the application's performance under *load*** — allowing some users to access and use the application to make sure it meets expectations
- ✔ **Tuning the application** — adjusting the application's configuration to optimize its performance under use
- ✔ **Tuning the virtual machine** so that it best supports the application

After the virtual server's test results meet the required performance goals, you can place it into regular service. Remember that end users should see the same performance whether they're accessing a virtual application or an application running on a physical server.

Replacing physical servers with virtual servers

The process of replacing physical severs with virtual servers includes the process of building a virtual server that we describe in the previous section. It also involves some decisions on the greenest way to deal with the servers you replace. We cover both these topics in this section.

Rev up the the virtual server

Here are the basic steps to replace a physical server:

1. Configure virtual machines for the applications that will be installed on the host or target physical server.

2. Test the virtual server to make sure that it supports the applications installed on it and that their performance meets expectations under real operating conditions.

3. Place the virtual server into production use.

4. Retire or repurpose the physical server or servers that the virtual server has replaced.

Here's where you also reap the benefits of more than ten year's industry experience with virtualization; suppliers such as VMware continue to work out bugs in the virtualization process, and the current virtualization software is easier to install and maintain than ever before. This is not to say that virtualization diminishes the importance of the administrator's experience, but many of the skills learned working with physical servers are directly transferrable to working with virtual servers.

Reuse or recycle the replaced server

What to do with the physical servers that you've replaced is an important decision. Depending on the age and performance capabilities of the server, you might find it useful in a different role — for example, you might use it as a file and print server, or as a workgroup document repository.

If the server is three to five years old, your decision may depend on how your company depreciates computer assets for accounting and tax purposes. Companies differ on when they consider an asset fully depreciated, so it's a good idea to understand your company's rules.

Another consideration is the server's *technological* age. A five-year-old server is way behind current server technology from performance and capacity standpoints. It may also be using more electricity and producing more heat than a more current model.

In either of these situations, the best choice may be to retire the server. If that's the case, you can recycle some of the components and dispose of the components that aren't recyclable responsibly. In this way, replacing physical servers makes two contributions to green:

- ✔ Building a virtual infrastructure that consolidates physical servers into virtual servers reduces power consumption and requirements for cooling.
- ✔ Recycling older or obsolete servers contributes to the overall health of the environment.

Enabling Virtual Disaster Recovery

Virtualization has affected both the cost of disaster recovery systems (see Chapter 7 for an overview of disaster recovery and business continuity approaches) and the way in which backup and recovery are performed. As mentioned earlier in this chapter, applications running on virtual servers each run in their own virtual machine. Virtualization software is usually capable of taking a *snapshot,* or *image,* of a virtual machine's current state, just as you'd take a picture of a tree or a sunset. All these snapshots represent a moment in time, but in the case of the virtual server, the snapshot contains the application and its current data.

This image of a virtual machine has some unusual properties:

- ✔ **It can be copied or moved.**
- ✔ **The image can be restored to the same or a different virtual server.**
- ✔ **If the image is captured in the right way, it can be restored to any computer, using a *bare metal recovery (BMR)* process.**
- ✔ **You can transfer the image to a remote location, such as a branch office.**
- ✔ **With the right software, virtual machine images can be captured automatically at preset intervals.** This capability — *continuous data protection (CDP)* — is very useful for protecting applications with a large transactional volume, but a large chunk of drive space is needed for each snapshot.

Exploring the financial and green benefits

Taking snapshots of virtual servers is a function of the virtualization software, not the underlying computer. This means it can substantially reduce the cost of building a disaster recovery infrastructure. In fact, disaster recovery is one of the main reasons companies build a virtual infrastructure, after server and application consolidation.

Is a virtualized disaster recovery infrastructure more green than a physical recovery infrastructure? The answer is, that depends. If you're incorporating disaster recovery into an existing server and thus replacing a physical server, the answer is yes. Otherwise, the net effect of using virtualization to green your disaster recovery may be neutral. If nothing else, it'll most likely be less expensive to acquire and maintain than a traditional recovery infrastructure.

Replacing physical tape with virtual tape

Physical tape has been the backup medium of choice for decades and it still continues to be used today. Unfortunately, physical tape has some characteristics that can make it undependable, such as incompatibilities between different types of tapes and tape readers. The physical tape itself can degrade over time, rendering it difficult or impossible to read. Of course, physical tape can be considered an inherently green solution because after a tape is put in the library, it doesn't consume any power. The tape drive doesn't consume any power either, unless it's in use.

Virtual tape is a technology that allows a specially formatted hard disk to emulate a tape drive. The emulation is accomplished by use of software and drivers that allow traditional backup software to use the same commands and protocols to write to virtual tape as does physical tape. In this way, virtual tape provides an alternative to traditional tape with few of tape's drawbacks. There are some significant advantages to virtual tape over its physical counterpart, including:

✔ Physical tape, even recent digital linear tapes (DLTs), will eventually run out of capacity, requiring the tape to be changed for the backup to continue. Because virtual tape is using the capacity of a hard disk or even a *pool* of disks — a storage area network (SAN), for example — it's unlikely that a backup to virtual tape will run out of capacity.

✔ A virtual tape can be scanned for duplicate files or records that are then removed — a *deduplication* process, we discuss in Chapter 11 — reducing the overall backup size. You can also perform deduplication on data before it is written to tape, but because it can be a lengthy process, deduplication is typically an *offline* process — that is, it's performed when no one is accessing the tape.

✔ Virtual tapes aren't susceptible to physical defects or degradation over time that can affect physical tape, although they are prey to problems that affect hard drives, such as bad sectors and so on.

✔ Virtual tape is easy to duplicate — simply perform a disk-to-disk copy. Most storage solution providers provide this facility in their disk management software.

✔ Virtual tape doesn't require a special, temperature-controlled environment — it can be used anywhere that a server can be used.

Adoption of virtual tape systems is still low, perhaps because most companies have an investment in physical tape systems. Also, the task of transferring archived data from tape to drive can be a lengthy process. Still, as tape systems are retired, adoption of virtual tape will certainly increase, but whether it will replace physical tape, only time will tell.

Part IV
Greening the Office

The 5th Wave   By Rich Tennant

"Good news—we found PCs that consume less energy."

In this part . . .

*O*utside the data center is plenty of IT left to green. In this part, we look at greener solutions for the computers and the monitors you need, how to reduce energy waste, and concrete ways to save trees (and money). We also tell you about nifty new gadgets that can help with your overall greening.

Chapter 14

Moving to Green Screens and Computing Machines

. . . .

In This Chapter

▶ Pursuing greener computer purchasing policies

▶ Becoming energy efficient

▶ Finding a green desktop machine and monitor

. . . .

These days every office worker has a computer monitor on his fixed desk, sometimes more than one. Those monitors and the computers they're connected to were once thought of as tools to enhance productivity. Today they're simply essential for workers to function at all. But these glowing lumps of encrusted silicon tie up corporate capital and consume significant amounts of energy. Computing technology keeps improving at a rapid pace and workers demand the latest gear, creating a constant flow of obsolete equipment that can clog landfills and create other environmental problems.

In this chapter, we give you tips for evaluating your purchasing policies and whether to extend the life of what you have or to buy new machines. If you need new desktop computers, take a closer look at how standards, which we introduce in Chapter 4, apply specifically to desktop computers. This chapter wraps up with tips and resources to help you compare green attributes of computers quickly and easily.

Developing wise, green policies for purchasing, using, and disposing of desktop computers can reduce your organization's environmental footprint while potentially saving money in the process.

Computer Purchasing Policies

Organizations differ in how they decide which office computing equipment to buy and when to buy it. Many have bulk purchasing agreements with specific vendors, whereas others allow individual departments or groups to make their own selections as long as they stay within their budget.

If you don't already know, find out how your organization buys computers and who makes decisions about purchasing policy. The following sections take a closer look at how to green current policies as well as how to add green criteria to purchasing decisions.

Adding green ideas to bulk purchasing

If you have a bulk purchasing agreement, you can work within this agreement by

- **Finding out how much wiggle room the agreement allows for selecting greener equipment.** What green equipment do the incumbent vendors offer? When you know what your options are, check out the "Finding Your Green Desktop Machines" section later in this chapter for easy ways to compare your options.

- **Researching what your current vendors' future environmental roadmaps look like.** Check vendor Web sites or query your sales representatives. If new, greener models are coming soon, you might delay purchases to get them.

Also worth knowing is when your agreements are up for renewal or re-bid, who is on the committee to draft new specifications, and when the committee meets. You may only have a chance to really green the process every couple years, so you don't want to miss the boat.

Greening decentralized purchasing

If your organization doesn't use centralized purchasing for computing equipment, you can still influence decisions in the green direction. One way, of course, it to establish centralized purchasing, but this is often unpopular and there's likely to be some history of past attempts.

Perhaps a better approach involves education and persuasion. The following list offers suggestions:

- **Enlist the help of facilities.** Greener equipment uses less power and could make a dent in your electric bill.

- **Develop guidelines.** Even if individual departments make purchasing decisions, you may be able to specify that purchases meet certain standards. Check out sections later in this chapter for details.

- **Educate the company.** Talk up the importance of green purchasing and the various guidelines at staff meetings. Write an article for the company newsletter.

✔ **Set up a green computing page on the corporate internal Web site.**
The page might include data, such as power usage by month compared
to the same month in the previous year, amount of material recycled,
stories about successful efforts to find new homes for old computers,
tips and links to other sites on home energy savings, and an online
suggestion box to collect employee ideas for reducing the organization's
environmental footprint.

✔ **Offer awards to departments that meet green goals.** Make the awards
themselves green, such as gift products made from recycled materials
or dinner at a restaurant that specializes in locally grown foods.

Making standards matter

One way to reduce your organization's energy and carbon footprint is to
require purchase of equipment that at least qualifies for the Energy Star
rating and preferably ranks high on the Electronic Product Environmental
Assessment Tool (EPEAT) rating as well. (See the "Finding Your Green
Desktop Machines" section later in this chapter for details.)

Portable device power supplies should meet the California Energy
Commission's efficiency levels or the European Union Code of Conduct on
Efficiency for External Power Supplies, or both.

If you have the clout, require an extra level of managerial sign-off on
purchase orders for equipment that isn't qualified under these programs.

Going green with what you have

Newer machines are faster, and many are more energy efficient. Flat panel
displays, in particular, use about a third of the power that older cathode
ray tube (CRT) monitors consume and free up a lot of desk real estate. An
employee with a three year old computer under her desk is likely to feel
underappreciated by the organization and might well be revising her
résumé on that bulky CRT display when no one is looking. Increased
energy efficiency might seem like one more reason to get that worker a
new machine. But hold on.

When you look at the bigger picture, keeping what you have might make
more sense. A new computer and display that costs $1,000 might take
1,000 kilowatt-hours to produce, package, and transport to your office
(this is a conservative figure; exact numbers are hard to come by). If the new
computer and display saves 40 watts, it could take 25 years for the total
energy savings to offset the energy embodied in the new computer, far more
than the life of the computer. And we haven't even considered the other

environmental impacts of producing that new computer or its eventual disposal.

In deciding whether to replace an older machine, consider how much it's used throughout the day. Energy is power × time. A desktop machine in the office of someone in outside sales or a field service who's on the road much of the time uses much less energy than a similar machine in the phone support center that's used two shifts a day. Also, major computer manufacturers are committed to making their products more green. By waiting another year before replacing an older machine, you'll likely get a greener replacement.

One approach is to replace the most used equipment first and then rotate the older machines through less demanding, less intensive uses. *Note:* It's especially important that older machines with high power consumption be configured to sleep after being idle. See Chapter 15 for more on this.

Perhaps the best way to find a green machine is to keep using the old one. Educating employees as to the environmental benefits of extending the life of the computing equipment they already have may be the highest payback green investment you can make.

Lengthening machine life with Linux

Older computers that can't run Windows Vista or that can barely handle Windows XP — or even those that are running Windows 95 — can often be repurposed by switching them to the Linux operating system. Unlike Windows, which ratchets up computer performance requirements substantially with each new release, Linux works quite well on older hardware. If you're already using Linux in the server environment, the additional support costs for adding Linux to the front office can be minimal, perhaps no more than letting your Linux support people get up to speed with Linux desktop programs. Linux people tend to be enthusiastic promoters of their favorite operating system. And you can expect Linux will be supported indefinitely, unlike Windows XP.

Popular versions of Linux for desktop computers include Ubuntu Linux and SUSE Linux Enterprise Desktop. All desktop Linux distributions (or *distros*) include Web browsers, e-mail, and instant messaging software. Ubuntu, for example, includes the Firefox Web browser, which is also popular on Windows machines. For more information on Ubuntu, see *Ubuntu Linux For Dummies* by Paul G. Sery.

One major problem with using Linux in the office environment is that Microsoft doesn't sell a version of its popular Office application suite for the Linux platform. You can get around this obstacle in three ways:

- **OpenOffice.org (that's their name and their Web address)** is a suite of applications that pretty much duplicates the most important features of Microsoft Office. OpenOffice.org is free open source software, so the price is right, and it runs on most popular Linux distributions (or *distros*), Windows, and Mac OS X.

- **Wine (`www.winehq.org`)** stands for *Wine Is Not an Emulator* and is another open software solution to the Office-on-Linux problem. Wine runs only on computers that use the x86-series CPUs from Intel and AMD. Wine provides all the system calls and application programmer interfaces (APIs) needed for Windows programs to run.

  Given the immense complexity and numerous variations of the Windows operating system, you may wonder how Wine can possibly get every interface right — well, it can't. Windows programs that try to run under Wine often exhibit bugs. The Wine developers concentrate on the most popular Windows applications and try to squish the bugs that come up in those apps.

  The good news is that Microsoft Office is at the top of most people's popularity charts, and Wine developers give it a lot of attention. The bad news is that Office is a sprawling software package, and it uses many obscure Windows features. The result is that Wine supports Microsoft Office but often not the latest versions. The best thing to do is set up a Linux machine and give Wine/Office a try. Of course you need a Microsoft Office license for each machine that's running it under Wine.

- **Google Docs (`docs.google.com`) and Zoho (`www.zoho.com`)** are free online suites of applications that include a word processor, a spreadsheet, and a presentation package. All you need to use it is a Web browser, such as Firefox, Internet access, and a Gmail or Zoho account. You set these up by visiting the respective Web sites. These services are currently free. Google Docs currently has a number of limitations as to size and the number of documents you can use, but it has important advantages, such as a collaboration tool and document creators that can allow anyone in their work group to access the document over the Internet from anywhere. Zoho is less well known but has been well reviewed.

There are free, open source Linux programs that provide capabilities similar to other popular Windows desktop applications. For example, the GNU Image Manipulation Program (GIMP) available from `www.gimp.org` offers many of the capabilities of Adobe's Photoshop, and Inkscape from `www.inkscape.org` is a vector drawing program similar to Adobe Illustrator.

We aren't saying the free Linux applications are every bit as good as their commercial counterparts, but they're good enough for many uses and are improving constantly. Setting up a test system with an old PC and giving them a try is a cheap investment that could save you a lot of money and extend the life of your computer investments.

Embracing Energy Efficiency

The main environmental impact from computers comes from their energy use, and you can trim that power drain in many ways. These ways range from buying more energy efficient equipment to reducing the average power consumed by the equipment you currently have. Reducing power consumption helps the environment but it also saves you money, in electricity charges for the computer and in reduced air conditioning costs. *Note:* Many large office buildings produce so much heat from internal operations that they're air conditioned year-round.

How do computers consume power?

A number of factors affect any computer's energy consumption. These include

- ✔ **Time the computer stays on:** Computers in sleep or hibernation mode use much less power. Computers that are turned off use even less.

- ✔ **Performance level:** Machines that boast the highest performance tend to be power hogs. Most office workers don't need that blazing performance to do their jobs, although super-speed comes in handy when playing online games. Unless you're in the computer game business (can we send you our résumés?), that's probably not something you want to encourage. Manufacturers often offer a particular model at several speeds, measured in gigahertz. The higher speed models are rarely justified.

- ✔ **Desktop versus laptop:** Desktop machines tend to use more power, — typically in the 100 to 150 watt range, versus about 25 watts for a typical laptop.

- ✔ **Power supply efficiency:** Each desktop computer includes a power supply that converts the alternating current coming from the wall outlet to the lower, direct current voltages the computer's chips consume. Higher efficiency power supplies cost a bit more but reduce total power consumption. (However, don't rush to replace your older computers just to save the planet, see the "Going green with what you have" section earlier in this chapter.) Look for an Energy Star (www.energystar.gov) or 80 Plus (www.80plus.org) certification. See the next section for more on these rating organizations.

- ✔ **Internal cooling:** Better computers use variable speed fans so they run at top speed only when the computer is really cranking, say on that *World of Warcraft* boss battle, *oops*, we mean that multimedia presentation you're working on. You may not find fan control mentioned on the manufacturer's spec sheet. Ask your vendor.

Wishing on Energy Star

The U.S. Department of Energy (DOE) and the United States Environmental Protection Agency (EPA) have a joint program — Energy Star, www.energy star.gov — that sets voluntary energy efficiency standards for a variety of products, from washing machines to new homes. They also rate products, such as computers, copiers, and fax machines, for businesses. They even rate water coolers. Products that comply can cite that fact in their marketing and sport the Energy Star logo, as shown in Figure 14-1. Chapter 4 introduces Energy Star, and in this section, we take a closer look at Energy Star ratings for computers and monitors.

Figure 14-1:
The Energy
Star logo.

For a computer to receive an Energy Star certification, the following elements need to meet the specified requirements:

✔ **Power supply:** The EPA's Energy Star certification requires computer power supplies to be at least 80 percent efficient at a range of operating loads — standby, idle, ordinary office work, and heavy cranking. Approved power supplies must also run at a power factor of .9 or higher. (A power factor of 1.0 is perfect; read about power quality in Chapter 5.)

✔ **Power consumption:** Energy Star also sets standards for maximum energy consumption when in sleep mode (less than 4 watts, 1.7 watts for laptops) and what Energy Star folks call standby. This isn't the Windows standby, but what the computer is doing when it's turned off but still plugged in. In that state, an Energy Star computer draws less that 2 watts, laptops less than 1 watt. (Many computers still draw a little power even when you think they've been turned off. In some cases, the *off* current is used by circuits that monitor a *soft* power button, one that doesn't directly control the power; in other cases, it's simply poor design.)

✔ **Power management:** Systems are to enter sleep mode after 30 minutes of inactivity or less.

The Energy Star program also rates computer displays. Here are the two levels:

✔ **Under the older tier 1 standard,** monitors draw 4 watts or less in sleep mode and 2 watts or less when off.

✓ **Under the newer tier 2 standard,** introduced in 2006, monitors draw 2 watts or less in sleep mode and 1 watt or less when off. Tier 2 also sets stricter limits on total power, in watts, of 28 times the number of megapixels, with a 23-watt limit for monitors less than 1 megapixel.

To check the ratings for a specific qualified monitor, go to the Energy Star Web site, www.energystar.gov. Click the Office Equipments link under Products and then click the Monitors link.

Looking Beyond the Star

As its name implies, the Energy Star program deals only with energy. Computers impact the environment in other ways besides the electricity they consume. The Institute of Electrical and Electronics Engineers (IEEE) has an IEEE 1680 standard that sets environmental performance standards for electronic products. This standard has 23 required criteria, and 28 more for extra credit. The IEEE 1680 standard looks at the following issues:

✓ **Hazardous substances in computer materials and manufacturing:** Required measures include meeting Energy Star and the European Commission's Restriction of the Use of Certain Hazardous Substances in Electrical and Electronic Equipment (RoHS Directive).

The European Union's RoHS currently restricts six chemicals: lead, mercury, cadmium, hexavalent chromium (remember Julia Roberts in *Erin Brockovich?*), and two flame retardants — Polybrominated biphenyls (PBB) and Polybrominated diphenyl ether (PBDE). There are proposals to expand the list to include up to 46 additional substances, including antimony trioxide, beryllium, cobalt, arsenic, and additional flame retardants containing bromine. Arsenic may sound like a no-brainer, but gallium arsenide is an important semiconductor that's used in everything from cell phones to light emitting diodes (LEDs). Also, the regulations cover what's in the final product, but some activists are concerned about chemicals used in the manufacturing processes for computing equipment.

Optional criteria include elimination of suspect materials in batteries.

✓ **Ease of recycling:** A minimum of 65 percent of the product must be recyclable. Extra credit is given if 90 percent is recyclable. The use of recycled materials in manufacturing is also a point-winning option.

✓ **The availability of a take-back service from the manufacturer:** This covers both the product and any rechargeable batteries. An optional criterion is a program for auditing the recycling vendors that the manufacturer uses. See Chapter 19 for more on take-back programs and recycling.

✔ **Packaging:** No toxins may be intentionally added to packaging materials, and the different material used must be separable. Additional credit for use of post-consumer waste in packaging and for the availability of a packaging take-back service.

The Electronic Products Environmental Assessment Tool (EPEAT) rates IT products based on their compliance with IEEE 1680 standard. For more information, visit the EPEAT Web site, www.epeat.net.

Finding Green Desktop Machines

A number of online resources help you find equipment that meets your needs. These include government sites and sites run by trade organizations and advocacy groups.

Sifting through Energy Star's Web site

The U.S. government's Energy Star Web site, www.energystar.gov, has a wealth of information on certified products. Click Office Equipment under Products on the left and then click Computers from the list on the left. The page you see has links to information on the Energy Star criteria as well as a search tool for finding rated computers.

Diving into the EPEAT registry

The U.S. Environmental Protection Agency has an Electronic Product Environmental Assessment Tool (EPEAT). EPEAT is designed to help institutional purchasers compare computer desktops, laptops, and monitors based on their environmental attributes and then select the ones best for their needs. EPEAT uses the IEEE 1680 criteria in its rankings. Devices are rated Bronze, Silver, or Gold, depending on how many optional checkmarks they get. You can find the ratings at www.epeat.net.

Tapping the source

Most major computer manufacturers are trying to green their image, at least, and many are making material progress toward helping the environment. Check their Web pages for more information on what they're doing and which products are certified under the various standards. Their Web sites are also the best places to find out about their take-back programs, if they have one, and how they recycle the machines they take back. For example, IBM has a substantive collection of pages on its green activities at www.ibm.com/ibm/green.

Buying green Apples

Though gaining in corporate popularity, Apple's Macintosh computers haven't been as popular in business as they are with consumers. But they have many green features including low power consumption, mercury-free LED backlighting, and easy-to-recycle aluminum enclosures. Apple's iMac one-piece desktop computers use half the power of a typical desktop tower plus flat panel display of comparable size. Microsoft offers a version of Office for Apple's OS X operating system, and all new Macs can run Windows. For more about the use of Macs in business see *Switching to a Mac For Dummies* by Arnold Reinhold.

Finding Greener Monitors

Newer monitors use light emitting diodes (LEDs) to light flat screens, which dramatically reduces the energy consumed and is greener for a variety of reasons.

Traditional flat screens use fluorescent lighting. Fluorescent lighting uses *mercury,* a toxic heavy metal, but LEDs are mercury-free. Environmental regulations restricting the use and shipment of products containing heavy metal are already beginning in Europe and California and will likely impact the rest of the world as we become environmentally-aware and environmentally-conscientious or want to do business in Europe or California.

Some monitors automatically adjust the backlight to save power depending on lighting conditions in the room.

Some monitors also come with features that let you see the screen's power efficiency, so you know more efficient energy habits. Monitors that can be monitored for energy efficiency at a distance and adjusted remotely allow for easier energy policy enforcement.

Chapter 15

Reducing Desktop Energy Waste

*I*n Chapter 14, we talk about buying greener equipment for the desktop. But we know your budget only lets you replace equipment every few years at best, and some may still have Windows 95 machines plugging away. Even so, you can introduce certain practices that help you reduce the energy use of the equipment you already have.

In this chapter, we tell you about simple energy-saving habits, such as setting computers to hibernate when not in use or turning off monitors at night. And you also find out about some of the technologies that are currently used to provide end users with their desktops. Finally, we look at some new technologies that may eventually replace the traditional PC.

Reducing Current Consumption (Pun Intended)

Saving on your electrical power consumption is an easy, effective way to reduce energy waste coming from your desktop computing equipment. Perhaps the simplest step toward your energy-saving goal is setting the computers and their monitors to go to sleep or hibernate after they've been idle for several minutes. According to Microsoft, activating your equipment's sleep settings prevents about 300 pounds of CO_2 emissions each year per computer.

Here are a number of other simple steps that reduce desktop computer power consumption:

- ✔ **Turn down the brightness of your display to the lowest setting you find comfortable.** The difference in power usage between the highest and lowest brightness can be 20 watts or more.

- ✔ **Turn off monitors at night and when you'll be away from your desk for a while.** Monitors consume some power, even on standby.

- ✔ **Put chargers for laptops, PDAs, Blackberry handhelds, cell phones, iPods, power tools, and other small devices on a power strip that you can turn off when the chargers aren't in use.** When buying new rechargeable devices, make sure the chargers meet the requirements of the California Energy Commission, limiting power used in standby mode. If you have windows that get sunlight for a good part of the day, consider getting a solar-power charger. Energy Star-rated devices meet the California standards.

- ✔ **Avoid using screen savers for long periods of time because they don't reduce energy use and may keep the computer awake when it would otherwise doze off.** A screen saver's purpose is to prevent monitor *burn-in* — the ghost image that appears when a static image is left on the monitor for long periods of time. Putting the display to sleep is just as effective for preventing burn-in. If you must employ a screen saver, at least select a pattern with a black background, which reduces the power used by the display a bit.

- ✔ **Find out where the computer fans and vents are located and make sure they're not blocked.** In particular, keep the back of tower computers at least three inches from the wall or another obstruction. Keeping the computer cool can reduce cooling fan use and reduce overheating failures. It's a good idea to remove the accumulated dust from the fan with a vacuum cleaner — doing this allows the fan to remove more heat from inside the case and prolong the life of the components inside.

While you're checking users' computer installations, keep your eye out for other energy wasters, such as halogen lamps and electric space heaters. A halogen lamp can consume as much power as a server blade; an office space heater can use as much as a five blades.

Saving Energy While You Sleep

Most modern computers have a sleep or standby mode that sharply reduces energy use when the computer is idle. Putting a computer to sleep should be a simple thing, but nothing associated with computers is ever simple, it seems (okay, maybe for Macs, but we get to that in the section "Letting sleeping Macs lie" later in this chapter).

Putting the computer to sleep is different from shutting it down. To use your computer after a shutdown, the computer must go through its entire boot-up procedure, which as we all know, can take awhile. Then you have to log in and open all your applications and work files. Time for a coffee break! As an alternative, the computer's sleep mode cuts power use without requiring a long boot-up when you get back to work.

Waking up alert

When you tell the computer to sleep, you want it to remember what it was doing at the time you gave the order. With that in mind, the computer can then go to a minimal power mode from which you can quickly wake it and resume working just where you left off. Maybe _napping_ describes this situation better than _sleeping_ does.

To accomplish this informed reawakening, the computer must have all the information it needs to re-create the exact state it was in when you said nighty-night. Oddly enough, we refer to that information as _state information_ (not to be confused with the state department or our state of mind).

Basically, a computer can keep state information in two places — in RAM (random access memory) or on its hard drive — and each one has benefits, as follows:

- ✔ **Storing data in RAM — what Windows calls Stand By — is the much faster method, but it's a bit risky.** If you lose power and the RAM contents disappear, the results are the same as if the computer lost power at the moment you requested it gets some z's. You'll have to reboot and endure the possibility that some data may get corrupted. The risk is less with laptops because they have an internal battery, but that battery runs down if you leave your laptop in standby mode for too long.

- ✔ **Writing all your state information to your hard drive — the hibernate method — is the safer route.** But your computer takes longer to wake up after you tell it to hibernate. Bears are no doubt familiar with this problem.

Windows Vista offers a hybrid sleep option that combines the standby and hibernate methods. The state information is kept in RAM _and_ written to the hard drive. If the RAM data is still intact at wakie-wakie time, the computer uses it for a fast recovery; otherwise, it uses the hard drive data and wakes up more slowly. Vista's hybrid sleep in enabled by default on desktop computers. To change settings, do the following:

1. **Open Power Options by clicking Start➪Control Panel➪System and Maintenance➪Power Options.**

2. **On the Select a Power Plan page, click Change Plan Settings.**

3. **In the Change Settings for the Plan window, click Change Advanced Power Settings.**

4. **On the Advanced Settings tab, click the plus boxes to expand Sleep and Allow Hybrid Sleep, as shown in Figure 15-1.**

5. **Click the On or Off buttons to get the configuration you wish.**

Figure 15-1:
The expanded options tree in the Power Options — Advanced Settings tab.

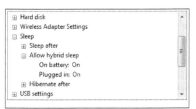

In Windows, tell your computer it's bedtime by choosing Start⇨Shutdown. Depending on your configuration, Windows either asks you what you want to do or just gives you options, such as Stand By, Shut Down, and Restart.

Hibernate is always enabled on Vista. To activate the Hibernate option on some Windows XP installations, hold down the Shift key while you choose Start⇨Shut Down. To see the Hibernate option, you may have to enable it from the Hibernate tab (as shown in Figure 15-2) in the Power Options Properties dialog box (choose Start⇨Control Panel⇨Power Options and then click the Hibernate tab).

Figure 15-2:
Enable hibernation from the Hibernate tab.

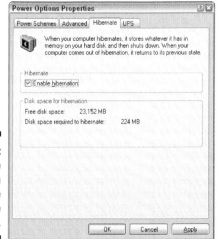

Automating sleep

You can tell your computer to sleep automatically when it's idle for a while. To see the various automatic sleep options in Windows, go to the Power Options Properties dialog box (choose Start⇨Control Panel⇨Power Options and then click the Power Schemes tab). See Figure 15-3. You can select different sets of settings, or *power schemes,* if you wish.

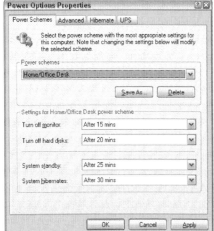

Figure 15-3: Selecting sleep settings from the Power Schemes tab.

Using software to manage sleep habits

In addition to the power management schemes already discussed, companies can use products, such as Verdiem's Edison software, to automate when PCs are on or off — Edison can also be downloaded for free for individual use. Both IBM and HP have comprehensive power management offerings intended for use in data centers, which can also be used to set the power profiles of a large number of PCs.

Avoiding troubled sleep

The sleep functions on computers running Windows have a reputation for experiencing problems. Sometimes a Windows machine will wake up in the middle of the night (suffering from digital insomnia), and other times it may not wake up when you try to rouse it (annoying you with digital narcolepsy). Computers may also lose network connectivity while slumbering. Often, any of these problems can trace back to specific peripherals and device drivers. The Microsoft support site has numerous articles on sleep and standby issues.

One thing your IT department can do to promote energy efficiency is to understand the various sleep and standby modes in the common software and hardware configurations used in your organization. Add any new driver and setting changes for reliable sleep to your regular system maintenance update schedule. Make sure that your help desk professionals know how to deal with sleep issues. Then, and only then, publicize internally the importance of having end users employ their computers' sleep function as an energy-saving tool.

Letting sleeping Macs lie

We must say something about Macs and sleep. The Apple Macintosh computers have had a sleep option for ages, and it pretty much just works. Simply select Sleep from the Apple menu (). The Mac comes set to sleep and blanks the screen after being idle for 15 minutes. If you want different delays, adjust as follows:

✔ Set the Mac idle time period before sleep starts from the Energy Saver control panel. Choose Apple⇨System Preferences and then click the Energy Saver icon. On the Energy Saver control panel (as shown in Figure 15-4), you find

 • Separate time settings for the computer and the monitor(s)

 • A check box that tells the system to shut down the disk drive whenever your Mac thinks that's okay

✔ Newer Macs running OS X version 10.4 and later have a safe sleep mode that combines sleep and hibernate, much like Vista's hybrid sleep. Safe sleep is the default when available.

Figure 15-4:
Saving
energy
with a few
settings on
your Mac.

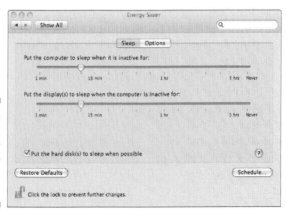

Disk encryption never sleeps

If you use disk encryption with your laptops — and you should if your laptop contains any sensitive data — avoid using sleep modes when the laptop is taken outside secure areas. That means this: Shut down your laptop when you're traveling with it and it isn't in your hands. Unscrupulous people can recover the encryption key from RAM if they find (or steal) your laptop when it's in sleep, standby, or hibernate mode. In these modes, your laptop isn't protected.

Full disk encryption can play a role in facilitating computer recycling. One obstacle to finding new homes for old computers outside the organization is the risk that hard drives may contain sensitive data. If the hard drive is encrypted with a high-quality encryption program (such as PGP Disk, www. pgp.com), as long as the encryption key isn't included, the computer can be donated safely. See Chapter 19 for more on computer recycling.

Figuring the Energy Consumed by Physical Desktop Computing

In Chapter 5, we talk about the conspicuous consumption of data centers — sometimes exceeding the power requirements of a small town. Part of the reason data centers consume so much power and cooling is their sheer concentration of computers and storage in a relatively small area. More processing power (unfortunately) leads to increased power consumption, increased heat production, and the related increased requirement for cooling.

In addition to the amount of power consumed by the average data center, each desktop computer probably consumes, on average, around 170 watts of power per hour. Keep in mind that this number can vary widely according to manufacturer, processor model, amount of memory installed, and so on. For this discussion, we use the 170-watt number for our calculations.

The formula for calculating energy consumption based on power rating and time in use is

```
(Watts × hours used) ÷ 1,000 watts per kilowatt = Energy consumption
                in kilowatt-hours
```

So, if a single desktop computer is on 24 hours each day, the energy it consumes is

```
(170 watts × 24 hours) ÷ 1,000 watts per kilowatt = 4.08 kilowatt-hours each day
```

Now think about how many desktop computers you have on your floor at the office, in your building, or even in your company. It's very likely that your company has at least one computer for every person, and if you work in a large enterprise, that number might be 10,000 or more desktop computers.

To illustrate our point, suppose we estimate the number of desktops at 1,000 and leave them on 5 days per week for a year. The amount of energy consumed each year in kilowatt-hours is

```
4.08 kilowatt-hours per day × 5 days per week × 52 weeks per year × 1,000
            computers = 1,060,000 kilowatt-hours per year
```

which is a sizeable amount of power consumed.

This number doesn't account for the impact of the sleep and hibernate features built into desktop computers (or even a 2-week vacation for your computer). If you have these features enabled on all your desktops, your annual desktop energy consumption will be perhaps half as much. But this calculation illustrates an important point: Desktop computers consume a substantial amount of power and thus present a real opportunity for reducing power consumption and cost. In fact, many experts believe that desktop computers represent one of the largest opportunities for companies to cut costs and contribute to green goals.

Reducing Consumption through Desktop Virtualization

We talk extensively in Chapter 13 about how virtualization works and how data centers can apply virtualization as a way of lowering the consumption of power for processing and cooling. The same virtual technology can apply to desktop computers, although you'll find several competing solutions that offer varying results, as we discuss in this section.

Virtualization describes a technology, usually implemented in a software application, which fools the applications into thinking that the organization has the exclusive use of a computer's resources. Under virtualization, applications run in a *virtual machine* — or *VM*. Each virtual machine and the applications running within the VM behave as though they're the only applications running on the computer; although many virtual machines could run on a single computer that has sufficient resources to provide acceptable performance.

Server virtualization has been widely adopted by companies of all sizes for the purpose of consolidating both physical servers and applications. Lowering the number of physical servers not only reduces the administrative burden but also has a substantial impact on power consumption for processing and cooling. Using virtualization to replace the traditional desktop computer is less widespread, although some industry sectors (for example, financial services) have used virtualization in the form of a terminal, which gets its data and services from a mainframe computer, since the 1970s.

Comparing terminals, stateless clients, and thin clients to PCs

A terminal has no computing intelligence and no internal processing power but, instead, is connected to a *host computer,* usually a mainframe with immense computational power and the ability to serve hundreds of directly connected users at once. The terminal transmits every keystroke on its keyboard to the host computer for processing, and the host transmits the result to the terminal for display. If you disconnect a terminal from its host, the connection is lost. Terminals running off a mainframe are really the first incarnation of the *client-server model* of computing. The *client,* in this case, a terminal, gets its intelligence from a *server,* which is the host computer. *Stateless clients* and *thin clients* are very similar to terminals, except that they don't connect directly to the host computer and they have enough intelligence when powered up to look on the network for a server.

Thin client has become the preferred term for the client part of client-server, to distinguish it from a *fat client,* a PC, which has its own computing intelligence and internal processing power. Thin clients, which usually consist of a display, a small chassis with connectivity, and a keyboard, have some advantages over PCs, including

- ✔ **Central administration:** Thin clients run only the software that's provided by the host server, which makes software administration faster and easier.

- ✔ **Simple:** Thin clients require very little installation and maintenance and are easy to replace if something goes wrong.

- ✔ **Workstation mobility:** The services provided on a thin client can move with the user; that is, wherever the user logs in is where the user's desktop appears.

- ✔ **Cost efficiency:** Most of the cost of this architecture is in the server infrastructure, not in the client.

✔ **Low power consumption:** Thin clients use very little power during operation, especially when compared to a PC desktop. Of course, this advantage is the one that contributes most to an organization's green IT goals.

The client-server computing model is really cost-effective only in large organizations — say, a company with more than 5,000 users. And even though this model might be economically compelling, PCs are still the dominant form of end user desktop computers, even in large companies. This fact dooms the PC to continue as a conspicuous consumer of power for some time to come.

Using terminal server, RDP, and remote desktops

In addition to PCs and thin clients, you have several other ways to supply end users with their desktops and applications. All these involve using a server as a repository for the user's data. You might think of these systems as variations on the client-server model, which we describe in the previous section.

A terminal server is almost like the terminal/host system from the previous section, except that the client is a regular PC running an operating system, such as Windows or Linux. The server, dubbed a *terminal server,* provides remote access to centrally administered applications and works something like this:

1. End users use their own PC to establish a connection over the Internet to the terminal server. Through this connection, they can access the files on their desktop at work or run a word processing application, such as Microsoft Word.

2. The users view and work with the applications in a separate window (the *terminal*) on their desktops. Also, the user still has use of their PC's desktop by minimizing the terminal window.

3. When users finish using a terminal application and close the connection to the terminal server, they still have their original desktops and all the computing power of their PCs.

The drawbacks to using terminal server are as follows:

✔ It requires a network connection, and the quality and speed of that connection has a great impact on how well the services or applications perform.

✔ Many applications don't perform well in a terminal window.

> ✔ The overhead required for serving a terminal server session to an end
> user usually limits both performance and the number of users that can
> use the server at one time.

The *Remote Data Protocol (RDP)* is the protocol on which terminal services
are based, and it's provided for informal use on Windows XP. For example,
PC service technicians use RDP to get remote access to your PC to fix a problem in Windows. In this instance, your computer acts like a terminal server
and grants access to your computer — with your explicit permission — for
the duration of the session. Implemented this way, the RDP session won't
support more than one user, as it would if RDP were running on a real terminal server.

The final variation on this client-server theme is a *remote desktop,* which is
nearly identical to the thin client model described in the previous section,
except that the client is a PC. The remote desktop model doesn't assume that
the PC is connected to a corporate network, although it could be. Similar to
the thin client, the remote desktop is centrally administered and distributed,
but the hardware is a PC or a laptop. Here are several drawbacks to this
approach:

> ✔ **No significant energy savings:** The client isn't thin or inexpensive; it's a
> regular PC, with all the energy requirements and administrative costs of
> a PC.
>
> ✔ **Potentially slow performance:** The end user's desktop performance is
> heavily dependent on the speed and quality of the network connection,
> which may degrade as more end users seek services.
>
> ✔ **Compatibility issues:** As with terminal server, not all applications work
> well under this scheme — applications that make frequent use of graphi-
> cal content perform poorly, if at all.

All these various client-server-type approaches attempt to provide end users
with a desktop, and they come with varying degrees of complexity (from an
administrative standpoint) and performance.

Utilizing Desktops on a Flash Drive

A recent development in desktop virtualization incorporates the idea of
putting some (or all) of an end user's desktop on a highly portable storage medium, such as a USB drive or a flash drive. Several companies (for
example, MokaFive or Sychron) offer software that enables virtualization of
some or all a user's applications and the personalization that make a user's
desktop unique.

You can set up a virtual desktop on removable media as follows:

1. **Create a desktop that includes the standard settings for all end users.**

   A system administrator or someone who has administrator privileges makes an image, or *snapshot,* of the standard company desktop — the desktop that's given to a new employee who's getting a desktop computer or laptop.

   This standard desktop becomes the *golden* image that's the basis for all user desktops.

2. **Customize the desktop image for a specific end user's needs and load the image on the USB or flash drive.**

   As each user's desktop is built and transferred to the portable media, the additional applications and settings unique to each user — the user's *preferences* — are also transferred. The result is an end user's desktop that can be transported anywhere.

Of course, the size of the portable storage medium will determine how many settings and applications can be virtualized. To transfer a full Microsoft Windows XP desktop requires a USB flash drive, but prices on these drives continue to fall while their capacity continues to increase.

This portable desktop technology has the potential to change the way IT delivers and maintains user desktops in a number of ways:

✔ **By saving time:** Desktop computers or laptops can be configured quickly because the portable media carries the desktop image, not the hard drive in the end user machine.

✔ **By enabling quick configuration and recovery:** The portable desktop image can be overlaid on *bare metal* — that is, a computer with no pre-installed operating system or software. This feature also allows quick recovery of an end user's desktop in the event of a disaster, such as a hard drive failure.

✔ **By facilitating remote computing:** A user can take his work home by simply removing the portable media and reinserting it in a computer at home. Of course, the task of moving business data to a laptop for traveling is made much easier.

✔ **By offering a secure environment:** The portable medium and the desktop image contained on it are secure and encrypted so that if the medium is lost or stolen, it can't be used by anyone else.

You could use the same technology to transport your MP3 song collection or photos of your last trip to the Grand Canyon to work, or to your cousin's house for that matter, without duplicating your desktop on someone else's computer.

You may be asking: "This is a great idea, but how does it support green IT goals?" The adoption of portable, virtualized desktops causes a corresponding reduction in the amount of power consumed by desktop storage, which this technology supplements and may eventually supplant. In order to maintain acceptable performance, CPU (central processing unit) power and memory requirements won't change, so the related power usage would stay the same. The eventual contribution of portable, virtual storage to green goals depends in large part on how widely IT departments adopt this technology — especially in larger organizations with thousands of desktops and laptops.

Chapter 16

Pursuing the Less-Paper Office

*P*aper for printing has yet to go the way of film for cameras, which is rapidly disappearing. But dramatically reducing printing and its associated costs is a green idea whose time has come. You can evaluate everything from the purchase of your printers, paper, and ink, to where you put your printer(s), to the reason people print, to the storage necessary for printed materials. And you can eliminate as much as 80 percent of your organization's paper and related costs by using and storing content in its original digital form.

In the sections that follow, you find information and tips to help you weigh your options and find solutions that are not only greener but also more beneficial to your operations.

Choosing Printers, Paper, and Ink

If you can avoid printing, do so. Using electronic forms and sticking with the digitized document will help. When you must print, make the greenest choices you can. Most printers come under the category of *always-on devices* — like network components, they're turned on and hardly ever turned off, except for changing ink cartridges, clearing paper jams, and periodic service calls.

When thinking about greening your office, you can find ways to benefit the planet and your bottom line by taking a look at what green printing might look like in your business environment. Examine not only the printer itself but also your paper and ink and how your equipment and supplies match your needs.

Checking out printer specs

Fortunately, most printers of recent vintage have the following green features:

- ✔ **Energy Star rating:** A new set of Energy Star specifications for imaging equipment went into effect in 2007. Energy Star–qualified devices cost about the same as standard imaging equipment, but use less electricity. In fact, qualified equipment that meets the new specification (a computer or monitor, for example) can save you $115 over the life of the product. Here are some other attributes Energy Star-qualified devices tout:

  - On average, 25 percent more energy efficient than traditional models.

  - Energy Star printers all print two-sided images, saving paper. (Read more about two-sided printing later in this chapter.)

  - Energy Star equipment is designed to run cooler and last longer, so using them may help with your air conditioning costs and replacement cycles.

  - Energy Star imaging products will save billions over the next five years and avert greenhouse gas emissions equal to four million cars.

  To read more about Energy Star, see Chapter 4.

- ✔ **Power saving mode:** In this mode, the printer effectively shuts down into an idle state that uses much less power until it gets a request to print something.

Equally important is matching the printer to your needs. Most people think about printers in terms of *speeds and feeds* — how many pages can the printer print per minute, does the printer handle photo quality printing, and so on.

In considering when to replace existing printers with greener options, you need to consider the frequency and usage your current printers get. Older, less efficient printers that are only used occasionally or only in back-up situations shouldn't be replaced. Older printers that won't print 2-sided copies that are in constant use probably should be replaced on the merits of saving paper alone.

These are important features, of course, but what is the printer's *duty cycle* — how many pages per month on average is the printer designed to print? You can find duty cycle information in a printer's specifications and then compare printer specs to the printing needs of your office. For example, consider the following scenarios:

- ✔ **The overloaded printer:** If a printer's duty cycle is 2,000 pages per month and the printer is being used by 50 people every day, printing 12 pages each on average, chances are good that the printer will wear out before it should. Frequent printer repair and replacement wastes money and resources and the printer may operate less efficiently than one designed for such a load.

- ✔ **Printer overkill:** It would be overkill (and unnecessarily expensive) to buy a printer that has a duty cycle of 10,000 pages per month for a four-person or home office that prints perhaps 50 pages a week. The *consumables* — ink and toner — are likely to be quite expensive for a printer designed to print 10,000 pages per month.

Considering ink and toner

Toner and ink emissions are toxic. Maybe knowing that can help you curb your dependence on printing. If not, maybe it can inspire you to stay as far away from your printer while it's printing.

Recycling ink and toner cartridges is one of the basic ways go green. If you're not recycling ink and toner cartridges, you're missing an easy opportunity to save some money — stores like Staples and Office Depot, as well as most printer manufacturers, offer rebates or discounts for recycling cartridges — and it's the right thing to do.

But it's also important to consider the cost of ink or toner in your printer selection. Many printers consume a lot of ink, especially when they're printing pictures or photographs. Unfortunately, photorealism has its price! The following questions can help you weigh what your color printing needs truly are:

- ✔ **Is color worth the cost?** Most office printing is black and white printing, and so buying a printer with exceptional color capabilities is probably a waste of money.

- ✔ **Am I willing to trade color for speed?** It turns out that color printers usually take longer to print in color, so if you're particularly concerned about speedily printing a large volume, forego color in favor of throughput.

✔ **What's my true business need for color?** If indeed you're an art house and most everything you print needs color, you'll need to make that call. If your need for color is occasional, a separate, smaller, color printer may be a better way to go.

Print, fax, fold, spindle, and mutilate: The multifunction device

Many manufacturers now make printing devices that combine printing, copying, scanning, and faxing — or some variation of these. *Multifunction,* or all-in-one, devices are usually based on ink-jet printers, which keeps their initial cost down. It also means that multifunction devices have a lower printing duty cycle (which we discuss in the previous section) than print-only devices. To a greater or lesser degree, multifunction devices are only as strong as their weakest function.

The message here: Make sure that a multifunction device doesn't represent a compromise on functionality that you really need. If you're scanning hundreds of pages into PDF files weekly, you might be better off getting a dedicated scanner. Similarly, if your business relies on a fax machine to receive customer orders, get a dedicated fax machine, or better yet a fax server that captures and stores fax transmissions electronically and prints no paper.

For a small business or home office, however, a multifunction device is really a great solution. By combining devices that would normally be separate, the multifunction device is a very green player in the office — it consumes less power and space than powering and providing space for two, three, or even four separate devices.

Buying based on your needs

Think about the points discussed in the preceding sections. Then you know the basics of what makes a printer green and suitable for your needs.

Ask yourself these questions as you consider what printer (or multifunction device) to buy:

✔ What is the printer's expected duty cycle? How many pages will I print on a daily (and monthly) basis?

✔ Do I need color printing or will black and white printing do?

✔ Do I want ink jet or laser printing? This one's kind of a gotcha:

- *Ink jet printers* tend to cost less than laser printers, and they may also have better color, but they often use ink at alarming rates.

- *Laser printers* have a longer duty cycle and cost less to operate, but not always. It pays to do your research on this one!

Online resources like CNET (`www.cnet.com`) often have printer *shootouts* — useful comparisons of printer functions and costs.

✔ Will this be a network printer, with its own IP address, allowing it to be shared directly over the network? Or will it be attached to a print server that handles the sharing? Networked printers tend to be more expensive to buy because they require additional electronics to handle the networking, but that's a one-time expense and eliminates the need for a print server.

✔ Does the printer have an Energy Star certification?

✔ What is the expected cost of operation: electrical, ink or toner, and service levels?

As in most things, the more you know about printers, the better choices you can make.

Picking greener paper

There are more kinds of paper than you can imagine. Or perhaps more than you would care to imagine. Trees are cut down to produce paper, and if not replanted, deforestation has dire consequences. When you clean up your act around paper, you're not just talking about reducing what you use and recycling your waste. We want you to understand what you're buying and the consequences.

You no doubt are seeing paper made with such-and-such a percentage of recycled content. What does that mean? Does it matter? Good questions.

There's a ton to learn about paper from a green perspective that goes beyond the simplistic moniker of "recycled." Considerations you can give to your paper purchasing decision include

✔ How paper is manufactured

✔ How the paper is recycled

✔ What percentage of a paper's content is recycled

✔ Whether the paper manufacturer works with the Forest Stewardship Council to ensure that forests are maintained

The Forest Stewardship Council (www.fscus.org) is a not-for-profit organization focused on maintaining and renewing forest resources. The council certifies paper, paper merchants, and paper manufacturers that align with responsible forest use.

To help you bridge the gap between a neophyte well-intentioned, responsible paper consumer to a well-informed paper purchaser, we recommend "Translating Recycled Paper Lingo into a Language You Can Understand" by Brian J. Cowie, CEO and Founder, The Paper Mill Store, www.thepaper millstore.com.

Start with what goes into paper:

- ✔ **Virgin fiber:** New fiber from trees; no recycled content.

- ✔ **Pre-consumer waste:** Scrap paper from industrial processes, such as the trimmings paper after a book like this is cut to size. There is nothing wrong with using pre-consumer waste — such scrap has always been used in paper making — but its use does not indicate new progress toward sustainability.

- ✔ **Post-consumer waste (PCW):** Paper that is collected from consumers after it has served its primary purpose. This is the stuff you put in your recycle bin.

- ✔ **Total recycled fiber (TRF):** The total amount of recycled content, including pre- and post-consumer waste.

A key factor in paper making is the average length of the individual fibers. Each pass at recycling tends to shorten fibers (they don't grow on their own). High grade paper typically needs some virgin fiber content, so don't expect all the paper you buy to have 100 percent post-consumer content. But routine printing needs can generally be met with high-recycled-content paper.

Different papers are appropriate to different usage and there's no such thing as 100 percent recycled paper — there's always some new paper content. Recycled paper that comes from the mill before consumer use reflects efficiencies in the mill's processes. Using post-consumer paper helps save landfill space.

Because paper is a commodity, the paper market is very sensitive to price variance. Manufacturers have to find simple, affordable ways that won't push their prices out of reach. Paper manufacturers that are trying to be more environmentally responsible are making choices; such as leveraging renewable energies, including wind; capturing methane from landfills; capturing the steam coming off paper machines to create power by turbine; and finding ways to reduce the water needed to create paper.

Not all paper fiber comes from trees — cotton, bamboo, and certain grasses all can be made into paper. New processes to make paper white include processes that are completely chlorine free, meaning there's no longer a need to bleach paper.

Simply put, you want to find the most affordable, environmentally friendly mix that does the job. The trick is to identify what's right for the job. The percentage of recycled content still doesn't tell you whether the paper's right for you. Chances are you'll need to see samples; if you'll be buying in quantity, your supplier should be more than happy to let you sample. Because so many different things get recycled into recycled paper — both pre-consumer waste fiber and post-consumer waste fiber — you don't know what you're getting without closer inspection.

There's nothing wrong with stocking more than one kind of paper — one kind that's fine for most tasks and a higher quality stock that's kept aside for such things as letterhead. It's no big deal to load different paper, as you know. And if you can work with lesser quality paper for routine documents, you'll save a lot of energy and trees consumed by paper manufacturers.

Changing Printing Habits

Too many folks are printing first, asking questions later. You can help people change their printing habits. The following sections offer some ideas.

Making printing less a part of daily life might take some time, but sending out organization-wide messages that educate, demonstrate, and reinforce the value change you seek can go a long way to expedite the change. That said, helping people become more aware of the costs and waste of unnecessary printing only goes so far. Reinforcing your message with some of the following strategies may help you change old habits.

When upgrading your company's monitors, keep in mind that older CRT monitors that flicker *do* make reading large volumes onscreen problematic. High-resolution screens make reading from a monitor more efficient.

Inconvenient printing

If you want to help people think about their printing habits, make it a little less convenient to just print everything:

- ✔ Have only the number of printers necessary for the task at hand.
- ✔ Put all printers in one location — don't distribute convenient printers throughout the building.

When folks actually have to get up and walk a few minutes to retrieve their printout, they may find it more convenient to read something on the screen — it may actually take less time than the round trip to the printer. Others will welcome the exercise. Folks at the IBM Corporation tell us that their printers are in a seldom-visited room, which is kept dark. Lights turn on by motion detector during the rare occasion someone must print.

In addition to reducing paper use, consolidating printers also offers the following benefits:

- ✔ **Reducing the number of printers being powered.**

- ✔ **Reducing energy costs.**

- ✔ **Taking up less space.** Instead, put in something green and living, like a plant. (Plants actually consume carbon dioxide and emit oxygen, so you might find your work place looks nicer and feels better with fewer machines and more plant life.)

Defaulting to duplex

Duplex printing is printing on both sides of the paper. Some printers are equipped to do this automatically; others allow you to reinsert a page so that the printer can print on the second side.

- ✔ Use printers that automatically enable duplex printing.

- ✔ Set printing to duplex by default.

Double-sided printing won't help with ink or energy costs per se, but the savings in paper is dramatic.

Presenting PowerPoints without printouts

PowerPoint presentations pervade our processes. Although PowerPoint presentations aren't a bad thing in and of themselves, we question the widespread *printing* and *distributing* of PowerPoint presentations. Period.

We're familiar with the popular reasons for printouts, and in Table 16-1, we present our case to the contrary. Find a way to avoid printing. Those copies will likely end up in the trash or, if trees are lucky, in the recycle bin.

Table 16-1	Refuting Popular Rationales for PowerPoint Printouts
Presenter or Company Rationale	**Our Counter-Evidence**
We want to avoid electronic copies to protect our intellectual property.	If you're disclosing proprietary information, distributing it on paper rather than electronically doesn't help you all that much. You can distribute them in PDF format. This helps protect against direct theft but enables readers to have your presentation for ready reference. Or if the material is really sensitive, don't distribute copies at all. That will get your audience's attention.
We're concerned the audience can't see the slides being presented.	If your slides are unreadable using a projector, maybe you should re-design them with larger fonts and less content per slide. Always check your presentation from the back of the room.
We want to enable note-taking.	What do folks do with those slides that you've so kindly provided in paper? Well, uh, maybe they file them in a file cabinet somewhere and can find them if they remember they have them. Or maybe they responsibly recycle them.
We want the audience to remember what we're saying.	A presentation filed electronically is ultimately a lot easier to retrieve. If it's on a laptop, it goes where you go. Unlike your filing cabinet.
The folks we're meeting don't have our slides in advance.	Put a copy on a thumb drive and allow them to copy them; or e-mail it to them right then and there.
Hey, we're printing more slides per page, okay?	That doesn't really help. The reduced slides are often totally unreadable, and all the reasons why printing them in the first place doesn't make much sense.

Switching to Digital Documents

Look around you. Chances are, the longer you've been in business, the more paper you have stored, the more manual your processes, the more paper and ink you use — unless you've made a conscientious effort to change not only your business processes but also the thinking endemic to your culture. Chances are, you're better off making that effort.

Paper documents are time-consuming and costly to create, process, distribute, file, store, retrieve, reproduce, and dispose of. But why focus just on paper's cons? The positives of digital documents may help you win the minds and hearts of people in your organization. And the benefits of digital documents outweigh the benefits of print in many cases. Consider the following:

- ✓ **You can search digital documents electronically.**

- ✓ **Digital documents are much more portable.**

- ✓ **Audio counts as digital, too.** Sometimes your message is better conveyed as an audio file than a document. Same for video. With digital, you can be more creative.

- ✓ **A non-paper method not only reduces paper but almost inevitably improves the process itself.** For example:

  - *When you fill out a form, chances are someone else has to interpret your handwriting and enter it into a computer for you.* However, if you register for something online, your registration is fed directly into a database without requiring an additional person to key it in.

  - *Service requisition done online allows for easy tracking and response through e-mail — no more physical requests.*

When processes change, IT is the critical enabler. Look for ways to cut costs and reduce time by eliminating paper processes throughout the organization. One study at a large commercial bank found a potential return on investment of over $36 million by just using the digital documents rather than printing them to paper. And this was in just six bank departments.

Handling contracts with digital signatures

A big hold-out in the paper-clinging world is the world of contracts. "We need a signature" is the mantra of the legal eagles tasked with safeguarding the organization's interests. Electronic signatures are our answer. Contracts can be exchanged with very high assurance that the sender who digitally signs and sends the documents is actually the person he says he is. What "proof" have you that that signature coming over the fax belongs to the person you spoke with on the phone or that the person you spoke to on the phone is the person they told you they were?

For more information on electronic signatures see *Cryptography For Dummies* by Chey Cobb.

Even if your legal department won't consider electronically signed contracts, you can still cut paper use dramatically by using electronic documents for all the drafts that precede the final signed version.

Improving data security

We don't want you to go all paranoid on us, but we question the argument that paper is safer:

- ✔ Paper must be filed, and filed correctly.
- ✔ Generally speaking, organizations don't have *backups* of their filing cabinets.
- ✔ Locking a filing cabinet is a good idea, but if documents are actually sensitive, what levels of protection and trust do you require of the person or persons who hold the key(s)?

Given the increased regulations around data privacy, chances are you're better off creating and protecting digital documents with the myriad tools at your avail, than risking sensitive paperwork finding its way into the wrong hands. Making a physical copy of paper documents leaves no trail — perhaps page counts on the copier, but no clue as to what's been copied. Data protection software can limit who can access what information and can actually limit where information flows, when, and how.

Going green here can help you stay on the right side of compliance and better protect your critical data.

Putting the E in forms

E-liminating paper by turning your paper-based processes into electronic processes greatly facilitates everything from sourcing and procurement, to benefits enablement, to provisioning access and equipment, to bill paying, payroll, expense accounting — you name it.

The software industry has rallied by providing a plethora of e-form software that makes creating e-forms simple.

Form creation itself is insufficient, however. You need to actually do the work to understand the business processes these forms support. *Business process optimization (BPO)* can be very, very green.

For example, processing a college application that's done by paper forms involves creating the original paper form itself and making many copies along the way. Often various forms including letters of recommendation, transcripts, and essays have to be copied to create packets of information that have to be reviewed by many parties.

Consider the same process the e-form way. The applicant fills out the e-form and subsequent copies are all electronic — no paper printed, copied, mailed, and filed. The admissions clerk can easily group and forward e-forms to all necessary reviewers. Personal student information, such as name, address, phone number, social security number, and names and contact information for parents, can all become part of the applicant's record automatically. If the student is accepted and matriculates, all this information can become part of the student's record without filling out new forms. All those important mailings will use information from that original e-form, all with entry done only once by the applicant at the beginning of the process.

Both green and BPO focus on eliminating waste, they both leverage reuse, and they both ultimately cut time and costs. Yet another win-win-win.

Scanning to reduce facilities costs and labor

Just how many filing cabinets does your organization use? Are there more on order? Whether they're full of sales contracts, patient medical records, architectural drawings, x-rays, or marketing collateral, chances are you could go a long way to cut the filing, storage, retrieval, and distribution costs by going digital. Libraries figured this out a long time ago when they started reducing stacks of newspapers to microfiche.

Depending on the legislation that applies to your stored data, you might find electronic systems makes economic as well as environmental sense sooner rather than later. You may find that scanning old paper documents and storing them

- Electronically frees up high-priced office space
- Simultaneously provides better protection and retrieval

Scanning documents is no one's idea of a good time but you might be helping both your organization's economy as well as your local economy by employing some folks who need the work. Of course, capturing and working with the original "born digital" document is even more efficient and also provides all the indexing and retrieval metadata you might need without having to scan paper.

Chapter 17

Evaluating Green Gadgetry

· ·

· ·

Much of Green IT focuses on racks of servers and vast disk storage arrays, and rightly so — these things consume lots of energy. But the computing world is shifting to the small and mobile. Tiny, intelligent devices proliferate along with their chargers; just look at any nearby power strip.

All this gadgetry has an impact on the green story, in several ways:

✔ **The good news:** Mobile devices can save energy and reduce IT's environmental effects — if you use them wisely.

✔ **The bad news:** The sheer number of devices and their always-plugged-in chargers require significant power.

✔ **The ugly news:** Dead batteries pose an environmental hazard, and disposing of them properly takes effort and energy. With a little planning and effort, however, you can make this impact less ugly. Read on. . . .

Powering Gadgets Intelligently

You can reduce the environmental impact of battery-powered electronic gadgets. Find better ways to supply them with power. Try better chargers, better batteries, and off-grid power sources.

Considering green chargers

The United States Environmental Protection Agency (EPA) estimates that American homes and businesses use some 230 million products that need battery-charging power adapters. The EPA estimates that Americans could save 1 terawatt-hour per year and reduce greenhouse gas emissions by 1 million tons by switching to more efficient chargers. According to the EPA, that's like taking 150,000 cars off the road.

Have you seen the Energy Star logo, as shown in Figure 17-1? The program doesn't just include refrigerators and washers. It also includes chargers and power adapters. Products with the Energy Star logo are 30 percent more efficient than conventional models.

Figure 17-1:
The Energy
Star logo
for power
adapters.

Another issue is the horde of power adapters people accumulate, each with its own plug style. Fortunately, many manufacturers of portable devices are standardizing their products to use mini-USB plugs as charging ports. (Figure 17-2 shows a charger equipped with a mini-USB plug.) These all use the same voltage, 5 volts, but can have different current capacities, ranging from 100 ma to 1 amp. Some manufacturers add special circuitry so their devices charge off their adaptors only, but most will charge off a charger with the same or higher current capacity. Other manufacturers claim using a different vendor's charger will void their warrantee. But in practice, compatibility is pretty good. And there's the added convenience of finding a suitable charger at your destination when traveling. Other manufacturers, such as Apple, have at least standardized the charger plug across their entire product line.

But just when it seemed like charger sanity was in danger of breaking out, the USB Implementers Forum (www.usb.org) has depreciated the mini-USB connector and introduced a still smaller microUSB for use in all new designs. We hope these will evolve into the long-sought universal charger.

When buying gadgets, look for the Energy Star logo and pick devices with standardized charging connections, such as a mini- or micro-USB (ask a salesperson or look at a display sample if the packaging isn't clear). You can also cut energy waste by collecting all your existing chargers on a single power strip that you can turn off during the day.

Figure 17-2:
A power
adapter with
a mini-USB
plug.

Using rechargeable batteries

According to the EPA, Americans buy some 3 billion dry-cell batteries each
year. These include the familiar AAA, AA, C, D, 9-volt, and button batteries
that power flashlights, radios, cameras, toys, and a myriad of other products.
Few of these batteries are recycled; most end up in landfills. In the past,
these batteries were a major source of mercury in landfills.

Most non-rechargeable batteries sold today contain no (or very little)
mercury. Even so, all those batteries represent a large stream of material
that must be manufactured, packaged, transported to end users, and then
transported to landfills after use. Each of those steps uses energy, produces
carbon, and has other environmental impacts.

You can reduce the number of batteries you use by employing rechargeable
batteries wherever possible. Although the initial unit cost is higher, rechargeable batteries quickly pay for themselves.

Charged up

In 1996, Congress passed the Mercury-Containing and Rechargeable Battery Management Act to phase out mercury in batteries. The law also helps ensure efficient collection and recycling (or at least proper disposal) of used nickel-cadmium batteries, small sealed lead-acid batteries, and others.

We know you're too sophisticated to try this, but please make sure everyone you know understands that trying to recharge a battery that's not designed to be rechargeable can result in undesirable consequences — namely, they can explode.

Recycling batteries

Do you live in the Golden State? If so, you have to recycle. California considers *all* batteries hazardous waste when they're disposed of (www.dtsc.ca.gov/HazardousWaste/UniversalWaste). Whether you live in the West or in West Virginia, recycling all those batteries seems like a no-brainer. But finding a place that *actually* recycles the batteries, as opposed to just sending them to landfills, can be challenging. Safe recycling is particularly important for rechargeable batteries, which may contain toxic of hazardous materials.

The *Rechargeable Battery Recycling Corporation (RBRC),* a non-profit organization created by the rechargeable power industry, collects and recycles rechargeable batteries and old cell phones through their Call2Recycle program. They don't accept non-rechargeable batteries.

The Call2Recycle program is funded by manufacturers of rechargeable devices, who get to display the RBRC battery recycling seal, and through the sale of refurbished cell phones. They claim that none of the material they recycle makes its way to landfills. They have collection sites at many major retailers, or you can check their Web site, www.rbrc.org.

Another vendor, Battery Solutions www.batteryrecycling.com, sells recycling containers that you fill and then send to them for recycling. For example, their *iRecycle Kit 35* is a plastic pail that holds up to 35 pounds and sells for $49. Return shipping is prepaid. They accept all types of dry-cell batteries, including AA, AAA, C, D, power-tool, laptop, camera, and cell-phone batteries. They also accept all handheld electronic devices, such as cell phones, music players, PDAs, and the like. Placing one of their kits in the cafeteria or the lobby is an easy way to encourage recycling with little expense.

Your local municipality may have a recycling program or special collection days for hazardous materials. Check their Web site.

Lead-acid wet rechargeable batteries require special attention. Lead-acid wet batteries are familiar items in cars and trucks, but sealed versions of them are also used in data centers for uninterruptible power supplies and emergency lighting. Lead-acid batteries are considered hazardous waste, with regulations that govern proper marking, transport, and disposal. You can get more information here:

`www.epa.gov/osw/hazard/wastetypes/universal/batteries.htm`

You can find a list of commercial-scale battery recyclers in the U.S. at `www.ehso.com/battery.php`.

Powering gadgets off-grid

Perhaps the ultimate green gadget doesn't depend on utility power at all. Solar-powered calculators were among the first. Now you can get solar-powered cell-phone chargers from companies like Solio (`www.solio.com`). Hand-cranked chargers are also on the market:

- ✔ The **Sidewinder** emergency cell-phone charger, available from `Amazon.com` and other retailers, claims to provide six minutes of talk time for two minutes of cranking.
- ✔ **Freeplay Energy** (`www.freeplayenergy.com`) offers a hand-cranked charger with a 12-volt cigar-lighter outlet that can be used with any car adapter to charge mobile devices.

Given how little power each gadget consumes, you can argue that the energy a separate solar- or hand-powered charger saves may be less than the cost of manufacturing the charger. However alternate power sources have other benefits, such as educational value and disaster preparedness.

Computing Green on the Go

You don't need us to tell you that mobile computing is taking off; it's long since reached orbit (so to speak). Information workers are no longer chained to their desks. They can get work done anywhere — or at least anywhere with wireless coverage. These days you can add green benefits to the list of advantages and conveniences that mobile devices bring.

Advantages of laptops

Cyberspace is a significant and growing part of your life these days. Some find this deplorable, but it's all too true. You feel a little disconnected when you're too far from your keyboard and display. Having a laptop lets you stay connected when you're out of the office. Everyone wants a laptop.

Using a laptop as your primary machine is a big step beyond just owning a laptop. The current crop of laptops can do most of the things that clunky desktops can, including process graphics. Considering chucking your desktop into the recycle bin but afraid of the small laptop view? Keep a big display at your desk and plug it into your laptop when you're working there.

Switching to a laptop as your sole computer reduces your environmental footprint in several ways:

- ✔ **Laptops contain less material than desktops (that's why you can hold one on your lap).** That means less metal to mine and refine, less oil from the ground to make plastics, less fuel to transport them across the ocean, and less stuff to recycle when their useful life is over.

- ✔ **Laptops use less power.** To get the EPA Energy Star rating, computers must have a typical annual energy consumption below certain levels, depending on the machine's capability category. The EPA has four such categories for desktops and three for laptops.

  - *For desktops,* the maximum annual energy consumption ranges from 148 to 234 kilowatt-hours (kWh).

  - *For laptops,* the EPA maximums range from 40 to 88.5 kWh.

Of course, non-Energy Star machines are likely to consume even more power, but the ratio of consumption is likely to be similar between laptops and desktops. So using just a laptop yields substantial savings, both in energy cost and in carbon emissions.

Getting by with less

The EPA's allowed power consumption for laptops ranges from 40 to 88.5 kWh — which suggests more energy savings are possible if you buy a laptop whose power consumption's at the lower end of the range. Do you really need a 17-inch screen, quad processors, and a separate graphics processor chip to put that PowerPoint presentation together?

Buying a smaller, less-souped–up laptop saves money, cuts the weight you have to schlep to and from the airport, and often means longer battery life.

Netbooks versus laptops

Smaller computers are getting more powerful and capable. For example, Asus launched a new category of mobile devices in 2007 — the *netbook* — when it introduced the Eee PC, with a 7-inch screen, 2GB solid-state disk drive, wiring for Ethernet networking, smaller keyboard, and Linux operating system. Later models added more storage, bigger screens, and Wi-Fi networking. Okay, these little guys were relatively wimpy in comparison to standard laptops, but they were comparable to the high-end desktops of just a few years ago and proved ample for many tasks. Their light weight and low cost resulted in instant popularity; hundreds of thousands were sold in the first year. Other vendors, including HP and Dell, have introduced competitive machines — and Microsoft has extended the life of its Windows XP operating system (which it planned to stop selling entirely in favor of Vista) so netbook vendors could use Windows instead of Linux on these smaller machines.

Limited battery life is one problem with the current generation of netbooks. The battery compartment shrank along with the machine; netbook batteries are much smaller than those in standard laptops, and the reduced power consumption of netbooks hasn't made up the difference. Yet.

Smartphones catch up

Although netbooks represent a step down from laptops, smartphones are a step up from standard cell phones. Smartphones add functions, such as e-mail and Web access, to the traditional voice and text messaging capabilities of cell phones. Most let you type text on a QWERTY keyboard instead of using multi-key-press codes on a number pad. The Apple iPhone has raised the bar on smartphones, with a relatively large (3-inch diagonal) color screen, 3G wireless and Wi-Fi connectivity, touch input, a serious, Unix-based OS-X operating system, high-quality browser, and a wide array of applications you can download from an online App Store.

Although smartphones are still clunkier to use than a laptop or a netbook, they're always with you — and they have much longer battery lives.

Off-grid computing

In large parts of the developing world, utility electric power is unavailable; in some other regions, it's unaffordable and unreliable. Cell-phone connectivity has proven easier to establish in the Third World than either landline phone or wired Internet infrastructure. After all, you don't need to string wire all over the place to get started; you just build a few cell towers and add more as demand builds. As a result, people in poorer countries often have their first contact with computers and communication technology through cell phones. Even the limited capabilities of a smartphone exceed anything they've experienced before and open a wide range of information resources to them.

Another initiative is the One Laptop Per Child (OLPC) initiative (www. laptop.org) at MIT. Their first laptop, the XO-1, has many energy-saving features (though the hand crank on early prototypes never made it into the production units). Each XO-1 can serve as a Wi-Fi repeater, creating a grid network that can cover a village. Outside connectivity in remote areas can be provided by a single server — at the local school, say — with an Internet connection via satellite or the cell network.

Everyone wants the developing world to have the benefits of IT, but if development produces levels of resource use that people in the North America and Europe have taken for granted, the impact on the planet could be intolerable. Taking a lower-energy path to IT can contribute to solving this conundrum. Supporting the OLPC project by subsidizing the sending of XO-1s to Third World schools may not have as crisp a carbon bottom line as other offset projects (such as planting trees), but the eventual environmental and human impact may be greater.

Greening the Data Center with Gadgets

A variety of gadgets can help you directly in meeting your green goals. These range from alternate energy sources to inexpensive devices that let you measure where the energy is going and find ways to reduce waste.

On-site power generation

Generating your own power from renewable sources can make a small dent in your electricity consumption — and its upstream impacts. Solar panels can be mounted on the roof of the data center and adjacent office space.

Solar roof

Averaged over the year, the sun can be expected to deliver about 4 to 7 kilowatt-hours per day per square meter in the U.S., with the lower values in the rainy Northeast and Northwest, and the higher amounts in the sunny

Southwest. Present solar-cells convert about 15 percent of the sun energy they receive into electricity. That translates to about 2.4 to 4.2 watts per square foot. Future technologies may double that efficiency. However, typical data centers have a *power density* — in the range of 100 watts per square foot (about a kilowatt per square meter) — so solar can only deliver a small fraction of the power required to run a data center, even if the entire roof is covered with panels. Still, such an installation would make a contribution and having an independent power source could have other benefits in terms of disaster recovery.

Small wind turbines

Full-scale wind turbines for power generation are mounted on towers as high as a 40-story building, with blades almost as long. If you're interested in wind power on this scale, it might be simpler to locate your data center near a wind farm. Smaller turbines are available for home and business use from a number of companies, such as Southwest Windpower (www.windenergy. com). They can mount on existing lighting poles in your parking lot or a smaller, free-standing tower, but they generate much less power, in the 500- to 700-watt range for a location with an average wind speed of 12 miles per hour (5.4 meters per second). Expect power output to be highly variable.

Roof-mounted wind turbines — maybe not

The roof, particularly on a tall office building, seems an ideal place to mount a wind turbine. The location is already well above the ground, and the air flowing over the windward edge of a roof gets sped up. However, here are the problems with this approach:

✔ **The airflow over the roof generates *turbulence* (chaotic air movements).** Turbines prefer smooth airflow for maximum efficiency.

✔ **The turbine mount adds weight to the building and produces structural loads that increase sharply at high wind speed.** Operating turbines vibrate and turbulence adds additional dynamic loads, all of which are transmitted to the building structure, causing damage and producing noise inside the building.

✔ **Most existing buildings aren't designed to handle all these extra forces.** Reinforcing the building can be more expensive than just buying a free-standing tower for the turbine. And the added vibration won't do your racks of electronic equipment any good.

If you want to try wind power, a free-standing tower, perhaps in the parking lot, may be a better approach.

Passive solar

Passive solar refers to systems that use sunlight directly, without converting it into electricity. Keeping home window shades closed on warm sunny days and open on cold sunny days is a simple form of passive power. Because data centers are large net generators of heat, passive solar in this context mostly means keeping solar heat from *adding* to the heat loads produced by the data center equipment — in other words, look for ways to add shade. Here are various ways to do this:

- ✔ **Landscaping:** Trees and shrubs planted in the right places can cut solar loads and, of course, trees extract carbon dioxide from the atmosphere (a few trees won't extract too much however). Using native flowers and grasses instead of manicured lawns can cut maintenance costs and attendant environmental impacts.

- ✔ **Automatic window shades:** Motorized shades can reduce heat load in buildings with large windows.

- ✔ **Green roofs:** Adding a layer of dirt and grass cools the roof by adding insulation and evaporating moisture. We know of one building built into a hill whose owners allow sheep to graze on its green roof periodically to keep the grass trimmed.

- ✔ **Paints and colors:** Silver and white reflect some of the sunlight falling on them. Black and dark colors absorb most of it. Light-colored roofing material cuts heat loads.

Smart power strips

The Colman Cable Smart Strip has a control outlet where you plug in a device (such as your computer) that you turn on and off. The strip senses when this happens and turns six other outlets on and off automatically, in sync with the control device. If you plug accessories (such as displays and USB hubs) into the smart strip and they're off when your computer's off, you save standby power. The strip also has three outlets that are always on for devices that need to stay on, such as a router that others use.

Grabbing Greening Tools

Improving your data center's energy efficiency is easier when you have reliable measurements of what's happening there. A number of vendors will sell you complete suites of instrumentation that collect data from dozens — or hundreds — of sensors scattered throughout your facility. Other vendors (or the same ones) will sell you elaborate software packages for analyzing that vast flow of data so you can get a real-time picture of what's happening. You could tie that output to an expensive computational fluid-dynamics simulation of your entire data center and produce impressive multi-colored air flow maps that may or may not reflect the reality of what's going on in your data center.

All this gathering of energy intelligence can be quite expensive — possibly beyond the reach of smaller installations. Fortunately, relatively inexpensive tools are readily available that can help you find out the ground truth of IT operations with little work. You don't really need minute-by-minute multidimensional data to figure out what's happening in you computer room, and even if you use the high-priced tools, you'll want to check their predictions against the actual conditions in your data center.

Thermometers

You'll want to measure temperature at multiple locations in your data center to check on your cooling system performance. Temperature is temperature, whether measured by a pricey networked digital sensor or a cheap, wall-mounted unit. You can buy a supply of simple thermometers from a scientific supply house or your local hardware store. Check them for accuracy by putting them in the same place with one well-calibrated thermometer. Then disperse them in strategic locations throughout the room — particularly near the air intake for equipment at the top of racks — and record the reading a few times each day, along with the time and outside air temperature. A week or so of readings will give you an idea of the temperature distribution in the room. Keep the thermometers in the same place, adding more if needed, and use them to test the effects of any changes you make.

Another approach is to go around the data center ever so often with a digital thermometer, but be sure to make measurements at the same locations and allow time for the reading to settle in. Hotspots, when identified, often can be quickly eliminated by the addition of a perforated floor tile.

Inexpensive home weather stations that monitor temperature, humidity, and dew point, by using a remote outdoor wireless sensor, are available from Radio Shack. You can mount the outdoor sensor in the data center and hang the weather station's display in your office.

 Don't use mercury thermometers. They're the ones with silvery bulbs. Analog thermometers that are filled with a harmless material, such as alcohol, are safe. Analog thermometers will have a red- or blue-colored filling, not silver. Digital and dial thermometers also aren't a problem. Mercury thermometers should be disposed of as hazardous waste.

Humidity gauge

Keeping humidity within recommended ranges is important for reliable operation of data center equipment, but humidity control takes energy and costs money, so you don't want to control humidity more than necessary. Most computer room air conditioners (CRACs) have built in humidity gauges, but having a couple of independent *hygrometers* (the fancy name for humidity sensors) isn't a bad idea.

Humidity at the air intake of equipment at the bottom of racks is what matters most for the well being of your equipment, so try to measure there. After the air is heated by the electronics, the humidity drops dramatically. A humidity sensor mounted on a perimeter wall can easily lull you into a false sense of security.

Power meters

You may know the total power consumed by your data center from its electric bills, but you'll want to know how much of that total power is consumed by the electronic equipment that's storing and processing all that data. Measuring the power consumption of individual electronic boxes is easy with the Kill A Watt EZ electricity usage monitors from P3 International (www. p3international.com). These cost about $50 and plug into a standard outlet or a power strip, as shown in Figure 17-3. You plug the unit to be tested (up to 15 amps) into an outlet on the front of the Kill A Watt. An LED display shows you the power usage since the last reset. The Kill A Watt can also display instantaneous power, voltage, current, and power-factor levels. (*Power factor* measures how closely a load comes to an ideal resistor; see Chapter 4 for more info on this tricky concept.) P3 International also sells a model with a built-in power strip, so you can test several devices at once.

Although most data centers may have row upon row of equipment racks, they generally contain at least some different types of equipment with different power requirements. Get power readings from your Kill A Watt on one unit of each type, along with the different models of desktops and laptops your company buys, to give you enough data to make a good model of your power usage. (For blade servers, check a couple of units with different populations of blades.)

The Kill A Watt works only on 120-volt circuits. Many data centers power rack equipment at 230 volts, as this allows higher power with standard wiring.

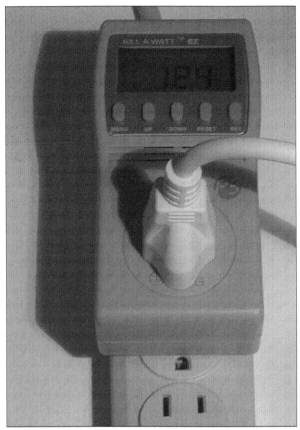

Figure 17-3:
A Kill A
Watt meter
measuring
power con-
sumption.

For 230-volt data centers, smart power-distribution units (PDUs) are available that measure power usage and include a network interface that lets you monitor power remotely. If money's no object, install these in all your racks; if cash is tight, you can buy one and move it from rack to rack over the course of a few weeks to get a good data set on power usage.

Data loggers

Keeping track of where energy goes requires a lot of measurements. Fortunately, *data loggers* will help you gather and coordinate all that data and download the data to your computer. For example, Onset (www.onsetcomp.com) sells Hobo data loggers that record temperature, relative humidity, and other parameters over time. Their inexpensive models, such as the one shown in Figure 17-4, cost under $80. The loggers save the data internally. You read them out into a PC over a USB cable. Onset also sells fancier models for monitoring power usage and other parameters, with options that can send the data collected over network connections.

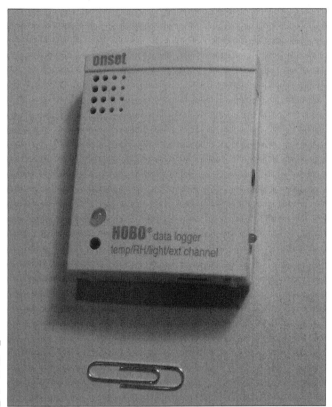

Figure 17-4:
A Hobo data
logger.

Infrared cameras

Knowing how the heat your computer generates is distributed can give you a better picture of how effective your cooling system is and help you eliminate hot spots, so you can make the system more efficient. One way to find those hot spots is to take and analyze many temperature measurements. A simpler way is to use an infrared camera, which produces pictures that directly show hot and cold areas. Infrared (IR) cameras aren't cheap; prices range from $5,000 to $25,000 and up, but they let you see surface temperatures directly.

Figure 17-5 shows an infrared camera in the $5,000 price class. IR cameras are available for rental, and if you're in a large organization, a lab somewhere might let you borrow one.

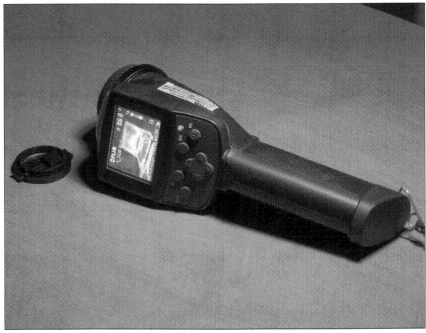

Figure 17-5:
An infrared
camera.

Photo courtesy of GreenStar Homes, LLC *www.GreenStarHomes.org*

Figure 17-6 shows an infrared scan of a laptop computer. Higher temperatures on the laptop show as a darker color (the original is color coded for temperature). The resolution is relatively low, 160 by 120 pixels, but you can easily see where the heat is coming from.

Figure 17-6:
An infrared
scan of a
laptop
computer.

IR image courtesy of GreenStar Homes, LLC
www.GreenStarHomes.org

Diffraction gratings

One simple way to save energy is to replace incandescent bulbs with more efficient units, such as compact fluorescent lights (CFLs). However, discovering what type of bulb is installed in a fixture can be a problem, particularly if the fixture is mounted in the ceiling or some other inaccessible location. An easy solution is to use a *diffraction grating,* which are sheets of plastic with numerous tiny lines molded into them — 13,500 to 25,400 lines per inch. The lines break light into colors, just like a prism. The sheets are transparent, but if you look at a light source, such as a lamp or a bulb, and then look to the side of the light, you see the light's spectrum.

So here's the trick: Different types of lamps give off different spectra of light. An incandescent lamp has a continuous spectrum with no lumps, just like a slice of a rainbow. A compact fluorescent shows up as several images of the lamp, one in each of the primary colors. Standard fluorescent fixtures and specialty lamps (such as sodium-vapor lamps) have distinctive patterns of bright spots. Looking through a diffraction grating, you can quickly scan an entire room for evil incandescents. Figure 17-7 shows a halogen desk lamp (left), a compact fluorescent bulb, and their spectra, as shown through a piece diffraction grating film. (Yes, you can take photos through the film as well — just hold the picture in front of you camera's lens.) The lower spectrum, typical of incandescent lamps, is continuous. The upper spectrum is characteristic of CFLs and shows discrete images of the lamp in different colors.

Figure 17-7:
A halogen desk lamp and a compact fluorescent light along with their spectra as shown through a diffraction grating film.

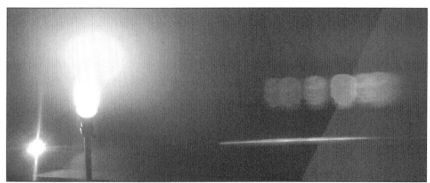

You can use a compact disc as a diffraction grating. The recorded tracks serve as the tiny lines, but you have to look at a reflection on the disc, which is awkward. The transparent diffraction grating film works much better and is really cheap. A pair of page-size sheets costs less than ten bucks at www. scientificsonline.com. Cut up one into credit-card–size pieces that you and your staff can keep in your wallets. The material is also sold as novelty *rainbow glasses.* (Your kid may have a set of those in a cereal box.) The glasses are cheap enough to give away to employees, perhaps as part of an environmental-awareness program, to use to check the lights in their houses. Of course, if you're insecure in your job, you may not want to be seen walking around the building wearing a pair of rainbow glasses. For the bold and the green, however, you can get them at www.rainbowsymphonystore.com and www.rainbowglasses.com.

Part V
Greening the Organization

The 5th Wave   By Rich Tennant

"I've never seen an office this green, Mr. Edmund.
As far as I can see, the paint's not flaking,
the exterior is pollinating."

In this part . . .

Going green is a process, not a destination. Green IT includes everything needed to make IT run, so we talk about how you can green your IT facility. Green IT also encompasses the entire lifecycle of all the IT you use. In this part, we explain what to do with IT equipment that you no longer want and ways IT can make your overall work-life greener.

Chapter 18

Greening the Facility

* *

* *

*E*lectronic equipment consumes lots of energy and creates many other environmental problems related to its manufacturing, materials, and disposal, but IT shops have other major opportunities for green improvements that don't involve stuff mounted in racks. To put things in perspective, take a look at how power for a typical IT facility is divided:

✔ Forty percent of the power consumed goes to servers, storage, and ancillary equipment (we talk about ways to green the data center in Part II).

✔ Another 40 percent goes to air conditioning the server room (we specifically address cooling in Chapter 10).

✔ Some 15 to 20 percent goes to providing conditioned power to the IT shop (UPS losses, PDU transformer losses) and to the other data center systems like lights and management systems.

In addition to lighting, we talk about other greenable elements you should tackle, including the heating and cooling of the facility as a whole and office recycling. By the way, these elements apply to the whole of your office environment — not just the data center — and your whole organization can be greener by applying these principles.

Lighting for Less

Office lighting usually burns all the time and, therefore, consumes considerable energy. In a typical office building (not a data center), *lighting is the largest single consumer of electricity.* In addition, all that energy gets converted to heat, which adds to the air conditioning load. You can take a number of simple steps that can reduce this energy use and often result in a more productive work environment.

Get to know your facilities person. Typically, IT and facilities report to different departments, making coordination difficult. A friendly visit to the head of facilities can work wonders. Ask what her biggest concerns are and find out where the electric meters are located. Talking to the janitorial and cleaning staff can also be a good investment, insuring that policies about turning lights out, appropriate recycling, and other green practices are in everyone's awareness.

Lowering lighting's energy consumption

In existing facilities, using more efficient lighting sources can make a significant dent in energy use. The following tips can help you ensure that lighting is as efficient as possible:

- **Replace incandescent bulbs with fluorescent ones.** Although incandescent bulbs are less common in office settings, those bulbs that are in use can be replaced with compact fluorescent units. A diffraction grating sheet or novelty rainbow glasses can be used to distinguish what types of bulbs are in use (see Chapter 17). Check your outside flood lights as these often use incandescent bulbs.

- **Upgrade older fluorescent bulbs.** For standard fluorescent ceiling fixtures, buy reduced power, low mercury bulbs. Older 40-watt T-12 bulbs can be replaced with 32-watt units, and some 30-watt bulbs are now on the market.

  A newer standard for fluorescent bulbs, *T-8,* can save significant energy. The T-8 bulbs are 1 inch in diameter as compared to the older T-12 bulbs, which measure $1^{1}/_{2}$ inches. The new bulbs fit in existing fixtures but require new ballasts. Never heard of a ballast before? Read on.

Upgrading ballasts

A *ballast* is a device used to maintain a constant level of current through a fluorescent or mercury light, protecting the light from changes in voltage, such as power spikes. Some ballasts may also provide the initial current needed to start a fluorescent lamp.

You don't need a ballast for an incandescent lamp. Incandescent lamps are simple to attach to the source of power:

✔ Connect the hot and neutral wires to the two contacts and *voilà,* you have light.

Or

✔ As seen by non-electricians, screw the light bulb into the socket where, hidden from view, the hot and neutral wires are put into contact with the power source and *voilà.*

Fluorescent lamps are more complex and while they need full power to start, after they're on, they must have some means to limit the current they draw, lest they burn out; hence the need for a ballast. Older fluorescent fixtures carry out these functions with a bulky, brick-like device — an *inductive ballast* — along with a small aluminum can — a *starter.* Electronic ballasts are available that replace these older units and offer a number of advantages. Not only do they consume less power, they can reduce the lamp's power consumption for a given amount of light output. They do this by operating at a higher frequency, usually 20–50 kilohertz, much like computer power supplies. (Both use similar switching technology.)

Reduced flicker is a side benefit of higher frequency. Regular fluorescent lamps go on and off at twice the power line frequency, 120 times a second in 60 Hz North America. A lot of people are bothered by this flicker — or by traditional fluorescent lighting without knowing about flicker — which can even cause seizures in sensitive individuals. So upgrading to electronic ballasts can make your work place better for flicker-sensitive people and save energy.

 Ballasts should be changed only by a licensed electrician, so check with your power company. Many will survey your existing lighting for free, and some will even subsidize a switch to more modern ballasts and higher-efficiency bulbs as part of their demand-reduction program.

Lighting the way out with LED exit signs

The lit exit signs mark the way out of the building in an emergency (in the U.K., they actually say *way out*). By law, they must be lit 24 hours a day, 7 days a week, 365 days a year. The oldest type of exit sign used incandescent bulbs and typically consumed 30–40 watts. Newer fluorescent designs take 14–22 watts. The latest signs use light emitting diodes (LEDs) and consume dramatically less power. As a result, the U.S. Congress passed a law requiring all exit signs manufactured on or after January 1, 2006, to use 5 watts or less per face.

Replacing exit signs with LED units saves money on your power bill and also reduces maintenance costs. LED lamps last longer than fluorescent lamps and much, much longer than incandescent lamps. LED retrofit kits are available for older signs, but it may be better to replace the older signs with newer ones. The low power draw of LEDs also makes it easy to include battery backup in each sign.

Exit signs are life-safety critical and only a licensed electrician should replace them.

Choosing green switches

Gadgets, devices, and switches appear throughout an office. Although you may not think about them very much, consider how you might incorporate them into your green strategy:

- ✔ **Timers:** Timers can insure that lights are out during off hours, but make sure there's an override for people working late and on weekends.

- ✔ **Motion detectors:** Many organizations have begun using motion detector switches in lavatories and other spaces that aren't occupied constantly. Using motion detectors to trigger lighting when needed as opposed to leaving lights on at night or always lighting conferences rooms and other areas with intermittent use can go a long way to reducing electricity consumption.

  Make sure the motion triggers the lights to stay on long enough. In particular, you don't want to lose people's favor for your initiative because they're regularly getting stuck in the dark in the bathroom.

- ✔ **Electronic plumbing and paper towel dispensers:** Encourage your facilities people to think twice about electronic plumbing and paper towel dispensers. Are they really saving water and cutting down on germs or are they trying to impress folks with their fancy fittings?

Letting the sun shine in

The most environmentally friendly lighting source is the sun, and it's often the most pleasant. The first step is to use what's already available. All too often blinds are closed on windows to prevent glare on computer displays. Sometimes all that's needed is a reorientation of workstations to allow the blinds to be opened. Strategically placed skylights can illuminate interior spaces and can have a positive effect on morale. Even fiber optic light-piping systems are available that bring sunlight to interior spaces.

Some areas of the globe have strong recommendations for the minimum amount of natural lighting that should be present in offices and classrooms. When considering new construction, talk to your architect about ways to maximize the use of indirect sunlight.

Less is more

The difference in the lighting you choose can have profound effects on the well-being and productivity of everyone in the workplace, can use energy unnecessarily, and can increase costs. Too much lighting can lead to the following problems:

✔ Irritating some individuals on a physiological level because it increases glare and eye fatigue.

✔ Unnecessary expense and energy use, which is gaining attention in the United States.

Too much lighting applies both to actually using more light than is necessary in a given environment and to lighting areas when they're unoccupied.

As you look at ways to reduce your lighting, consider the following:

✔ As we write this book, researchers are working to understand why people seem to need less natural light than artificial light to do the same tasks. See "Letting the sun shine in" earlier in this chapter for ways to improve your use of natural light.

✔ Full-spectrum bulbs can simulate natural light, so often less light is needed and people get some of the benefits of natural light in interior spaces without windows.

✔ An electrician can add switches that allow users to turn off some of the overhead lights.

✔ Desk lamps can provide stronger light where it's needed without flooding all the cubicles.

✔ Less lighting means less heat is produced, which cuts air conditioning costs.

Landscaping the Sustainable Way

Take a walk around the outside of your building on a sunny day. Look for places where plantings can reduce building heat loads due to direct sunlight. Plants will help the overall air quality, too. Here are some examples:

✔ If air conditioning units are mounted on pads at ground levels, shading them can improve efficiency as long as plantings don't interfere with air flow.

✔ *Deciduous* trees, the type that shed their leaves in the fall, can provide shade in the summer, while allowing the sun to heat the building in the winter.

Another green concern about greenery is whether it's suitable for the local climate. A manicured grass lawn in the desert requires large inputs of water and chemical fertilizers, which can pollute water sources. Selecting ecology-friendly plants that are native to your locality can reduce the need for extra amounts of water and fertilizer and save on gardening and other maintenance costs at the same time.

Improving the Indoor Environment

The world inside your building is its own environment, and what you do and bring inside can affect the quality of life and sometimes the health of people who work or visit there.

Setting the thermostat

You can get significant savings in heating and cooling costs by widening the office temperature range, say 68 degrees in the winter and 78 degrees in the summer. Under the new American Society of Heating, Refrigerating and Air-Conditioning Engineers (ASHRAE) recommendations (see Chapter 4), computers can take temperatures up to 81 degrees. Don't let the relative humidity get above 60 percent, lest you encourage corrosion.

Encourage workers to keep a sweater in their desks in the winter and encourage casual dress in the summer.

If you see employees wearing sweaters in the building during summer, you're probably wasting money keeping indoor temperature too low.

Supplementing heat with solar

When you have the opportunity to build from scratch or to make architectural changes in your current structures, determine what you can gain by incorporating solar designs. If you're starting from scratch, you can include passive solar-design criteria in choosing the site for construction. Passive solar buildings rely on the design of the building, not on technology, to harvest the benefits of the sun. Some fundamentals to consider for office facilities include

✔ Maximizing good exposure to the sun throughout the day

✔ Orienting the building to maximize solar collection

✔ Locating windows in accordance with optimal solar collection

✔ Shading appropriately to prevent overheating in summer

For data centers, the opposite advice is appropriate. Because data center equipment generally creates more heat than is needed to keep the building warm in winter, the buildings that house the equipment are best designed for minimal exposure to direct sunlight. Natural light admitted into the building should be indirect to minimize heat load.

For more information about building a green facility, check out www.buildinggreen.com. *Green Building & Remodeling For Dummies* by Eric Corey Freed (Wiley) offers a more in-depth look at building materials, systems, and sustainability practices.

Minding indoor air and water quality

The quality of the environment in which people work has an impact on the overall health and well-being of employees who, in turn, are ultimately responsible for the overall health and well-being of your organization. To this end, it's important to pay close attention to the quality of the air, lighting, temperature, and anything that adversely or positively affects your working environment.

When it comes to air quality, buildings need to supply adequate levels of ventilation and outside air. Make sure that the air intake for a building is actually taking air from the best possible place, avoiding loading areas, vehicle idling areas, parking areas, waste disposal, or exhaust areas that might contaminate the air.

The heating, ventilating, and air-conditioning systems (HVAC) must control humidity and prevent the moisture that enables the growth of mold and fungi in the system. HVAC filters must be changed regularly to ensure their effectiveness.

Indoor Environmental Quality (IEQ) looks not only at air quality (including airborne contaminants) but also at lighting, acoustics, water quality, and electromagnetic frequency levels. Here are additional aspects for you to consider:

- ✔ **Use a permanent air-quality monitoring system to make sure that the internal environment doesn't exceed acceptable levels of carbon dioxide (CO2) or carbon monoxide (CO).** Carbon monoxide is highly poisonous, and CO detectors are required in many localities. Although low levels of carbon dioxide are normal and harmless, high levels are a sign of inadequate fresh air intake and can indicate that other air pollutants are present at too high levels.

- ✔ **Ensure the quality of water by filtering or providing safe water.**

- ✔ **Use sound-absorbent materials and perhaps sound masking to dampen noise pollution in the workplace and provide a degree of privacy.**

- ✔ **Provide exhausting for copying areas and any area where chemicals, including cleaning chemicals, are used regularly.**

- ✔ **Use environmentally safe cleaning products.** For information and suggestions on alternative cleaners, visit www.womenandenvironment.org/campaignsandprograms/SafeCleaning or www.thegreen office.com.

- ✔ **Limit exposure to Electric and Magnetic Fields (EMF).** Electrical currents, transformers, microwaves, and radio waves are thought to have detrimental effects on health. Some people seem more sensitive to these effects than others, but building designers should keep moving electrical charge at a distance from employee work areas. For the World Health Organization's fact sheet, including guidelines, go to www.who.int/mediacentre/factsheets/fs322/en/index.html.

- ✔ **Look at the ASHRAE guidelines.** The American Society of Heating, Refrigerating and Air-Conditioning Engineers (ASHRAE) provides guidelines for HVAC systems, air quality testing, thermal conditions for human occupancy, indoor air quality and ventilation, building energy efficiency, and more. Check them out at www.ashrae.org.

- ✔ **Be aware of paints and building supplies that exude toxic substances into the air — known as *offgassing* or *outgassing*.** Choose paints and materials engineered to minimize this hazardous effect.

Recycling throughout the Office

Of course, no green IT program would be complete without office recycling. No, we don't mean putting new employees in former workers' cubicles. We're talking about diverting a large portion of discarded work material (and beverage consumption) from the trash stream to better uses. The simplest step is placing recycling containers alongside trash containers all around the office. This should be accompanied by efforts to educate workers on their proper use. Overzealous employees who insist on putting every scrap of plastic in the container bin, even if it's food soiled or un-coded (see the sidebar, "Know your plastics"), can be as much of a problem as those employees who just dump everything in the trash. Be clear about what is wanted and what isn't.

Although paper and containers are the most common items collected for recycling in offices, IT should consider setting up collection points or special times for discarded electronics. E-waste can be recycled effectively, but it's a source of pollution if it isn't. This is particularly true of older electronics, which more often contain hazardous substances.

Reducing and recycling water

Another way to reduce your environmental footprint is to make better use of water. H_2O is becoming a scarce resource in many places and capturing, producing, and purifying it consumes quite a bit of energy and other resources. Water bills are getting bigger each year. You can reduce water use by simple steps, such as helping facilities set up an intranet site to report faucets and toilets that don't shut off.

In some cases, waste water that's lightly polluted *(gray water)* can be used to water decorative plants. The gray water movement has many creative ways for doing this, but you must make sure local codes allow such re-use.

In the data center, you may be able to store supplies of fresh water for the cooling system, reusing it to the extent possible. This not only conserves resources but adds to security because in an emergency, such as a power failure, municipal water may stop running.

Buying green

Buying recycled supplies helps sustainability by creating markets for such products. Recycling doesn't have to be 100 percent. Even 10 or 20 percent recycled content helps. Paper products are obvious candidates but so are printer cartridges and even office furniture. Buying locally manufactured products and locally grown food offers another green-buying opportunity by reducing transportation costs and impacts. For instance in the United States, most produce travels at least 1,500 miles before it gets to a store where you can buy it. That's bad for a number of reasons — the cost of transportation, the amount of time it takes to get to you (what do they mean by *fresh?*), and the focus given to producing *durable* produce over *edible* produce. If you've ever watched one of those so-called tomatoes sit on a shelf without deteriorating for months on end, your desire to get your food from a local farmer will likely increase substantially. Using a network of local suppliers also aids security as local suppliers are more likely to be able to re-supply your facility in an emergency.

Know your plastics

Recycling symbols have been placed on the bottom of plastic containers in the U.S. since 1988. Not all recyclables are recycled equally, and your access to recycling may be restricted by what materials a given recycling company or town will take. Developed by the Society of the Plastics Industry (SPI), recycling symbols are commonly referred to as *SPI codes* or *resin identification codes.* Each triangular *chasing arrows* symbol has a number inside that identifies one of seven different plastic resin types:

1. Polyethylene Terephthalate (PET)
2. High Density Polyethylene (HDPE)
3. Vinyl/Polyvinyl Chloride (PVC)
4. Low Density Polyethylene (LDPE)
5. Polypropylene (PP)
6. Polystyrene (PS)
7. Other

You may also see a triangle symbol with ABS — Acrylonitrile Butadiene Styrene — inside, which is often used in electronics enclosures.

The most valuable types are clear PET and HDPE because they can be incorporated in a broader range of recycled products than colored plastics.

See www.earthodyssey.com/symbols. html for a more complete description of these materials.

Using Greener Facilities Management and Security Systems

Ironically, IT is simultaneously a big power consumer and a great enabler of greener systems or greener ways of approaching problems. Facilities management and security systems are a good case in point. Electronically controlling thermostats, humidity, and lighting can have huge dividends. Not relying on an individual to remember to turn the heat down or the lights off can go a long way toward consistent energy savings. Newer systems that allow temperature, humidity, and lighting to be monitored and adjusted remotely means someone doesn't need to be physically present to watch over and correct things, which is more cost-effective.

Despite the big-brother implications of having cameras everywhere, much surveillance activity is being performed by electronic equipment that really can be everywhere at once and isn't reliant on a guard walking around or driving around hoping to catch goings-on in the act. Likewise, recorded surveillance has the added benefit of going back and seeing what happened after the fact. Although surveillance technologies aren't innately green, reducing the transportation, lighting, and heating necessary to accommodate surveillance personnel is.

For help with more ideas about how to create and manage a green facility, check out www.facilitiesnet.com for ideas about lighting, HVAC, water, building automation, security systems, and more. Also see www.thegreenworkplace.com for a blog about green facilities management and everything having to do with a green working environment.

Chapter 19

e-Waste Not, e-Want Not

*F*ew things are more universal in the IT industry than the constant replacement of hardware by new machines, each cooler in concept and hotter in performance (and often in thermal dissipation) than the last.

Along with new technology's coolness factor comes a serious problem — what to do with the stuff you don't need anymore. Here's what you mustn't do — just throw them away. Computers are full of hazardous material that, if disposed of improperly, creates serious health problems. This chapter offers some better alternatives and talks about what you can do to live a green IT lifecycle.

The good news is that no organization is too small to do the right thing. We help you figure out some of the ways that might be right for you. Developing a better approach to this cycle of obsolescence can yield one of the biggest and most lasting impacts you can have in reducing your organization's environmental footprint.

Your organization probably has a range of equipment, from stuff that just arrived on your loading dock, to a Windows 95 machine in a closet that no one uses. An ideal asset retirement plan addresses the entire equipment lifecycle from purchasing to trash pickup.

Buying Wisely

Take some steps now to ensure a cleaner tech death a few years from now.

Take-back (recycling) programs are easier to find when your machines are only two or three years old. At five years old, they're fossils. Yet, if you *can* get useful life out of your computers, use them. The mere manufacture of new equipment is a carbon-producing process.

A *take-back program* means a manufacturer or seller accepts old equipment for recycling. Better programs supply you with the shipping materials and pay shipment costs. Others expect you to pack and ship, and some are restricted to consumer purchases only.

Consider this before you purchase:

- ✔ **Give preference to manufacturers that have a take-back program for their equipment.** This can be either an absolute requirement or a weighting factor that reflects the full cost of eventual disposal — use it to adjust upward bids by vendors who lack a take-back program. Some sellers are beginning to offer take-back as an option you can buy at the time of purchase.

- ✔ **Buy equipment made from materials that are easier to recycle.** For pointers, read the rest of this section.

- ✔ **Label machines that are covered by a take-back program.** Include the necessary contact information so they're less likely to end up in a dumpster.

- ✔ **Look for equipment you can upgrade without replacing the entire mechanical assembly.** Replacing a server blade has a smaller impact than replacing a 1U pizza-box server.

- ✔ **Use disk encryption from the beginning.** Not only is this sound security practice, but it also facilitates the eventual disposal of the computer with its hard drive, making the computer more attractive for reuse.

Some materials recycle more easily than others. A key indicator is the price of that material on the scrap market. Prices for scrap material fluctuate widely with changes in economic conditions, but here are some typical prices as of this writing, when markets are very low. All these materials are commodities, and as supply and demand fluctuate, so does their worth. Prices are higher for truck-load quantities. Visit scrapindex.com for current prices.

- ✔ **Aluminum:** Aluminum is one of the easiest materials to recycle. It doesn't corrode and can simply be melted down to produce new products. Scrap aluminum sells for around 20 cents a pound.

- ✔ **Copper wiring:** Copper is also an easy material to recycle, with scrap selling for over $1 a pound. However, computer wiring is covered with plastic insulation and removing the wire is labor intensive.

- ✔ **Steel:** The steel industry is heavily dependent on recycling. Much of the steel consumed in the U.S. comes from scrap metal. Scrap steel is traded in much larger quantities and sells for $50 to $200 per ton.

- ✔ **PC boards:** Electronic circuit boards are difficult to recycle. The precious metals can be removed (particularly the gold that is used to plate connector contacts), but the processes tend to be less than environmentally friendly.

- ✔ **Paper:** Scrap paper is widely recycled. Prices range from $10 to $300 per ton. Prices are higher when the paper is sorted by grade; office paper, newsprint, corrugated cardboard, and so on. Mixed paper commands the lowest price.

- ✔ **Plastic:** Although all polymer plastics consist of long chains of molecular subunits strung together, those chains go together differently depending on the type of plastic. Some plastics can be melted down more easily than others, but all must be segregated by type to produce any useful result. Consumer products made from plastic, particularly containers, are marked with a triangle symbol containing a number that indicates the type of plastic used. Plastics used in computer equipment aren't always so marked. Chapter 17 takes a closer look at office recycling to help you look for certain types.

Knowing What You've Got

Although setting up an equipment-recycling policy is a good first step, your plan should have measurable targets to be most effective. That means not only trying to do the right thing with retired equipment, but knowing what you have and tracking what happens to it.

All too often, obsolete equipment is stuffed into a closet somewhere on the theory it may be needed again. When the inevitable move, reorganization, or downsizing takes place, that storage space is needed immediately. No one claims responsibility for the old machines, and they're simply tossed in a dumpster.

An electronic asset-tracking system allows decisions to be made about old equipment before the cleanout crew arrives. A small to medium-size organization can get a pretty good inventory just by sending somebody walking around with a clipboard or (better) an inventory-tag scanner. But a one-time inventory has only limited value. Without a system for tracking the equipment over its life, material will make its way to the dumpster. Larger organizations likely already have a capital-asset management system in place. Adding a disposal component can make the process automatic.

An alternate approach is to add a disposal fee to internal budget accounting for new equipment, and then offer a bounty when equipment is returned to the retirement program. The bounty might be paid to an office-morale fund or donated to a charity of the employees' choosing.

Extending Lifecycles

The best form of recycling is reuse. IT equipment typically has a three-to-five-year working life. Keeping equipment in service for even a year longer reduces — by as much as 33 percent — the environmental cost of manufacturing, transporting, and disposing of new hardware.

Reassigning old equipment to new tasks

Perhaps the simplest way to extend the life of IT equipment is to find new uses for it within the organization.

- ✔ Older servers can be kept as standby units for use during periods of high demand, such as the holiday season or new product introductions.
- ✔ Older desktop equipment can be handed down to users who don't need blazing-fast machines.

A switch to desktop virtualization can greatly extend the service life of older computers as can the installation of Linux, which performs quite well on older PCs. See Chapter 15 for details.

In larger organizations, it might be easier for users to buy new equipment than to find suitable older stuff that has been made surplus by another department. An equipment-exchange site on the company's intranet can save a lot of money by helping donors and receivers find each other. Find a way to give credit to employees who make such matches.

For some more creative ways of reusing old equipment, see Chapter 22.

Donating machines to worthy causes

Offering equipment donations to a nonprofit group — school, library, job-training program, or other charity — that can use your old computers provides another way to extend their life.

But this isn't as easy as it sounds. Many groups that could potentially use previously owned computers have been approached before by someone who was just after a tax write-off and left a pile of unusable junk on the doorstep.

If your machine is nearly dead, not working, or otherwise a disaster, a nonprofit doesn't need that problem either. Restore it to operating condition, recycle the beast, or dispose of it properly.

Here are some things to consider in setting up a donation program:

- ✔ **Nonprofits only want reasonably recent machines in good working order.** That means machines must boot up with a current (and *licensed*) operating system *installed.*

- ✔ **Windows XP or Mac OS-X Tiger or later are probably okay.** Some groups may accept donations that use a Linux desktop operating system variant, such as Ubuntu, but call them first to verify.

- ✔ **Machines with functioning hard drives — minus the previous owner's data — are much preferred.** (See the section on sanitizing your hard drive later in this chapter.)

You may find a group that accepts computers that lack a hard drive but have a live-CD/DVD-based operating system (such as Knoppix) — but you'd better bring the organization a sample machine so they can try it. A group is unlikely to understand the benefits and limitations of such a system without seeing one in action. An agreement to accept diskless systems, negotiated over the phone, may unravel after the equipment is delivered.

Make sure the group that receives your donations understands proper ways to dispose of the equipment after it's no longer needed — and agrees to responsible disposal. If the computer is eligible for a take-back program (see "Taking advantage of take-backs," later in this chapter), either from the original manufacturer or from your company, put a label to the machine with the necessary details; otherwise the equipment may end up in the landfill or shipped to the Third World by an unscrupulous recycler. This step is especially important if the charitable group plans to redistribute the machines to needy individuals.

The U.S. Environmental Protection Agency has a list of organizations that accept used computer equipment: epa.gov/osw/conserve/materials/ecycling/donate.htm.

Reselling systems for profit

There's a market for used computer equipment, but it isn't terribly attractive for sellers. Bargains abound. Used equipment dealers seem to turn over often. Finding a nearby reputable dealer can take some leg work. Be sure to ask how the equipment they can't sell is disposed of.

Consider these options:

- ✔ **eBay:** eBay has an entire category devoted to Computers & Networking, with subcategories for the following:

    - Desktop PCs

    - Laptops and notebooks

    - Apple computers and components

    - Drive and storage

    - Monitors and projectors

    - Networking and communications

    - Servers — both branded and *whitebox* (built from parts)

    Several additional subcategories exist for accessories and software, plus a subcategory for wholesale lots, broken down into sub-subcategories matching the list you see here. Finally, there's a category for vintage equipment in case you have some real old clunkers around. PDP-11s come up for sale quite often.

    You may want to seek some policy guidance from your management before listing your company's name as an eBay seller. Some firms may shun the publicity, and there are tricky questions on whether you have warrantee obligations and how to handle them. eBay has a culture of its own, so start with small sales to gain some experience if you haven't used it before. For more information about eBay, get a copy of *eBay For Dummies*, by Marsha Collier.

- ✔ **Craigslist.org:** Listings are free, and there's an emphasis on local cash sales, eliminating the need for packing and shipping. Craigslist might be ideal for smaller firms and field offices of larger firms. Again, you might want to get some policy guidance before listing your company on Craigslist.

- ✔ **Local flea markets, especially those that specialize in electronics:** You may be able to recruit volunteers from within your organization to staff a flea market table if you agree to donate the proceeds to the employee morale fund or a charity.

Recycling Safely and Legally

All good things must come to an end and that includes the useful life of electronic equipment. What was once a miracle of technology becomes a nasty trash disposal problem.

Trash can take three routes:

- ✔ **The worst solution is to transfer the equipment to a recycler who ships the stuff to a third-world country,** where cheap labor, often children, exposes themselves to hazardous materials to extract valuable material and components, and dumps what's left over in an empty field or waterway.

- ✔ **The bad route is to the local landfill.** At least U.S. and European authorities supervise active landfills. Still, old computer equipment takes up landfill space and dangerous substances, such as lead and mercury can leach out.

- ✔ **The right way is through a service that recycles as much of the materials as possible.** Although much of what's recovered in the recycling process has value and can be sold, the money earned by selling the recycled material isn't usually enough to cover the costs of extracting it in the first place. That means someone has to subsidize this recycling effort.

The U.S. Environmental Protection agency says that 66 million PCs, 42 million monitors, and 25 million hard-copy computer peripherals (including printers, scanners, and fax machines) were in storage as of 2007. The EPA estimates that only 18 percent of these will be recycled, with the rest disposed of in landfills. Not all electronics shipments for offshore recycling are irresponsible. For example, the EPA estimates that 60 percent of computer monitors shipped overseas are rebuilt to serve as functioning monitors for local markets. However, the EPA doesn't discuss what happens to the other 40 percent.

Taking advantage of take-backs

Many major IT equipment manufacturers offer to take back their products when they reach the end of their useful life. These *take-back* programs aren't to be confused with *trade-in* programs, where the old equipment is accepted as part of a new purchase from the vendor. A true take-back program is valid even if you don't continue to buy from the original manufacturer.

The take-back programs of most of major manufacturers are backed by a well-thought-out recycling and disposal protocol. You can usually find details on the manufacturer's Web site. The availability of a proper take-back-and-recycle program is one of the elements required under certification programs such as the Electronic Product Environmental Assessment Tool (EPEAT) developed by the Green Electronics Council. (For more about products that meet EPEAT standards, see Chapter 4.) Be sure the manufacturer that takes back your equipment isn't dumping it in other countries — check to see if they comply with the Basel Action Network's requirements. You, the buyer, can greatly impact what manufacturers do. Insist on *total transparency* — the ability to see what the manufacturer does during the whole disposal process.

Finding a green recycler

Although manufacturer take-back programs are an ideal solution to e-waste, in all likelihood you have some equipment that isn't covered by such a program. Some of the hardware in your closet may be from manufacturers that don't offer take-backs; others may be from firms that failed.

The key again is to find and vet a reliable firm that will recycle and dispose of the equipment properly, without shipping it overseas. Figure 19-1 offers a bird's-eye view of what you have to gain.

Both recycling and reusing electronic components contribute greatly to more sustainable computing. A responsible asset-disposal company can give you a detailed accounting of what happens to your assets. Take a look at a report from Redemtech (www.redemtech.com or, for that matter, at Figure 19-2) to get a sense of the junk and gunk that have to be managed.

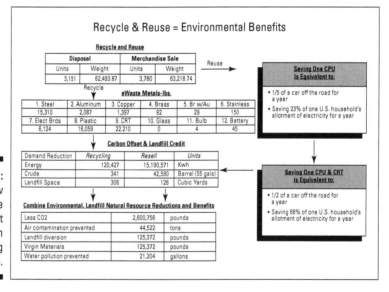

Figure 19-1: An overview of the benefits that come from recycling and reuse.

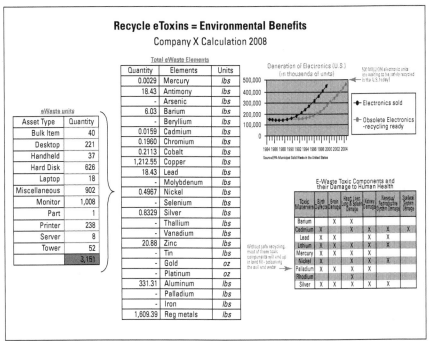

Figure 19-2:
Beware of
e-toxins.

Devices have e-waste-soluble elements. Redemtech tracks the scrap metal and total e-waste toxins that pose proven health risks. When e-waste reacts with air or moisture, it becomes hazardous to the health of human beings and other Earthlings. Figure 19-3 shows how proper handling can reduce the risk.

Many electronics vendors are doing their best to create take-back programs and asset recovery systems. The IBM corporation started some 20 years ago and now processes some 40,000 machines a week around the globe. In 2006, it processed more than 108 million pounds of end-of-life products. They don't limit themselves to IBM equipment and there's no minimum number of assets you need to collect before they'll help you.

Here are several good starting points for recycling old IT tech:

- ✔ The EPA Web site lists recycling firms, along with state and local e-waste disposal efforts: `epa.gov/osw/conserve/materials/ecycling/donate.htm`.

- ✔ Another useful site for disposal is `computerhope.com/disposal.htm`.

- ✔ The U.S. government has a checklist for selecting an electronics recycler at `federalelectronicschallenge.net/resources/docs/select.pdf`.

TTLC	Elements		STLC
0.0029	Mercury	lbs	-
18.43	Antimony	lbs	0.0258
-	Arsenic	lbs	-
6.03	Barium	lbs	0.0067
-	Beryllium	lbs	
0.0159	Cadmium	lbs	-
0.1960	Chromium	lbs	-
0.2113	Cobalt	lbs	-
1,212.55	Copper	lbs	0.0216
18.43	Lead	lbs	0.0093
-	Molybdenum	lbs	
0.4967	Nickel	lbs	0.0036
-	Selenium	lbs	
0.8329	Silver	lbs	-
-	Thallium	lbs	-
-	Vanadium	lbs	-
20.88	Zinc	lbs	0.0133
-	Tin	lbs	
-	Gold	oz	
-	Platinum	oz	
331.31	Aluminum	lbs	
-	Palladium	lbs	
-	Iron	lbs	
1,609.39	Reg metals	lbs	0.0802

Ewaste Processors

Primary Lead Smelter

U.S. Wire Choppers

U.S. Steel Mills

U.S. Aluminum Mill

Precious Metal Refiners

Plastic Processors

Pre-Consumers Products for:

Steel

Copper/Brass

Aircraft

Automotive

TOXICITY CHARACTERISTIC CONSTITUENTS AND REGULATORY LEVELS

Waste Code Conatinments Concentration

Regulated Toxins	Fed Haz Waste Levels	Circuit Card
	ppm	ppm
D005 Barium	100.00	17.7
D006 Cadmium	1.00	21.2
D007 Chromium	5.00	28
D008 Lead	5.00	31,900
D011 Silver	5.00	202

Figure 19-3: Proper handling results in appropriate reuse.

The Basel Action Network (`ban.org`) runs an e-Stewards certification program for recyclers of electronic waste. The program forbids accredited firms from doing the following:

- Dumping toxic e-waste in developing countries, local landfills, and incinerators
- Using prison labor to process e-waste
- Releasing (without authorization) private data contained in discarded computers

Making a difference one person at a time

Here's a real-world example of the quest for a greener IT — the story of Bob and Jim. Bob is Bob Houghton of Redemtech, an asset-disposal company; Jim is Jim Regan, a former employee of a large health-maintenance organization. The year is 1999, and Jim is the controller for the HMO's Y2K initiative.

"We were a big organization," says Jim. "Some 9 million members, 38 huge hospitals, umpteen hundred clinics, and our excess IT equipment was piling up. It was overflowing everywhere. 'What are you going to do with all this equipment,' I asked. Since he asked, he was told to figure it out. And Jim began his research. He had a lot of requirements:

- ✔ His company had a whole range of devices to dispose of — servers, mainframes, storage systems, routers, switches, laptops — and they wanted one vendor to take care of everything . . . *responsibly.*

- ✔ The HMO is a nationwide organization and wanted a vendor that would help them in the various different states and do everything right.

- ✔ Many devices held patient health information; proper disposal meant ensuring complete erasures.

- ✔ As an organization, the HMO already had a culture of handling things properly. They had extensive experience with disposing of medical waste and were very sensitive to regulations.

Jim got help from the Silicon Valley Toxics Coalition (etoxics.org), and you can read more about this organization in Chapter 21. He made his decision to find a vendor who would work hard to meet their core principles:

- ✔ No exporting of e-waste to another country — no exploitation of other countries with less stringent regulations.

- ✔ No use of landfill for disposal — coming from the healthcare industry, they were well aware of the dangers of dumping toxic substances into a landfill where the substances can leach into the water supply.

Jim says now that he didn't realize at the time that what he was asking for wasn't common practice. That's because common practice then wasn't exactly green: Disposal companies put e-waste on a slow boat to nations that couldn't protect themselves. When Bob agreed to take the business, he didn't know quite what he was signing up for. To meet Jim's requirements and go on to establish strict guidelines for Redemtech took time and investment. These, days, however, Redemtech makes some important guarantees:

- ✔ They don't export e-waste.
- ✔ They don't use a landfill.
- ✔ They don't incinerate.
- ✔ They don't use prison labor.

Jim says that doing things the right way has proven cost effective as well. Because they chose a vendor that takes their problems seriously, they say the added benefit of thorough asset reporting made the finance and accounting departments happy. At $20 a square foot, every bit of space they freed up saved money. Today they dispose appropriately of thousands of assets a month.

Protecting people who do the recycling

Our friend, Sarah Kuhn, PhD, who teaches a course in e-waste at the University of Massachusetts in Lowell, Ma., points out that in addition to the problems of contaminating the land when electronics are exported or when they're land-filled in the U.S., there's also the serious issue of worker protection. U.S. worker protection laws aren't always enforced and may not be up to date with the latest hazards embedded in the latest technologies. Historically, recycling has been done with prison labor, endangering the health of prisoners. Abroad, people who melt or disassemble old electronics in primitive ways are directly poisoned in the process.

 Beyond ethical IT asset disposal, the organization makes efforts to recycle and reuse everything wherever possible. When they move data centers or remodel buildings, they find ways to reuse floor tiles and recycle cement. All this is a big deal because, believe it or not, creating cement produces an inordinate amount of carbon.

Disposing Safely and Legally

The only thing inconvenient about an ever-so-convenient lifestyle is what to do with all the stuff when it's no longer useable. Electronic equipment and the batteries that power it are a lot more difficult to get rid of (ethically) than they are to acquire. Here are some basics.

Batteries

The IT sector generates a constant stream of worn-out batteries: from tiny silver-oxide or lithium cells (used on computer motherboards for battery backup) to large lead-acid units used in uninterruptible power supplies. Lead-acid batteries and older nickel-cadmium batteries contain hazardous materials (lead and cadmium are only the obvious ones). Older, disposable cells contained small amounts of mercury, but the use of mercury has been phased out. Alkaline and lithium cells no longer contain those particular hazardous materials, but they must still be protected from accidental short circuits, particularly the batteries used in laptop computers.

 A number of businesses recycle batteries. For a list of these — along with other essential information, such as proper shipment procedures — see ehso.com/battery.php.

Employee equipment

Your organization is primarily responsible for the computers it buys and eventually disposes of. But if you're looking to increase your organization's environmental standing or to offset some of its unavoidable impacts, consider extending your recycling umbrella to computers and other electronic equipment owned by your employees.

Even if you don't think you can afford to accept employee e-waste, providing education and information about local recycling options can make a difference.

Data Security and Recycling

Sensitive information stored on computer hard drives and non-volatile memory presents a major obstacle to reuse and recycling IT equipment. A common solution is to remove the hard drive from each computer before it's allowed out of the building. This makes the computer much less usable and greatly increases the likelihood of it ending up in a landfill.

A better solution is to get your organization involved on two fronts:

✔ Develop a procedure for sanitizing hard drives. Those in charge of security (and your legal department) should find the procedure acceptable.

✔ Place protocols that ensure that the sanitizing is carried out on all machines transferred out of the organization.

Safely removing files from a computer isn't just a matter of deleting them. When an operating system, such as Microsoft Windows, deletes files, it only removes information from its file directory and makes the space on the hard drive available for reuse. It doesn't erase the data. Software utilities, such as Norton Unerase, can recover deleted files if they've just been deleted.

Disposing of business IT equipment without first removing sensitive data can have serious legal consequences. A partial list of U.S. laws that require steps to prevent the unauthorized disclosure of data from IT systems include

✔ Health Information Portability and Accountability Act (HIPAA)

✔ Identity Theft and Assumption Deterrence Act

✔ Children's Online Privacy Protection Act

✔ Fair and Accurate Credit Transactions Act of 2003 (FACTA)

✔ Personal Information Protection and Electronic Documents Act (PIPEDA)

 ✔ Payment Card Industry standards (PCI)

 ✔ Gramm-Leach-Bliley Act (GLBA)

 ✔ California Senate Bill 1386

 ✔ Sarbanes-Oxley Act (SBA)

 ✔ SEC Rule 17a

The European Union has even stricter requirements.

iPods, thumb drives

You'll find many statements on the Internet and in older publications that data on hard drives must be rewritten multiple times to prevent it from being accessed by advanced laboratory methods. This is usually based on a now-obsolete U.S. Department of Defense directive, DoD 5220. However, this document has been replaced for civilian use by a more current source, the National Institute of Standards and Technology (NIST) Special Publication 800-88, Guidelines for Media Sanitization, available online at csrc.nist.gov/publications/nistpubs/800-88/NISTSP800-88_rev1.pdf.

According to NIST, for ATA hard drives manufactured after 2001, typically those with 15 gigabytes or more of storage, a single overwrite is enough to purge all data so it can't be recovered even by an advanced laboratory.

If you're working with classified defense information, your friendly security officer will tell you what procedures to follow. Follow their advice; if it conflicts with what this book tells you, follow their advice, not ours.

 ✔ Post-2001 ATA drives have a built-in secure erase feature that overwrites all data using a command built into the drive's firmware. You need special software to execute this secure erase feature, as most operating systems don't support it. You can download a NIST-approved freeware utility called HDDerase for this purpose from the University of California San Diego's Center for Magnetic Recording Research at cmrr.ucsd.edu/hughes/SecureErase.html.

 ✔ HDDerase is much faster than conventional erase utilities, wiping a disk in a couple of hours; a conventional program takes a day or more. The CMRR site also has a good tutorial on disk-drive data sanitization at cmrr.ucsd.edu/people/Hughes/DataSanitizationTutorial.pdf.

Some drives lack a "secure delete" feature, such as SCSI drives and older units. In those cases, get a program that erases files by rewriting them with patterns of 1s and 0s.

Here are some examples of reliable erase programs:

- **Darik's Boot and Nuke:** This Linux-based program is free and distributed as a self-contained boot-disk image that you can load on a CD, diskette, or Flash drive. It can automatically wipe contents of any hard drive it can detect — including IDE, SCSI, and SATA hard drives, even if the computer is a Windows or Macintosh system. You can download it at `dban.sourceforge.net`. A commercially supported version, EBAN, is available at `www1.techwayservices.com/eban-data-destruction`.

- **SDelete:** Microsoft suggests using this free command-line program on Windows 95, 98, NT 4.0, and Win2K. You can see instructions and a download link at `microsoft.com/technet/sysinternals/utilities/SDelete.mspx`.

- **Mac OS X's built-in file-wiping utility:** When you drag files to the trash, you can choose Secure Empty Trash from the Finder menu. In addition, the OS X Disk Utility can erase all your free space, securely cleaning out any deleted files you did not securely erase.

- **The U.S. EPA list:** The EPA maintains a list of file-wiping programs, along with other computer recycling tips, at `epa.gov/epawaste/partnerships/plugin/pdf/pcthing-bus.pdfm`.

- **RCMP's list:** The Royal Canadian Mounted Police (RCMP) lists file-wiping programs at `rcmp-grc.gc.ca/tsb/pubs/it_sec/b2-001_e.pdf`.

These programs are also good for erasing thumb drives and camera memory modules.

Making diskless machines usable

If you can't get corporate acceptance for data-sanitization procedures that don't destroy the hard drive, there are still ways to keep those old computers usable.

- **Install new hard drives.** These can be older, lower-capacity models that you buy at a steep discount. If you're working with a nonprofit that wants used computers, the cost of the new drives might be subsidized as a part of your organization's community service effort.

- **If the computer has a working optical drive, run a live CD or DVD operating system, such as Knoppix (knoppix.org).** These CDs/DVDs come loaded with desktop software such as the free OpenOffice.org program, which performs the most common function of the Microsoft Office suite and can read and write to Office files. Users can keep files they create on USB thumb drives, or on other machines such as a central server.

Dealing with dead drives

You can't use software to erase a hard drive that has completely failed. But that doesn't mean the data on that drive is inaccessible. Data-recovery firms have a good success rate in extracting data from failed drives, and criminals potentially have access to their methods. Also, drive failures are often intermittent. A drive you discard as failed may fire up just fine in the hands of its next owner.

Many recycling firms confirm erasing your drive before recycling it, but most lack the resources to indemnify a large firm for the risk of wholesale data loss, which can run into tens of millions of dollars or more.

It's often worth making one last effort to resuscitate a failed drive to recover any data that wasn't backed up, and then to erase it. I've had good success dropping a hard drive onto a table from an inch or so as it starts up. Another method is to remove the drive's cover and give the disks a nudge to get them spinning.

Educate employees about the signs of impending drive failure, such as occasional failures or strange noises, and encourage them to contact tech support to get their machine fixed before their hard drive fails totally. One data recovery firm, DataCent, provides recordings of failing drive sounds at `datacent.com/hard_drive_sounds.php`.

Destroying disk drives

When a hard drive fails completely, or if your organization won't accept overwriting by itself as a secure method of erasure, you must sanitize the dead drive by other means.

The National Security Agency (NSA) recommends sanitization with an automatic *degausser,* a device that erases data in bulk using a very strong magnetic field:

1. **Remove the hard drive from the chassis or cabinet.**

2. **Remove any steel shielding materials or mounting brackets that may interfere with magnetic fields.**

3. **Place the hard drive in an NSA-evaluated degausser and erase.**

NSA provides a list of evaluated degaussers at `nsa.gov/ia/government/MDG/NSA_CSS-EPL-9-12.PDF`.

NSA highly recommends that the hard disk drive be physically damaged prior to release. UCSD's Center for Magnetic Recording research recommends bending the disks; however, this requires disassembling the disk drive. Others suggest drilling a hole through the drive at a place where the hole goes through the disks themselves. Show your boss this chapter when you put in that requisition for a drill press.

Again, some firms offer this service, but the risk of data loss may well justify taking initial steps in house.

Sanitizing laptops and other portable devices

Despite the convenience, portability, and (often) smaller carbon footprint of laptops and other digital gadgets, they do have their own disposal issues. This section gives you an appropriate heads-up.

Laptop security concerns

Laptops have two advantages over desktop computers when it comes to end of life. Laptops are smaller, which means less material to deal with; used units tend to be in greater demand. On the other hand, they're more subject to wear and tear as they're transported around; they tend to fail sooner, resulting in a shorter lifespan. When it's time to send a laptop to the great beyond, keep these issues in mind:

✔ **One concern with laptop reuse and recycling is the risk of compromising sensitive information stored on them.** To be safe, configure all laptop hard drives to use disk encryption from the beginning of their use; you never know what data might end up stored on those portable hard drives.

✔ **Information in random access memory (RAM) can be extracted if the laptop hasn't been completely powered down for several minutes.** This information can include the cryptographic key than can unlock the encrypted hard drive. As a result, remove the laptop's batteries for at least an hour before the laptop is turned over to an outside organization for reuse, recycling, or disposal. (Yes, you can and should put the batteries back in before you transfer the laptop.)

✔ **Inspect the laptop visually to make sure the disk-encryption password isn't recorded on it somewhere; look inside the battery compartment and under other removable covers.**

Disposing of all those other little gizmos

Other electronic devices, such as cell phones, fax machines, network routers, PDAs, and the like may contain sensitive data. For example, routers may contain network passwords; cell phones may have customer contact information. Many of these devices have a reset procedure that restores the device to its original state. You can usually get the necessary information from the device manufacturer. Memory devices, such as thumb drives, camera memory modules, and the like can be purged using the software we describe in the section, "Sanitizing laptops and other portable devices" earlier.

Compile reset information for the devices most widely used in your organization into your sanitization manual, so information is available to each user.

Chapter 20

Virtually There: Collaboration Technologies for a Greener World

*T*he Internet has changed our world in countless ways, not the least of which is how and where we work. This network of networks (and the applications now available on it) has freed both organizations and individuals from the ties of any specific work location. That freedom carries with it some profoundly green consequences, including not polluting by commuting and reducing the need for physical media. And so, we use this chapter to share the hows, the whys, and the greens of various collaboration, telecommuting, and telepresence systems and programs.

Virtually Yours

The *virtual world* came into vogue as the Internet became mainstream in people's lives (over the past 15 years or so). The implication of this term is: The world that's connected through the Internet is somehow a world apart, and anyone's presence in it is a *virtual* presence. You can be anyone, anywhere in cyberspace — virtually — without leaving the comfort of your home. (Remember the cartoon — captioned "On the Internet, no one knows you're a dog." — with a hound at the computer?)

But the somewhat derogatory connotation to a virtual existence is being replaced by a widespread acceptance of various Internet-related technologies that foster new kinds of relationships, new kinds of collaboration, new kinds of innovation, and new ways of doing business. In particular, these technologies carry with them the benefit of reducing travel — be it on an airplane to a business meeting or simply a daily commute to the office. All the technologies we discuss in this chapter have the real potential for reducing carbon while simultaneously expanding your world view, reducing overall business costs, and improving employee morale and productivity.

Collaborating for Fun and Profit

We use *collaboration* to cover all the ways that folks work together to create, understand, and accomplish much more than any individual can do alone. Teams inside organizations collaborate whether their teammates sit next to them or in another country. Organizations collaborate to define new standards and share best practices. Companies collaborate to leverage special skills, such as artistic design and translation, to buy supplies, or to sell and distribute products.

Thanks to the miracle of communications networks, the same kinds of tools that can help team members collaborate locally can also perform effectively across the globe. This section introduces some of the basic (and not so basic) technologies and techniques that enable business collaboration while reducing the related carbon footprint.

Ever-ready e-mail

You probably take it for granted, but e-mail was one of the first collaborative technologies to take root. Some of you might remember when not everybody had e-mail, but it's now the communication mechanism of choice and is mission-critical to most organizations everywhere. And when you think of the paper and postage saved by using e-mail instead of snail mail or the courier charges and physical media costs avoided by sending files electronically, you know that e-mail has a very green upside.

Here are common business communications done by e-mail that are harder, less efficient, and costlier to do other ways:

- Sending files and messages to more than one person at the same time
- Keeping complete records of the files and messages sent and received

✔ Sharing the information received with other people

✔ Carrying on conversations with people *asynchronously* — conversations that span time zones, days, weeks, and months and include as many that want to participate

If folks have access to the Internet, they have access to e-mail, which is a great place to start collaboration.

Most think of e-mail as basically free — it costs next to nothing to send, and sending something to 20 people is no costlier than sending it to one. However, we want to alert you to greener e-mail usage. Here are some things to consider sharing with the e-mail users in your company:

✔ **Don't print hard copies** of your e-mail messages unless you really, truly need to.

✔ **Delete e-mail** you don't need and aren't required to keep (by organizational policy or by law). E-mail you keep is archived, and e-mail archives take up constantly growing, digital storage space somewhere — typically, on a disk that, by design, consumes power.

Keeping less e-mail means that less storage is needed to back up your e-mail and, ultimately, less power is being consumed. Because the amount of information that businesses store can double every 18 to 24 months, do your best to get rid of what you don't need. Here are specific ideas to help you decide what you don't need:

  • *When replying to or forwarding e-mail, delete whatever is no longer necessary to the conversation.* Remember that most e-mail is being archived. The less you send, the less has to be stored, the less storage space is needed, and the less power is needed to support it.

  • *Clean out your often forgotten Sent folder.* Delete everything you're not required to keep or won't need.

  • *Offload old e-mail onto media that's not always on.* You may want to keep some messages *just in case,* but you don't need countless copies and you don't necessarily need them on your computer. Storing to a flash drive, CD, DVD, or other device that isn't always powered on makes a lot of sense.

✔ **Use secure/managed file transfer for attachments,** especially large attachments or attachments sent to more than one person. Here's why: Large attachments are problematic to e-mail — it wasn't designed to support them, and many e-mail gateways won't allow attachments larger than 10MB (some have an even smaller threshold).

Sending attachments to a large number of people translates to a large number of copies of the same attachment getting archived and increasing storage demand. Not everyone you send to necessarily wants or needs to see all your attachments, so basically you're doing the equivalent of making a lot of extra paper copies and handing them out whether folks want them or not. You know that extra paper copies are wasteful — it's equally true that extra electronic copies are wasteful, too. We talk more about the value of using file transfer in the next section.

Secure/managed file transfer

Transferring files directly from one computer to another without using the arcane routing system designed by the Department of Defense to ensure message delivery in case of attack — the routing system used by e-mail — is not a new functionality. What's new is that you can now find a whole lot of easy, cost-effective, even *free,* ways to transfer files. And you have a whole lot more reasons than ever to do so.

Here are some of the biggies:

- ✔ **Files are getting bigger.** The kinds of files used in everyday work are a lot bigger than they used to be and can prove problematic for e-mail. For example, audio files, video files, PowerPoint presentations, graphical design files, medical imaging files, check images used by banking — all these files are good candidates for file transfer.

- ✔ **File transfer can be a lot faster than e-mail.** The bigger the file, the more you should consider using a file transfer technology.

- ✔ **File transfer is a lot faster and cheaper than shipping physical media through the mail or courier services.** We know of lots of collaborative processes that save time and money this way, including

  - The distribution of feature length films — or the collaborative work involved in creating them — both of which used to rely on shipping reels of film from place to place.

  - The sharing of medical imaging electronically rather than creating and transporting x-rays.

  - The use of electronic images instead of paper checks allows banks to avoid handling and shipping the paper artifacts.

  - The distribution of software releases. We know of a company that used to regularly buy seats on overseas flights just to get its latest software release from its U.S. office to its European office and back.

- ✔ **File transfer involves only the folks who truly want or need the file.** Unlike e-mail, which arrives unsolicited with all its attachments, file transfer users choose what they want to receive.

The benefits of file transfer over e-mail attachments are many fold — and largely green. You can avoid creating all those unsolicited copies of files that get archived — thereby, saving oodles on storage. And even for those folks who choose to download a transferred file can store that file outside the e-mail archive and lessen the storage burden that way as well.

Even companies the size of Aberdeen Group — roughly 110 employees — can save a bunch by using their intranet for file transfer rather than e-mailing files to all employees. For daily reports, we now receive a short e-mail with a link to the posted report, and those who need to can download it whenever they want.

Web conferencing, WebEx, GoTo Meeting and Unyte

Classic collaboration tools leverage the Web to minimize the need for travel and to enrich what would otherwise be just an ordinary phone conversation. Organizations use a host of online conferencing platforms to guide their listeners through PowerPoint presentations, show product demonstrations, and use a virtual whiteboard to brainstorm ideas across the ether. All these tools can be very helpful and are critical in environments that have truly embraced remote employees' full inclusion and enablement. Collaborative experiences can be enriched by using Webcams that give the folks at the other end a glimpse of a real human.

Our caveat to the use of Web-meeting tools is that not all organizations are equally equipped to support these technologies; these tools have actual system requirements and use bandwidth. If you're going to make Web conferencing part of your green strategy and overall corporate culture, make sure you're ready to provide and support the necessary software and hardware, and have sufficient bandwidth to support these applications across the organization. If you expect your customers and business partners to use these tools, you need to determine if they have the resources necessary to support these technologies in their environments.

Unified communications

Unifying voice, video, and data transfer is sometimes called *unified communications* (UCC) and refers to moving all the methods of traditional communications to integrated digital communications that are managed together. For some businesses, this integration is a real competitive advantage; for others, it might not be so imperative. For example, a company that does a lot of video conferencing and voice communications might find that unifying communications saves loads of time and money by bringing the management of these separate systems to one "unified" view.

The potential of unified communications warrants an investigation into what you're spending in each category (voice, video, and data) and how you can best minimize your costs. If you're being charged for all your telephone usage on a per-call basis, we can tell you that you're likely paying too much. However, we'd never recommend that *all* your communications go over the same wire (what if that wire failed?).

Vidddeeeovvo ccccconnfffeerrrennnnnciiinnngg

We use *video conferencing* to encompass everything from the wide spectrum of Webcams focused on individuals to the fancy video conferencing equipment stationed in conference rooms. We do not include the idea of *telepresence* (which brings high-definition technology to bear, making it another horse of a different color) in the scope of this term.

Reviews about the effectiveness of video conferencing and the comfort level of video-conferencing users are mixed. Folks who go to work and find themselves under the electronic eye often feel a lot better when they know they can cover up the thing. Most people don't readily embrace even the thought (let alone the practice) of somebody watching them all the time. It's basically creepy. However, using cameras to bridge the lack of face-to-face contact certainly helps boost the feeling of connectedness.

If you're thinking about adding or enforcing video conferencing as part of your travel-reducing (greener) business practices, be sure to find out about potential shortcomings. Escalating from an individual camera to the conference room tends to exacerbate the limitations of video — too often the lag between picture and sound, as well as the jagged images, stand between the promise and the reality of video conferencing. For this reason, video conferencing hasn't seen the widespread adoption that was anticipated by many, and organizations often see usage fall off rather than gain acceptance over time.

Telepresence, on the other hand, can be nirvana. Stay tuned for "Coveting Telepresence," a section you find later in this chapter.

Green document management

Most teams that collaborate to create business documents — reports, presentations, budgets, and so on — understand that they need some sort of central repository for storing these documents as well as some system for managing versions. We want to point out that document management systems can obviate the need for paper storage while enabling team members from across the hall (or across the planet) to collaborate without undue cost or constraint.

And how do document management systems affect your plans for greening IT? You can save as many versions as you like electronically without printing and storing every one. The less you print, the less paper and ink and electricity you use.

Tools in the cloud

We touch on *cloud computing* (computing done in a remote, perhaps hosted environment — think of IT being done for you somewhere outside your physical environment) in various places in this book, and not every cloud is green just because it's a cloud. (See Chapter 7 for more on cloud computing.) However, availing yourself of the following *functionality in the cloud* can aid in your collaborative efforts and in your efforts to be green:

 ✔ Storage
 ✔ Document-processing
 ✔ Super-duper, high-end–processing

Processing may serve to keep your own costs and carbon footprint small by shifting the processing to the cloud provider. The cloud provider's footprint has the potential of lessening the overall carbon footprint produced by many organizations by consolidating hardware, employing virtualization, and using other greening strategies.

Twitterific

If instant messaging is an insufficient distraction for you, you can now connect to *Twitter,* an online service by which you get and send *tweets* (brief online messages). A social networking tool that's limited in scope (140 characters per tweet) allows users casual comment (and conversation) in kind of a micro log. Follow these steps:

 1. **Sign up for a Twitter account and invite your friends and colleagues to follow your messages at** www.twitter.com.

 2. **Send a tweet.**

    Any friend and colleague that's following you can read your tweet.

 3. **Your friends may or not tweet in response, so you may or may not have a tweet to read and respond to (or not).**

In a virtual working environment where colleagues may not physically lay eyes on each other for weeks or months at a time, Twitter can add a dimension of chatter that lets participants keep up with each other's doings without undue effort. If you have paranoid tendencies, Twitter may not be for you. As Twitter sends you messages telling you that so-and-so is now following you, you may regret Twittering impulses.

Auspicious avatars

In the first section of this chapter, "Virtually Yours," we talk about the virtual world of the Internet in which the opportunity for fiction and fantasy in an online presence may not fully reflect the reality of the physical world. Well, from the fiction comes a contribution to mainstream business that still may baffle many.

As part of this contribution, an *avatar* is a pictorial representation of a user. In virtual worlds, avatars represent game players and members of the virtual society, giving them form and "life." In *Second Life,* www.secondlife.com, the residents (some 16 million strong) create avatars of themselves, and a half-million residents are active within the virtual world in any given week.

As organizations embrace virtual real estate, many are turning to avatars as embodiments or incarnations of actual or concocted spokespeople. For example, the U.S. Army uses Sergeant Star as its recruiter on its site.

And beyond the fantasy, real-life organizations purchase space on *Second Life,* create avatars for their managers, and do all kinds training — as well as trading — in this virtual land.

So, from the point of view of reaching lots of people with no one needing to travel, *Second Life* certainly is green. However, considering the electricity powering *Second Life* servers, *Second Life* can't exactly be considered carbon-free. We mention this to illustrate that as organizations use all available technologies to embrace remote members and collaborators, new ways of interacting are emerging, and the lines between fantasy and reality seem to be blurring at the same time.

Getting on board your social network

As social networking in the virtual world takes root, you, too, can have greener networking events by meeting and connecting to new people through social networking sites, such as LinkedIn.com and Facebook.com. The demographic barriers between these sites seem to be eroding as *older* people start to leverage the collaborative and community aspects of Facebook (just don't befriend your own kids) and the professional silos start to erode on LinkedIn.

Transcendental Telecommuting

All that glitters is not telework. *Telecommuting,* or *teleworking,* or working remotely — also known as working from home — has shifted from the occasional perk in a liberal organization, to the way many individuals work at industry giants, such as IBM, Cisco, Sun Microsystems, and Nortel, and at mainstream organizations, such as the federal government. Other companies have tried telework and failed so miserably that working at home is *verboten* (that's German for, *no way*). What have organizations with successful telework programs figured out that others are slower to adopt? Frankly, a bunch of things.

Arriving at successful telework programs takes time, work, and investment on the part of the organizations that embrace this path. But the benefits, including very green ones, are widespread. Here are the reasons telework is popular among those in the know:

✔ Telework can reduce bundles of carbon emissions by allowing employees to work from home instead of commuting to work.

✔ When fully rolled out with a concrete plan, including optimizing the use of seldom-used office space, organizations reduce the amount of office space they need and cut facilities expenditures to boot.

✔ Employees value their remote work environment, enjoy more time with their families, and prove highly productive and loyal.

Discovering telework

Before diving off into telework for everyone, learn, plan, create policy, and educate everyone about the opportunities, responsibilities, and expectations around telework. The U.S. federal government has put together guidelines for federal agencies that you might find helpful. At www.telework.gov, you can find help for how to manage teleworkers and how to be a teleworker. You also find policies and procedures that may or may not be right for your organization, but at least give you a place to start.

Knowing the tricks of the trade

Organizations that go beyond sanctioning telecommuting to enthusiastically embracing it understand that in order for workers to be highly productive, they need appropriate tools. Remote workers also need to be actively engaged and feel part of the whole — not like folks relegated to the sidelines.

Instant same-time messaging messengers

AIM, Lotus Sametime, Yahoo! Messenger, — all those pesky little messages that pop up to create direct, instantaneous communication on your screen — seem to be the salvation of many and the bane of others. The pros, to a certain extent, come from a younger demographic and from organizations that have fully integrated *instant messaging (IM)* into their corporate culture. The cons often come from generations that didn't grow up juggling 16 simultaneous online conversations with their high school chums. Even so, instant messaging seems to be pervasive in organizations that are successfully implementing telework. (More about telework, or telecommuting, later in this chapter.)

Stay connected

It's important that remote employees be *full* employees in every sense of the word — that you enable their full participation. Create appropriate e-mail distribution lists so that everyone's kept in the loop and provide all the access to communications needed to be highly productive from a remote site.

Fully equip the remote employee

Make sure remote employees have all the productivity tools (hardware and software) they need to do their jobs and that these tools all work over their Internet connections. If your culture embraces instant messaging, Webcams, and other collaboration tools, ensure that all your remote users are fully trained in their use.

Make meetings count

If you call a meeting or participate in a meeting, make sure the meeting stays on track, is punctual, and succinct. As well as everyone's valuable time you're spending, you're likely racking up minutes on your conference call account or hogging bandwidth that might be better used elsewhere. The real risk, of course, is that you'll bore your listeners who will no doubt begin multitasking — you know, reading their e-mails, surfing the Web, and cleaning their houses.

We're big fans of John Cleese's training videos on how to run meetings. (Check out www.videomedia.net/catalogjohncleese.html.) And here's one big take away: Running effective meetings is a skill that can be learned. Every organization needs good meeting management, and with a highly distributed team, it's vital.

Make good use of office space

Larger organizations make hay from telecommuting by capitalizing on the diminishing demand for office space, which can translate into a huge decrease in operational costs. Effective teleworking programs help organizations avoid costly build-outs or new construction, and over time, prove to palpably reduce costs.

Because employees do occasionally come into the office — we hear "every couple weeks or so, for a day" — organizations do need space for folks to use on those days. And those spaces must enable the telecommuters to be highly productive when they're not in the meetings they came in to attend. People who are accustomed to working at home complain that coming into the office is very wasteful of their time — they often have a hard time making good use of commuting time, and they're much less effective in the office than they are at home.

These tools and practices seem to help:

✔ **Have phones that go where you go:** Being able to tell the phone wherever you happen to be that it is your phone — that is, your number will ring there — is a great help. Folks trying to reach you don't need to know where you are exactly and don't have to keep track of your schedule — your number is yours. They call it; you answer. Simple and effective. Current technologies go beyond simple call forwarding. Making the phone next to you your phone means that when you dial out, you're dialing from your phone, your credentials appear on the caller id regardless of whether you're in Tulsa or Taiwan.

✔ **Know where you can hang your hat:** Some organizations have assigned offices for remote workers but astutely share offices between at least two, the idea being that if each is only in the office every couple weeks, there won't be a lot of conflict over the space. Others have designated areas with plenty of open office space that's unassigned and available for anyone who needs a place to work on a given day. However you arrange the workspace for remote employees, make sure that it's ready to go with a working phone, electrical outlets, and Internet connectivity.

✔ **Optimize for greener practices:** Newer collaboration tools put more focus on using less energy and disk space. New Lotus Domino and Notes require less hardware and, in turn, use less energy. The software developers did a lot of work to make these products more efficient. They put a big focus on data compression, which reduces the amount of disk storage needed, the network traffic produced, the backup costs incurred, and the actual physical space (with its attendant facilities costs) needed for data storage.

Telecommuting stars

Take a look at (and a lesson from) some of the businesses who have made telecommuting a successful part of their corporate (and green) strategies.

Forty-two percent of IBMers work from home

Many of the IBMers we've met over the last several years work from home full-time. The 42 percent of the nearly 400,000 employees who don't regularly come into an office saves IBM $100,000,000 in real-estate costs every year. They go to real, live, physical (as opposed to virtual) conferences — which is how we can attest to their actual existence — but do their day-to-day work from home. In 2006, in the United States, IBM's work-at-home program, which leverages IBM's collaboration tools, conserved more than eight million gallons of fuel and avoided more than 68,000 tons of CO_2 emissions. By using collaboration, last year IBM was able to save $97 million in travel costs. In addition to the full-time, work-at-home program, IBM has a mobile employee program that enables employees to work from home a designated number of days each week. IBM claims another $16.5 million in cost savings from using instant messaging instead of the phone. And using voice communications over the Internet (technically known as Voice over Internet Protocol, or VOIP) can dramatically reduce phone usage charges as well.

Cisco

A great many Cisco employees also work from home, leveraging Web conferencing, virtualized phones, office sharing, and a corporate culture that makes green a high priority. Visible throughout the Boxborough facility we visited are recycling bins for paper, plastics, aluminum, discarded electronics, and batteries — a responsible way for disposing of everything. Posted on a bulletin board was a notice of a community event that allowed folks to bring in their electronics from home for responsible disposal. This convenience is no small thing when folks are faced with the cost and hassle of disposing of electronics responsibly.

Cisco employees are adept at leveraging a spectrum of Web-conferencing and telepresence tools, and have other collaborative and supportive tools at their disposal, including phones that go where they go. (See the section, "Making good use of office space" for details on such phones.)

Sun Microsystems

Sun Microsystems is another winner in the gaining-by-teleworking front. If you need help stating your case, borrow some ideas from their "Top 10 Myths about Mobile Work" at www.sun.com/aboutsun/openwork/top_10_myths.pdf.

Coveting Telepresence

We've had enormous help in writing this book, but we'll all tell you that one of the high points in our research was a trip to the Cisco offices in Boxborough, Massachusetts. Our host Mark Leary introduced us to Lisbet Sherlock in the U.K. via *TelePresence*. Now, some of us had not such happy memories of early video conferencing, some had experienced the joys of a Webcam, but none of us was prepared for what we experienced that day.

In a room with high-definition TV screens, at the push of a button, we met a crystal clear, life-size Lisbet. No video distortion, no time lag. We had a terrific meeting, feeling we had genuinely met Lisbet — not just talked with her. On her end, she had a smaller system, so she couldn't see us all at the same time, but while we spoke, the camera followed our voices. The meeting had been scheduled through their calendaring program, just they way they'd book a conference room.

We were, in fact, truly taken by this technology — so much so that we herald its widespread adoption. How many companies that now spend thousands to travel for face-to-face meetings when offered an alternative that doesn't seem like a compromise in quality won't say yes? For those who can't yet justify a full system, we look forward to local telepresence rooms available by the hour springing up much the way Internet cafés have — by demand.

Cisco has eliminated a huge amount of business travel through the use of telepresence and other collaborative technologies; consider these statistics:

- ✔ Cisco employees hold about 1,200 meetings using telepresence every week.

- ✔ In just two years, Cisco deployed 284 systems with a utilization of about 50 percent and climbing. (Compare that with video conferencing, which started out with lower utilization figures that fell when it failed to meet expectations.)

- ✔ At least 25 percent of the telepresence meetings saved a trip that would've had to have been made otherwise, saving millions of cubic meters of carbon emissions and more than $68 million in travel costs.

Mark says he used to travel monthly to San Jose, California for a few days, but because of telepresence, he hasn't needed to make that trip in more than a year. Simple arithmetic says that saving 12 trips for one individual alone will scale to dramatic savings for the organization and a lot less disruption both on the work and home fronts.

Beyond saving the wear, tear, time, expense, and carbon of business travel, Cisco says their telepresence helps them speed time to market. They use it for virtual meetings being held around the globe and even boast of an in-person speaker (CEO John Chambers) sharing the stage in Bangalore, India with a hologram of another speaker (Marthin DeBeer) from a remote location in California. (Check it out for yourself at www.youtube.com/watch?v=rcfNC_x0VvE. Or watch the King of Saudi Arabia get a telepresence demo at www.youtube.com/watch?v=FI2kqt3KNxA and practice your Arabic at the same time.

Green distance learning

Nowadays, you can easily continue your education or beef up on what you once knew with online distance learning. Doing so saves the costs of driving to class (for you) and the costs of lighting, heating, cooling, and maintaining classroom space for the educational institution. Our hope is that in-person teaching isn't replaced entirely by virtual teachers, but we do appreciate the green savings. Another round of savings comes from training videos that students watch on-demand while saving the time (and potential travel costs) of the trainer as well as the facilities costs for the training room, coordinating schedules, and on, and on.

Part VI
The Part of Tens

The 5th Wave

By Rich Tennant

"I don't know much about alternative energy sources, but I'll bet there's enough solar power being collected on those beach blankets to run my workshop for a month."

In this part . . .

We figured out early in our experience writing *For Dummies* books that we shouldn't get too literal when it comes to this part. We offer you tens of ideas for help with green objectives, computer recycling, and green home offices but please don't count too carefully.

Chapter 21

Ten Organizations That Can Help with Green IT Objectives

. . . .

In This Chapter

▶ Helping you with greener IT strategy and management

▶ Helping you make responsible IT purchases

▶ Managing the reuse and proper disposal of electronics and technology products

. . . .

*O*ne great thing about green is that nobody expects you to do it all on your own. Green is all about working with other people, and plenty of people are ready to help. The following sections introduce you to our top picks for organizations that can help you with green planning, buying, and disposing of information technology systems and equipment.

Thinking and Planning Green

When you're in the initial stages of planning for green IT, the following resources can help you develop green goals and strategies to meet those goals.

Alliance to Save Energy (ASE)

```
www.ase.org
```

ASE is a worldwide organization supporting the adoption of energy efficient strategies by providing information and support to consumers, policy makers, private industry, and educators. ASE is active in over 20 countries and is well-versed in the regulations and tech deployment strategies for organizations of all sizes. ASE specializes in energy strategies that promote a healthier environment, economy, and energy security and is supported by over 150 organizations including those representing industry, government, trade associations, non-profits, non-governmental organizations (NGOs), and others. (NGOs are typically, but not necessarily, not for profit organizations with a social, cultural, or environmental agenda that's not government funded. Many United Nations organizations that exist outside nation states fall into this category.) You'll find white papers and reports on a variety of energy-related topics in the Energy Professionals section.

The Green Grid

`www.thegreengrid.org`

The Green Grid is an industry consortium focused on improving energy efficiencies in data systems and computing environments. The Green Grid is working to define metrics, models, measurement methods, processes, and new technologies, and its members span the globe. They have a wealth of information you can download for free. Here are some of the topics The Green Grid covers:

- Organizational behavior issues in optimizing IT and facilities for energy efficiency
- Metrics for data center infrastructure efficiency
- Ways to reduce data center server power consumption
- Data center power efficiency metrics
- Guidelines for energy efficient data centers

See Chapter 1 for an interview with the Green Grid.

The American Society of Heating, Refrigerating and Air-Conditioning Engineers (ASHRAE)

The American Society of Heating, Refrigerating and Air-Conditioning Engineers is an organization created to "serve humanity and promote a sustainable world." As cooling is of major concern to data centers and is a huge consumer of power, ASHRAE has been invaluable in its efforts to define standards and to provide insight and guidelines.

ASHRAE produces a journal and a newsletter and sells books, tools, and design guides at www.ashrae.org.

The Global e-Sustainability Initiative (GeSI)

www.gesi.org

The Global e-Sustainability Initiative (GeSI) aims to further sustainable development in the Information and Communications Technology (ICT) sector. GeSI works with the United Nations Environment Programme (UNEP) and the International Telecommunication Union (ITU) to support businesses and organizations. The current initiatives focus is on

- Best practices in how to make the supply chain sustainable
- Addressing climate change, which is the result of environmental negligence
- Keeping organizations accountable to a sustainability agenda
- Responsibly disposing of e-waste

You find interesting reports on this site, including the *SMART 2020: Enabling the Low Carbon Economy in the Information Age,* which details how changes in business use of technology could reduce annual human generated global emissions by 15 percent by 2020, with potential savings of over $800 billion.

NetRegs

www.netregs.gov.uk

This U.K. consortium of environmental government agencies from England, Wales, Scotland, and Northern Ireland supports small and mid-sized businesses on following the various environmental regulations, including the European Community regulations on the Registration, Evaluation, Authorisation and Restriction of Chemical substances (REACH), Waste Electrical and Electronic Equipment (WEEE), and Restriction of Hazardous Substances (RoHS). This helpful Web site provides free guidance by business type, legislation, and environmental topic. The site also functions as a handy gateway to learning tools, permit issues, trade associations, regulations, and business support organizations.

Buying Green

The following sites offer buying guides: some general and others with a focus, such as energy efficiency or minimizing toxic components. You might find them helpful while you shop around.

Climate Savers

www.climatesaverscomputing.org

This non-profit, coalition of consumers, businesses, and conservationists is dedicated to reducing computer power consumption by 50 percent by 2010. The Climate Savers Web site provides helpful resources and an online directory for purchasing energy efficient servers, desktops, and more. The organization has also partnered with the U.S. Environmental Protection Agency (EPA) to help spread adoption of Energy Star-rated products.

Energy Star

www.energystar.gov

The U.S. Department of Energy (DOE) and the EPA provide guidelines and tips for energy efficient purchases for businesses and homes. They provide guidelines for green buildings and energy management, a library of resources, and directories of services and products. We talk a lot about Energy Star in Chapter 4 and Chapter 14.

Silicon Valley Toxics Coalition (SVTC)

www.etoxics.org/site/PageServer

SVTC is a grassroots research and advocacy organization focused on reducing e-waste and toxins in technology products. Surprise, surprise; high-tech giants have left behind enough waste to create 29 EPA *Superfund* sites — heavily contaminated toxic waste sites so bad that the government has to step in to clean up — and it's really just the tip of the iceberg. For more than 25 years, SVTC has been monitoring hazardous materials and is active locally, across the U.S., and internationally.

This site provides a buying guide for organizations and individuals who try to buy responsibly, an electronics recycling guide, and a whole lot more.

Disposing Responsibly

Improper disposal of *electronic waste (e-waste)* is a major environmental problem. These sites help you do the right thing with your retired equipment.

The Electronics TakeBack Coalition

www.computertakeback.com

Technology equipment becomes obsolete faster than most other kinds of goods, and just throwing that equipment away is not only wasteful but also hazardous. Pressure from consumers on their electronics providers to assume responsible take-back (and appropriate recycling or disposal) of their obsolete equipment is proving a win-win. Consumers responsibly get rid of their obsolete equipment, and the providers gain customer loyalty as well as the recovery of recyclable components.

This site provides an interactive map to help locate a responsible recycler in your area and ways to take action against irresponsible disposal.

International Association of Electronics Recyclers (IAER)

www.iaer.org

IAER is an international trade organization that offers membership to private, public, and non-profit entities of all kinds that are involved in the recycling of any and all electronic products and materials. IAER offers information, events, and a world-wide directory of recycling and reuse services. The organization also developed the first certification standard for electronics recyclers. Additionally, the recyclers are supported through a research and an education program.

Tech Soup Global

www.techsoupglobal.org

Tech Soup Global is an international group dedicated to supporting social benefit organizations and charities outside the U.S., with information and donations of technology and tech-related services. By 2012, Tech Soup Global will be active in over 60 countries. They don't currently accept used equipment directly, but their recycling page, www.techsoup.org/recycle, offers a number of recycling resource recommendations.

The Basel Action Network (BAN)

The Basel Action Network (BAN) is a global organization that addresses environmental injustice and toxic trade. This very important organization has created criteria to credential 3rd-party–audited recyclers that adhere to "the world's most responsible environmental and social justice criteria for electronics recyclers. These criteria include no toxic e-waste dumped in landfills or incinerators, exported to developing countries, or sent to prison labor operations and no release of private data." For more information on e-Stewards, check out www.e-stewards.org.

See what BAN is doing and join or support them at www.ban.org.

Other helpful organizations

Great new organizations are coming into existence all the time, and we may have missed some important ones. We want to know about them! Please write to tell us about them at greenIT4D@yahoo.com. Here are some more we've already found:

✔ **Green Technology, www.green-technology.org/about.htm:** A California-based non-profit aimed at influencing government to effect sustainability and further green initiatives. A great source for connections to other green initiatives and events.

✔ **World Computer Exchange, www.worldcomputerexchange.org:** An organization created to match donated computers with need schools and libraries.

✔ **Ceres, www.ceres.org:** U.S.-based coalition of environmental experts and investors committed to supporting companies in their sustainability efforts.

✔ **EPA — EPEAT, www.epeat.net:** U.S. Environmental Protection Agency Tool designed to help entities in the public and private sectors make responsible and sustainable technology choices.

✔ **Federal Electronics Challenge, www.federalelectronicschallenge.net:** Program supporting the efforts of having government agencies purchase greener electronic products, adopt greener practices associated with electronics, and responsibly manage obsolete electronics.

✔ **Green Computing Impact Organization, www.gcio.org:** A U.S.-based organization dedicated to supporting the sustainable transformation of IT infrastructures by providing education, audits, strategy, advocacy, and networking for IT organizations and green technology vendors.

✔ **International Institute for Sustainable Development, www.iisd.org/infosoc:** Canadian-based non-profit organization that works internationally with multiple stakeholder groups around sustainable development. IISD has a special focus area on the role of IT in sustainable development.

✔ **Natural Resources Defense Council, www.nrdc.org:** NRDC is an American grassroots environmental action group with over 1.2 million members.

✔ **Rocky Mountain Institute, www.rmi.org:** American non-profit organization that works with multi-level stakeholders to provide research and consulting support related to responsible resource use and management. RMI has also been one of the greatest champions of systems thinking.

✔ **World Business Council for Sustainable Development, www.wbcsd.org:** International organization comprised of CEOs from over 200 companies, worldwide, dedicated to sustainability.

✔ **National Renewable Energy Laboratories (NREL), www.nrel.gov:** The U.S. government's primary laboratory for renewable energy and energy efficiency research and development.

✔ **Lawrence Berkeley National Laboratory (Berkley Lab), www.lbl.gov:** Former nuclear weapons lab now devoted to energy research.

✔ **National Energy Research Scientific Computing Center, www.nersc.gov:** Main scientific computing facility for the U.S. Department of Energy's Office of Science.

✔ **Green Power Network, www.eere. energy.gov/greenpower.**

✔ **American Council on Renewable Energy (ACORE), www.acore.org.**

✔ **Oak Ridge National Laboratory — Energy Efficiency and Renewable Energy program, www.ornl.gov/sci/eere:** Works on expanding energy resource options and improving efficiency in energy production and use.

✔ **Sandia National Laboratories — Renewable Energy office, www.sandia.gov/ Renewable_Energy/renewable. htm:** Develops commercially viable energy technologies based on solar, wind, and geothermal resources.

✔ **Renewable and Appropriate Energy Laboratory, http://rael.berkeley. edu:** A research, development, project implementation, and community outreach facility based at the University of California, Berkeley.

✔ **Renewable Energy Research Laboratory (University of Massachusetts Amherst), www.ceere.org/rerl:** Promotes education and research in renewable energy technologies.

✔ **Idaho National Laboratory, www.inl. gov/renewableenergy.**

✔ **Natural Energy Laboratory of Hawaii Authority, www.nelha.org:** An industrial park on the island of Hawaii that offers renewable energy tenants unique facilities, such as supplies of both warm surface-sea water and cold deep-sea water.

✔ **Renewable Energy World, www. renewableenergyworld.com:** A magazine, trade show, and online information source dedicated to Renewable Energy World.

✔ **Distributed Energy, www.distributed energy.com:** A free trade magazine that covers local power generation, including wind, solar, and cogeneration.

✔ **National Association of Energy Service Companies, www.naesco.org:** A trade association that promotes the benefits of energy efficiency.

✔ **Environmentally Preferable Purchasing (EPP), www.epa.gov/epp:** Offered by the U.S. Environmental Protection Agency.

✔ **Database of Environmental Information for Products and Services, http:// yosemite1.epa.gov/oppt/ eppstand2.nsf/Pages/ Homepage.html?Open:** Also offered by the U.S. Environmental Protection Agency.

Chapter 22

Ten Creative Computer Recycling Tips

. . . .

. . . .

*V*eteran readers of *For Dummies* titles know that when it comes to *The Part of Tens, For Dummies* authors don't take "ten" too literally. When it comes to recycling tips, we certainly don't want to hold back.

Now, about those computers you're about to retire: They can still be productive for others. Although some effort is involved in finding new uses for old equipment, having such a reuse program in place can not only boost your company's image but also offer perks for your employees or the community. This chapter briefly introduces you to a number of ideas for recycling computers, from tips for removing sensitive information to ways to reach out to your community.

Plan for Reuse

Many obstacles to reusing older IT equipment can be avoided by taking care when new equipment is purchased. Save the software — the restore discs and any operating system license certificates — in a standardized way, either in a central location or, perhaps, in a shipping-label pouch attached to the machine.

Also, plan how you'll remove data from equipment you'll eventually retire so that you can prepare machines for reuse in a streamlined way. Use disk encryption from the beginning to reduce problems with removing sensitive data from machines before recycling. Develop a corporate policy on hard drive sanitization that allows machines to be recycled with their hard drives (see Chapter 19).

Set Up an Equipment Exchange Site on Your Intranet

Finding out about surplus equipment in large organizations can be hard. A simple blog or Wiki-style internal Web site can allow people in one group to get machines that are surplus in another group.

Load Linux on Older PCs

Older PCs that are too wimpy to run a reasonably current version of Windows can still be useful if reconfigured with the Linux operating system. See Chapter 14 for suggestions on how to do this and which office applications are available for use under Linux.

Use Knoppix

If corporate security policy won't allow even sanitized hard drives to leave the company, surplus disk-less PCs can be made quite usable with a live CD- or DVD-based operating system, such as Knoppix (www.knoppix.org; click the U.S./U.K. flag for the English version of this site.). These Linux distributions (distros) boot directly from the computer's CD or DVD drive and include a Web browser and office applications. Files can be saved on a USB (Universal Serial Bus) thumb drive or by mailing the files as an attachment to an e-mail account at Gmail or Yahoo. (You can open such an account for free at `mail.google.com` or `mail.yahoo.com`.)

Make Some Hot Carts

Install several surplus PCs on office carts that can be rolled out for special needs, such as training courses, visiting employees from the field, or temporary replacements when equipment fails.

Use Old PCs for Bulletin Boards and Kiosks

Set up a computer and a monitor in the cafeteria or other public gathering places as a quick way to spread corporate information, perhaps by offering access to selected parts of your intranet. Use them in the entry-way to welcome guests with access to your public corporate Web site and perhaps local services, such as hotels, transportation, and local attractions. For information on building kiosks with the Linux operating system, visit `kiosk.mozdev.org`.

Build an Old Media Center

If your organization has been around long enough, you probably have archives stored away on Zip disks, floppies, and other oddball media. You may need to read them someday. Save a couple old PCs that support these media and set them up as a data recovery station. You'll want two machines in case one dies right when you try to use it. Keep them powered off and disconnected from the Internet until you need them.

Offer Older Computers to Employees

Letting employees purchase retired PCs and laptops at a discount is an inexpensive perk that builds loyalty and improves staff skills. Also consider a donation program for workers with special situations. Our esteemed editor, Becky, purchased her laptop this way and says such programs are great.

Equip a Disaster Recovery Center

Disasters — natural or human-made — that can shut down a corporate center seem to happen more frequently these days. Planning for such possibilities has become an important IT role. All too often, disaster plans are limited by budget constraints to the minimal needed to keep operations going (or less). Older IT equipment can beef up the disaster plan. Set up a computer room in an offsite location, perhaps a warehouse or a field office with backup servers and desktops. For more on disaster recovery plans, check out *IT Disaster Recovery Planning For Dummies,* by Peter Gregory (Wiley).

Start a Computer Recycling Club

People in charities and schools can often use older computers, but they're often inundated with offers of obsolete equipment in poor condition that are more trouble than they're worth. Getting employees to volunteer time to check out and configure surplus stuff and provide initial support to recipients makes equipment donations truly usable. Some things a club might take on include

- Configuring working systems, perhaps taking parts from different machines

- Erasing hard drives to meet corporate security standards

- Loading new operating system and application software

- Collecting documentation, software discs, cables, and other accessories needed

- Packaging machines for shipment or pick-up

- Evaluating requests for donations

- Running training classes for new users

- Visiting sites where the donated equipment is being used to check on how things are working out. Such visits can be rewarding if the equipment is being used effectively and can be a learning experience if not.

Here's one story that describes a recycling group effort: `http://escrap indiana.org/pdfs/community/VSPCaseStudy.pdf`.

Run a Tag Sale

Hold a weekend *tag sale,* where you sell used equipment at a reduced price (traditionally each item is marked with a price tag so buyers don't have to keep asking what items cost). The company parking lot might be good place. Some or all proceeds could go to a local charity. You'll move equipment and generate goodwill in the community. Advertise the event on Craigslist.org and in community newspapers. Extra credit for running extension cords to power machines so buyers can see they're working.

Pick a fixed time each year (or quarter) for the tag sale and you'll soon have a following.

Find a Green Disposal Path for Equipment You Can't Reuse

In configuring working systems from old equipment, you end up with some hulks that have to be cannibalized for spare parts. And some older equipment is truly worthless. Don't use just any old scrap dealer or waste hauler to get rid of the useless junk. Make the effort to verify that they dispose e-waste in a responsible way. Chapter 19 covers recycling equipment safely and legally.

Chapter 23

Ten Tips for a Green Home Office

*M*uch of this book addresses the greening of medium and large organizations. But many people work in their homes, and many large enterprises have some staff working out of their residences, at least part of the time. (Remember all those miles you don't travel in a daily commute contribute to a greener world.) This chapter suggests ways to reduce your home office environmental footprint.

Buy Only What You Need

Your home office impacts the environment in a big way when you buy new equipment. The energy that went into making it and transporting it, along with the accompanying pollution, often in third-world countries, is substantial. Using what you have another year, perhaps adding some more RAM (random access memory) and an external hard drive (the drive you can then use with your next machine) may be the greenest steps you can take. And when you do buy, get a machine that matches your real needs. A super-duper 500-watt 8-core dual graphics tower may win you points on *World of Warcraft,* but you waste too much time playing those games. And if you have kids, they'll take it over anyway (so get a machine your kids won't covet).

When you do buy, check environmental ratings. For starters, get an Energy Star rated machine. Some manufacturers go beyond those ratings. Give them a look. For more on finding a green desktop machine, see Chapter 14.

Corral Power Adaptors

Get all those little power adaptors on a single power strip, or a couple daisy-chained power strips, so you can shut them down at night with a single switch. Use a separate strip for chargers that you'll leave on at night while your cell phone, PDA, iPod, Bluetooth headset, and electric toothbrush are plugged in. Turn these off during the day.

Also, turn off your router at night. You're not using it, and the boot-up is fast. Just add the router's power adaptor to the others on your shutdown power strip. We hear that in some parts of the world, routers are configurable to *go to sleep at night (when you tell them to),* making one less thing you have to remember.

Enable Power Management

Enabling the power management options of your operating system and lowering the brightness setting for your display can make a big difference in power usage. For instance, Arnold's 24-inch iMac uses 148 watts at full brightness, 118 watts at minimum brightness (he can hardly tell the difference in use), 63 watts with the screen blanked, 4 watts in sleep mode, and 2 watts when turned off.

Energy savings with a laptop are less because their overall power consumption is much lower, but the savings are still worthwhile. Your operating system will automatically blank the display and put your computer to sleep if you select the proper options. In Microsoft Vista, select Control Panel➪Hardware & Sounds➪Power Options. In Mac OS X, select System Preferences➪Energy Saver from the Apple Menu ( ). We discuss the power-saving features of your operating system in detail in Chapter 15. Chapter 17 tells you about the inexpensive Kill A Watt power meter that Arnold used to make these measurements.

Set Up for Natural Lighting

Many people commandeer a nice room for their home office and then close the curtains and pull down the blinds on all the windows. Consider rearranging your office furniture so you can take advantage of natural lighting without having a glare on your computer display. This generally means pointing the back of the display roughly toward the window and making sure no reflective objects are behind you. As a bonus, you get to look out the window while working.

Use Energy Efficient Lighting

In Chapter 18, we discuss the ins and outs of evaluating lighting in office buildings, and many of the same principles apply in the home, too. The easiest thing to do, of course, is replace incandescent bulbs with compact fluorescents or LED (light emitting diode) lighting. Avoid high-power halogen lamps.

Try Solar Power

If you live in a sunny location, you can use solar panels to charge your laptop's battery. However most laptops run only a few hours on their internal battery, so you won't get much work done at night or on cloudy days. EarthTech Products (www.earthtechproducts.com) sells a solar panel and a battery pack kit that gives you more hours of use. You can also find solar and hand-cranked chargers for small devices, such as cell phones and iPods. See Chapter 17 for details. If you're really ambitious, get a copy of *Solar Power Your Home For Dummies* by Rik DeGunther and free yourself from the power company.

Manage the Shades

You don't need expensive technology to use the sun's energy. If you're working at home during the heating season, you can easily take advantage of passive solar heating. Open blinds and curtains when the sun is out and shining in, but close them at other times to keep in heat. The energy you save can be more than what your computers use. Keep sun-facing shades closed when the air conditioner is in use, of course.

Buy Recycled Products

Look for printer paper with substantial post-consumer scrap content. Paper with 100-percent recycled content is best, of course, but even partial recycled content paper makes a contribution and often costs less. Most office supply companies carry recycled paper or you can order on line from sites like www.thegreenoffice.com.

When you're working on a draft and need to print, use the back side of the page. If you have a printer that prints 2-sided copies, print 2-sided whenever you can.

Recycled printer cartridges generally work fine, and there's often a significant rebate for your old cartridge when you buy new cartridges at major retailers, such as Staples, which often uses recycled cartridges.

Save Good Printing Scrap

If you don't reuse all your print scrap by printing on the back for drafts, you can use it for scrap paper. Arnold saves only the sheets with relatively little printing, say a last blank page with headers and footers. A few minutes with a paper cutter produces a nice stack of note paper.

Dispose Old Equipment Properly

Make sure you do the right thing when it's time to get rid of that old machine. Giving it to a family member or a friend may be the easiest solution, but you may end up getting a lot of calls as their free tech support. Unless you *want* to be their tech support, you might rather give your computer to someone who won't call you at any hour.

Chapter 19 covers disposal tips in detail, and Chapter 22 offers some more creative ideas for disposing of a computer.

Make Your Home Green

Putting effort into saving a few watts in your home office when your house is a big energy waster won't get you very far. Make sure you've done the easy things, such as weather stripping, installing compact fluorescents throughout the house, changing you heating system air filters, cleaning your refrigerator coils, and the like. See *Green Living For Dummies* by Yvonne Jeffery, Liz Barclay, and Michael Grosvenor (Wiley) for more ideas.

Appendix

Consumption and Savings Worksheets

. . . .

In This Appendix

▶ Establishing your baseline

▶ Logging data center conditions

▶ Calculating facility power with meter readings

▶ Estimating your IT power consumption

▶ Calculating DCiE and PUE

▶ Using quickie watts calculation

▶ Filling out your data center green report card

. . . .

Establishing a Baseline

As you begin your green IT program, collect as much of the following information as you can and keep it where you'll be able to find it years from now. It will help you document how much progress you've made. See Chapter 5 for more on getting started with a green program.

Floor space

If you can't get this from architectural plans, get out your tape measure and measure the room. Remember area = length × width.

Raised floor area _____ ft^2 or meter^2 (circle one)

Total floor area _____ ft^2 or meter^2 (circle one)

IT equipment

Number of server cores _____

Online data stored _____ terabytes

Online storage capacity _____ terabytes

Network connection bandwidth _____ gigabytes/second

Utility meter

Location of data center utility meter _____

Date _____ Time _____ Reading _____

Power cost per kWh (kilowatt-hour)

Use your recent utility bill, if possible. Check with your accounting department if you don't regularly see the bill.

Bill date: Month _____ Year _____

Base $ _____ /kWh

Peak $ _____ /kWh

Night $ _____ /kWh

Billing period duration _____ (such as 30 days)

Power used in last billing period _____ kW (if broken out for data center)

Total corporate power usage in period _____ kW

Chiller capacity

Type _____

Manufacturer _____

Cooling capacity per chiller _____ tons

× number of chillers _____

= Total cooling capacity _____ tons

× 3.5 kW/ton

= _____ kilowatts

Date _____ By _____

Data Center Conditions Log Sheet

Fill out this form on a regular basis to track the performance of your data center air conditioning equipment. See Chapter 17 for suggestions on measuring equipment. Temperature and dew point readings are in Fahrenheit or Celsius (circle one).

Measurement date _____ Time _____ By _____

Perimeter

Temperature _____ Relative humidity _____ % Dew point _____

CRAC set points

Temperature _____ Relative humidity _____ % Dew point _____

Outdoor conditions

Temperature _____ Relative humidity _____ % Dew point _____

Computer room temperature distribution survey

Aisle	Rack	Height	Temperature

Calculating Facility Power from Two Meter Readings

Use this section to estimate your total facility power usage.

Date_____ Time _____ Meter reading 1 _____ kWh

Date_____ Time _____ Meter reading 2 _____ kWh

Ideally, meter reading should be a week or more, or at least several days, apart.

Meter reading 2 – meter reading 1

= Period energy usage _____ kWh

To calculate power usage, we need the time difference in hours between meter readings. Use the following section to convert days, hours, and minutes into decimal hours:

Number of days _____ × 24 = _____ hr

Hours _____ hr

Minutes _____ / 60 = _____ hr (decimal)

Total hours between readings (add entries above) _____ hr

Period energy usage (kilowatt hours)
÷ Total hours
= Average total facility power during measurement period _____ kW

Estimating IT Power Consumption

You'll want to know how much power the electronics in your data center draws to calculate power utilization efficiency and other performance metrics. (See Chapter 8 for an explanation of these metrics.) If direct measurements of IT equipment power draw aren't available, you can estimate it by counting devices in the data center and adding their power consumption. Use actual measured power for devices, not rated or nameplate power. ***Note:*** This bottom-up methodology tends to underestimate power usage and inflate PUE scores.

Server units

Manufacturer	Model	Quantity	Average Power Usage (Watts)	Combined Power Usage (Quantity X Average)

Server subtotal: Watts/1000 = _____ kilowatts

Storage units

Manufacturer	Model	Quantity	Average Power Usage (Watts)	Combined Power Usage (Quantity X Average)

Storage subtotal: Watts/1000 = _____ kilowatts

Miscellaneous equipment

This includes networking, operator monitoring console, firewall appliances, and so on.

Manufacturer	Model	Quantity	Average Power Usage (Watts)	Combined Power Usage (Quantity X Average)

Miscellaneous subtotal: Watts/1000 = _____ kilowatts

Total IT equipment power: server+storage+misc. = _____ kilowatts

Calculating PUE and DCiE

You are now ready to calculate the important performance metrics PUE and DCiE as described in Chapter 8.

Average total facility power during measurement period (from Calculating Facility Power from Two Meter Readings, above) _____ kW

Average total IT power during measurement period (from Estimating IT Power Consumption) _____ kW

Average total facility power during period _____

/Average total IT power during period _____

= **Power Utilization Effectiveness (PUE)** _____

100

/PUE _____

= **Data Center infrastructure Efficiency (DCiE)** _____ %

PUE Scoring

3.0 or more: Poor

2.0–2.9: Average

1.7–1.9: Fair

1.4–1.8: Good

1.3: Very good

1.2: State of the art

1.0 or less: Recheck your calculations (your equipment can't use more power than is going into your building)

Quickie Watts Consumption

This section describes some common calculations, from the number of watts that a single piece of equipment uses to the number that a whole facility uses, on the basis of daily, weekly, and yearly energy consumption. See Chapter 4 for the basics of energy and power.

(_____ watts × hours used)/1,000

= _____ Consumption in kilowatt-hours

To compute daily energy consumption:

(_____ watts × 24)/1,000

= _____ kilowatt-hours consumed per day

To compute yearly energy consumption:

_____ kilowatt-hours per day × 7 days × 52 weeks

= _____ kWh of yearly energy consumption

For the following, we use the example that a server consumes an average of 300 watts per hour. First, we calculate the daily consumption:

(300 watts × 24 hours)/1,000

= 7.2 kilowatt-hours per day

After calculating the daily consumption, calculate the yearly consumption, as follows: 7.2 kilowatt-hours per day × 7 days/week × 52 weeks

= 2,620 kilowatt-hours per year

Use five days per week in case equipment is shut down over the weekend.

Data Center Green Report Card

Consider filling out this form annually, quarterly, or even monthly as a way of tracking your progress toward green goals. The way to calculate some of the information is described earlier. Other data will require using your ingenuity.

Energy consumed by data center _____ kilowatt-hours

Power expense $ _____

Average power load _____ kilowatts

Average power cost $ _____ /kW

Power Utilization Effectiveness (PUE) _____

Data Center infrastructure Efficiency (DCiE) (100/PUE) _____ %

Power cost at PDU (average power cost × PUE) $ _____ /kWh

Data center floor area _____ (ft²)

Power density _____ W/ft²

Number of server cores _____

Online data stored _____ terabytes

Online storage capacity _____ terabytes

Storage utilization _____

Server utilization _____

Bandwidth available _____ gigabytes/second

Total Internet data transmission _____ terabytes

Total intranet data transmission _____ terabytes

Index

• *N* •

• *O* •

BUSINESS, CAREERS & PERSONAL FINANCE

Accounting For Dummies, 4th Edition*
978-0-470-24600-9

Bookkeeping Workbook For Dummies†
978-0-470-16983-4

Commodities For Dummies
978-0-470-04928-0

Doing Business in China For Dummies
978-0-470-04929-7

E-Mail Marketing For Dummies
978-0-470-19087-6

Job Interviews For Dummies, 3rd Edition*†
978-0-470-17748-8

Personal Finance Workbook For Dummies*†
978-0-470-09933-9

Real Estate License Exams For Dummies
978-0-7645-7623-2

Six Sigma For Dummies
978-0-7645-6798-8

Small Business Kit For Dummies, 2nd Edition*†
978-0-7645-5984-6

Telephone Sales For Dummies
978-0-470-16836-3

BUSINESS PRODUCTIVITY & MICROSOFT OFFICE

Access 2007 For Dummies
978-0-470-03649-5

Excel 2007 For Dummies
978-0-470-03737-9

Office 2007 For Dummies
978-0-470-00923-9

Outlook 2007 For Dummies
978-0-470-03830-7

PowerPoint 2007 For Dummies
978-0-470-04059-1

Project 2007 For Dummies
978-0-470-03651-8

QuickBooks 2008 For Dummies
978-0-470-18470-7

Quicken 2008 For Dummies
978-0-470-17473-9

Salesforce.com For Dummies, 2nd Edition
978-0-470-04893-1

Word 2007 For Dummies
978-0-470-03658-7

EDUCATION, HISTORY, REFERENCE & TEST PREPARATION

African American History For Dummies
978-0-7645-5469-8

Algebra For Dummies
978-0-7645-5325-7

Algebra Workbook For Dummies
978-0-7645-8467-1

Art History For Dummies
978-0-470-09910-0

ASVAB For Dummies, 2nd Edition
978-0-470-10671-6

British Military History For Dummies
978-0-470-03213-8

Calculus For Dummies
978-0-7645-2498-1

Canadian History For Dummies, 2nd Edition
978-0-470-83656-9

Geometry Workbook For Dummies
978-0-471-79940-5

The SAT I For Dummies, 6th Edition
978-0-7645-7193-0

Series 7 Exam For Dummies
978-0-470-09932-2

World History For Dummies
978-0-7645-5242-7

FOOD, GARDEN, HOBBIES & HOME

Bridge For Dummies, 2nd Edition
978-0-471-92426-5

Coin Collecting For Dummies, 2nd Edition
978-0-470-22275-1

Cooking Basics For Dummies, 3rd Edition
978-0-7645-7206-7

Drawing For Dummies
978-0-7645-5476-6

Etiquette For Dummies, 2nd Edition
978-0-470-10672-3

Gardening Basics For Dummies*†
978-0-470-03749-2

Knitting Patterns For Dummies
978-0-470-04556-5

Living Gluten-Free For Dummies†
978-0-471-77383-2

Painting Do-It-Yourself For Dummies
978-0-470-17533-0

HEALTH, SELF HELP, PARENTING & PETS

Anger Management For Dummies
978-0-470-03715-7

Anxiety & Depression Workbook For Dummies
978-0-7645-9793-0

Dieting For Dummies, 2nd Edition
978-0-7645-4149-0

Dog Training For Dummies, 2nd Edition
978-0-7645-8418-3

Horseback Riding For Dummies
978-0-470-09719-9

Infertility For Dummies†
978-0-470-11518-3

Meditation For Dummies with CD-ROM, 2nd Edition
978-0-471-77774-8

Post-Traumatic Stress Disorder For Dummies
978-0-470-04922-8

Puppies For Dummies, 2nd Edition
978-0-470-03717-1

Thyroid For Dummies, 2nd Edition†
978-0-471-78755-6

Type 1 Diabetes For Dummies*†
978-0-470-17811-9

---

* Separate Canadian edition also available
† Separate U.K. edition also available

Available wherever books are sold. For more information or to order direct: U.S. customers visit www.dummies.com or call 1-877-762-2974.
U.K. customers visit www.wileyeurope.com or call (0)1243 843291. Canadian customers visit www.wiley.ca or call 1-800-567-4797.

INTERNET & DIGITAL MEDIA

AdWords For Dummies
978-0-470-15252-2

Blogging For Dummies, 2nd Edition
978-0-470-23017-6

Digital Photography All-in-One Desk Reference For Dummies, 3rd Edition
978-0-470-03743-0

Digital Photography For Dummies, 5th Edition
978-0-7645-9802-9

Digital SLR Cameras & Photography For Dummies, 2nd Edition
978-0-470-14927-0

eBay Business All-in-One Desk Reference For Dummies
978-0-7645-8438-1

eBay For Dummies, 5th Edition*
978-0-470-04529-9

eBay Listings That Sell For Dummies
978-0-471-78912-3

Facebook For Dummies
978-0-470-26273-3

The Internet For Dummies, 11th Edition
978-0-470-12174-0

Investing Online For Dummies, 5th Edition
978-0-7645-8456-5

iPod & iTunes For Dummies, 5th Edition
978-0-470-17474-6

MySpace For Dummies
978-0-470-09529-4

Podcasting For Dummies
978-0-471-74898-4

Search Engine Optimization For Dummies, 2nd Edition
978-0-471-97998-2

Second Life For Dummies
978-0-470-18025-9

Starting an eBay Business For Dummies, 3rd Edition†
978-0-470-14924-9

GRAPHICS, DESIGN & WEB DEVELOPMENT

Adobe Creative Suite 3 Design Premium All-in-One Desk Reference For Dummies
978-0-470-11724-8

Adobe Web Suite CS3 All-in-One Desk Reference For Dummies
978-0-470-12099-6

AutoCAD 2008 For Dummies
978-0-470-11650-0

Building a Web Site For Dummies, 3rd Edition
978-0-470-14928-7

Creating Web Pages All-in-One Desk Reference For Dummies, 3rd Edition
978-0-470-09629-1

Creating Web Pages For Dummies, 8th Edition
978-0-470-08030-6

Dreamweaver CS3 For Dummies
978-0-470-11490-2

Flash CS3 For Dummies
978-0-470-12100-9

Google SketchUp For Dummies
978-0-470-13744-4

InDesign CS3 For Dummies
978-0-470-11865-8

Photoshop CS3 All-in-One Desk Reference For Dummies
978-0-470-11195-6

Photoshop CS3 For Dummies
978-0-470-11193-2

Photoshop Elements 5 For Dummies
978-0-470-09810-3

SolidWorks For Dummies
978-0-7645-9555-4

Visio 2007 For Dummies
978-0-470-08983-5

Web Design For Dummies, 2nd Edition
978-0-471-78117-2

Web Sites Do-It-Yourself For Dummies
978-0-470-16903-2

Web Stores Do-It-Yourself For Dummies
978-0-470-17443-2

LANGUAGES, RELIGION & SPIRITUALITY

Arabic For Dummies
978-0-471-77270-5

Chinese For Dummies, Audio Set
978-0-470-12766-7

French For Dummies
978-0-7645-5193-2

German For Dummies
978-0-7645-5195-6

Hebrew For Dummies
978-0-7645-5489-6

Ingles Para Dummies
978-0-7645-5427-8

Italian For Dummies, Audio Set
978-0-470-09586-7

Italian Verbs For Dummies
978-0-471-77389-4

Japanese For Dummies
978-0-7645-5429-2

Latin For Dummies
978-0-7645-5431-5

Portuguese For Dummies
978-0-471-78738-9

Russian For Dummies
978-0-471-78001-4

Spanish Phrases For Dummies
978-0-7645-7204-3

Spanish For Dummies
978-0-7645-5194-9

Spanish For Dummies, Audio Set
978-0-470-09585-0

The Bible For Dummies
978-0-7645-5296-0

Catholicism For Dummies
978-0-7645-5391-2

The Historical Jesus For Dummies
978-0-470-16785-4

Islam For Dummies
978-0-7645-5503-9

Spirituality For Dummies, 2nd Edition
978-0-470-19142-2

NETWORKING AND PROGRAMMING

ASP.NET 3.5 For Dummies
978-0-470-19592-5

C# 2008 For Dummies
978-0-470-19109-5

Hacking For Dummies, 2nd Edition
978-0-470-05235-8

Home Networking For Dummies, 4th Edition
978-0-470-11806-1

Java For Dummies, 4th Edition
978-0-470-08716-9

Microsoft® SQL Server™ 2008 All-in-One Desk Reference For Dummies
978-0-470-17954-3

Networking All-in-One Desk Reference For Dummies, 2nd Edition
978-0-7645-9939-2

Networking For Dummies, 8th Edition
978-0-470-05620-2

SharePoint 2007 For Dummies
978-0-470-09941-4

Wireless Home Networking For Dummies, 2nd Edition
978-0-471-74940-0

Printed in Great Britain
by Amazon.co.uk, Ltd.,
Marston Gate.